Las Vegas: *The Social Production o*

# Las Vegas
## *The Social Production of an All-American City*

M. Gottdiener,
Claudia C. Collins,
and David R. Dickens

BLACKWELL
*Publishers*

First published 1999

2 4 6 8 10 9 7 5 3 1

Blackwell Publishers Inc.
350 Main Street
Malden, Massachusetts 02148
USA

Blackwell Publishers Ltd
108 Cowley Road
Oxford OX4 1JF
UK

*Library of Congress Cataloging-in-Publication Data*
Gottdiener, M.
    Las Vegas : the social production of an all-American city / M.
Gottdiener, Claudia C. Collins, and David R. Dickens.
        p.      cm.
    Includes bibliographical references and index.
    ISBN 1–57718–136–0 (hc : alk. paper). — ISBN 1–57718–137–9 (pbk.
: alk. paper)
    1. Las Vegas (Nev.)—Social conditions. 2. Las Vegas (Nev.)–
–Economic conditions. 3. Las Vegas (Nev.)—Politics and government.
I. Collins, Claudia C.  II. Dickens, David R.  III. Title.
HN80.L27G67   1999
306'.09793'135—dc21                                    99–22551
                                                            CIP

*British Library Cataloguing in Publication Data*

A CIP record for this book is available from the British Library.

Typeset in Palatino 10.5 pt on 12 pt
by Avocet Typeset, Brill, Aylesbury, Bucks
Printed in Great Britain by T J International, Padstow, Cornwall

This book is printed on acid-free paper.

# Contents

vi   *Contents*

# Tables

# Maps

# Figures

The authors and publisher would like to thank the *Las Vegas Review Journal* for permission to reproduce all the above figures.

# Acknowledgments

We have benefited enormously from assistance we received, both technical and intellectual, from a number of colleagues and local Las Vegans and we wish to take this opportunity to thank them for their generous support. They include Dixie Allsbrook, Stavros Anthony, Robert Antonio, Michael Bowers, Donald Carns, J. J. Charis, Nora Cooper, Bob Faiss, Linda Faiss, Mark Fine, Michael Green, Russell Guindon, Jeff Hardcastle, Laura Bourne Hernandez, Terry L. Hicks, Richard Holmes, A. D. Hopkins, Veona Hunsinger, Dean Judson, Jim Laurie, Christina Majik, Chris Mele, Gustavo Mesch, Gene Moehring, Richard A. Nielsen, Jeanne Palmer, Robert Parker, Fred Preston, John Schlegel, Paul Shapiro, Ron Smith, SNAPPE (the Southern Nevada Area Population Projection and Estimation Committee), Kathy Somers, Edward Steinfeld, Janet Usinger, Melissa Warren, Richard Wassmuth, Jon Wellinghoff, and Garth Winckler.

# Preface

This book concerns Las Vegas, a town about which almost everyone has an opinion, most often derived from tourist visits or mass media images on television and in Hollywood films. For many, Las Vegas is "Sin City" or "Lost Wages," a glitzy fantasy town devoted entirely to gambling and entertainment. Without denying the continuing salience of Las Vegas' image as a tourist mecca, our primary focus here lies elsewhere: on what we term the normalization of the Las Vegas area, its development into a fully fledged metropolitan region with a growing number of permanent residents whose everyday life involves concerns that mirror those of other large Sunbelt cities.

At the same time, this is also a book about the rest of America, insofar as we argue that in many ways Las Vegas represents, though often in exaggerated form, several important trends in contemporary American society as a whole. Some of these new trends are political-economic in nature, such as the prominent role of what Henri Lefebvre refers to as "the second circuit of capital," i.e., real estate investment, in driving urban development and supporting contemporary urban elites. Others are more cultural, including the spread of legal gambling across the country and the increasing reliance of older metropolitan areas on tourism, with the accompanying use of Las Vegas-style boosterism to attract visitors. In this sense, we argue that Las Vegas is more avant-garde than aberrant, albeit in ways that are not always particularly positive, but which nonetheless demand serious study by scholars of contemporary urban life.

Certainly we are not the first to put forth such an argument. The first and perhaps still the most famous commentary on the broader cultural significance of Las Vegas is Tom Wolfe's discussion of the town in *The Kandy-Kolored Tangerine-Flake Streamline Baby* (1965). Noting that the important thing about Las Vegas is not that its builders were gangsters but that they were working class, Wolfe goes on to argue that:

> long after Las Vegas' influence as a gambling heaven has gone, Las Vegas' forms and symbols will be influencing American life. ... Las Vegas' neon sculpture, its fantastic fifteen-story high display signs, parabolas,

boomerangs, rhomboids, trapezoids and all the rest of it, are already the staple design of the American landscape outside of the oldest part of the oldest cities. ... They are the new landmarks of America, the new guideposts, the new way Americans get their bearings.   (1965: viii)

Nearly as significant in its impact, at least in certain academic circles, was the celebration of Las Vegas-style architecture in the late 1960s by the Yale architects, Robert Venturi, Denise Scott Brown, and Steven Izenour (1972). Promoting what they saw as Las Vegas' vibrant, populist celebration of postwar American mass culture as an antidote to the sterile formalism of high modernist design, the Yale architects urged their colleagues to "learn from Las Vegas."

More recently, still others have commented on Las Vegas' role as a pioneer of sorts in regard to new national trends (see Findlay 1990; Hess 1993). Architectural critic Alan Hess in particular has provided an update of Venturi, Scott Brown, and Izenour's classic work, chronicling more recent developments in what he refers to as Las Vegas' commercial vernacular style, which, he argues, has "catapulted Las Vegas to the leading edge of American urbanism" (1993: 114).

None of these observers, however, have tried to document the point sociologically, as we do here, by means of an in-depth analysis of the region and the tremendous changes it has recently undergone. This book, therefore, is not about Las Vegas, or "Vegas," the seedy gambling haven for adults, but about the area as a developing metropolitan region of permanent residents with an enviable quality of life. In chapter 1 we provide an historical overview of the development of Las Vegas from its origins as a sleepy railroad town through its emergence in the decades following World War II as a major tourist destination. We also analyze this development in terms of a relatively recent approach in urban sociology, the socio-spatial model, which is a regional approach that emphasizes capital investment in real estate and the actions of powerful elites.

In chapter 2 we discuss the most recent era in Las Vegas' history, characterized by the advent of giant megaresorts and the prominence of multinational corporate ownership. Chapter 3 describes the origins and development of Las Vegas' glitzy image, focusing especially on the role of advertising and other forms of media hype in creating that image. One factor that is especially relevant here is the melding of the get-rich-quick glamor of gambling with that of Hollywood celebrities. As a location, Las Vegas promises a new, spectacular form of happiness and entertainment.

In chapter 4 we examine the advent of development on a regional scale, detailing the metropolis's explosive population growth as well as its booming economy. While the region has become more diverse racially and ethnically, and has attracted a large influx of senior citizens, questions are raised concerning its continued heavy reliance on gambling.

Chapters 5 and 6 address a central theme of the book: the transformation of Las Vegas from a predominantly tourist town of transients into a diverse region that also contains a growing number of residential communities with conventional families and suburban lifestyles. In chapter 5 we focus especially on the development of master-planned communities and other new suburban areas whose residents have formed local identities largely removed from the glitz and glitter of gambling and tourism. We also raise the crucial question of the effects of uneven development on class and racial inequality as well as on spatial growth patterns. In chapter 6 we continue our discussion of the normalization process in Las Vegas by examining the region's emerging civic culture as manifested by its public activities in libraries, parks, churches, and educational institutions.

Chapter 7 provides a portrait of everyday life in Las Vegas, emphasizing the colorful contradictions of living in what is both a typical Sunbelt metropolis and a 24-hour entertainment town. In chapter 8 we focus on the unusual nature of local politics and the impact of a variety of community concerns such as growth, inequality, education, and the environment on the local political agenda. It is the change in this agenda that best characterizes normalization.

Finally, in chapter 9, we offer a summary evaluation of our thesis that Las Vegas is becoming a more typical American city, while the rest of the country is changing in ways that make it more like Las Vegas. We conclude by discussing a list of some of the problematic aspects of growth and the growing contradiction that lies at the very heart of normalization, between a politics based on promoting the interests of business and the need for government that better serves the needs of the increasing number of residents. In so doing we hope to encourage readers to look past the neon façade that has traditionally defined Las Vegas and appreciate the dynamics of community formation in its midst.

M. GOTTDIENER
CLAUDIA C. COLLINS
DAVID R. DICKENS

# 1 From Desert Oasis to Glitter Capital of the World

Las Vegas, Nevada, is located in the middle of one of the most forbidding deserts on earth. It is a most unlikely place for a city, yet, in 1995, the population of the Las Vegas metropolitan region passed one million and Nevada's state demographer predicts a population of two million for the Las Vegas Valley by 2007. The average annual temperature is 66.3 degrees Fahrenheit, but after May relentless heat sears the summer months. There is little variation in temperature once the hot weather arrives, at midnight in July the temperature can be 90 degrees. Millions of gallons of water must be pumped uphill each day to Las Vegas from nearby Lake Mead and most other necessities such as food, clothing, building supplies, and construction equipment must be transported in from other states. How this improbable metropolis developed in the midst of such a forbidding environment hundreds of miles from any large urban center is truly a remarkable story.

## The Early Days

One of the key issues in urban analysis is to explain how land acquires value through location. While agricultural land derives value from its intrinsic worth as a natural resource, city land derives value from its location. The area of southern Nevada within which Las Vegas is located possesses no intrinsic worth as an agricultural resource. Even today the Bureau of Land Management classifies most of the area surrounding Las Vegas as arid wasteland. In the 1800s, however, the region was highly valued as a site of mineral deposits, especially gold, bringing the first Europeans to the area, although the Paiute Native American tribe had lived in the region for centuries.

The Las Vegas site also had one other precious resource. Water regularly bubbled up through the ground from artesian wells. Prior to the 1820s, those few hearty souls seeking to go west followed a trail carved out by the early Spanish explorers between what is now New

Mexico and California. The Old Spanish Trail stayed close to water, following the Colorado River south and then due west below the Mojave Desert to the Pacific Ocean. This L-shaped trail was the easiest but not the most direct path, so explorers searched for a quicker route. In November 1829, a sixty-man merchant party led by the Spanish explorer and trader Antonio Armijo, and his scout, Rafael Rivera, discovered a verdant oasis while searching for water midway on their trip. They named the site Las Vegas, the Meadows, and it proved to be a valuable alternative to the longer trail by cutting days off the journey west. As one historian observed: "The abundant artesian spring water at Las Vegas shortened the Spanish Trail to Los Angeles and eased the rigors for the traders who used the route" (*Las Vegas Review-Journal* 1989: 19A). Others, such as the fur trapper Jedediah Smith, soon used the route to reach California. Without its naturally occurring ground water, the early settlement of Las Vegas never would have begun.

By the 1850s, the Utah-to-California route via Las Vegas was so well established that Congress created a regular mail run between Salt Lake City and San Diego (Moehring 1989: 1). A significant Anglo population moved into the area for the first time when a Mormon expedition from Utah arrived. After establishing the city of San Bernardino at the east end of the Los Angeles basin, the Mormons "put in a settlement at Las Vegas to supply travelers going to and from San Bernardino and Salt Lake City" (Moehring 1989: 2). They also constructed an adobe fort near what is now the city's downtown. Consequently, Las Vegas became an early general provision site in the expanding settlement of the southwest.

In the 1860s gold strikes in the vicinity of Las Vegas, at Mt Potosi north of town and another in Eldorado Canyon, drew prospectors already working the gold fields of California and northern Nevada. As gold seekers streamed into the Las Vegas area, the city's role as a center for provisions expanded, bringing others who cashed in not by mining directly but by catering to the needs of prospectors. In the 1860s, for example, a former prospector named Octavius Gass took over the old fort abandoned by earlier Mormon settlers and converted it into a large general store and ranch. This building anchored the town's early settlement. He also bought a large abandoned farm site and founded the Las Vegas Ranch, which was cultivated until the early 1900s. By the turn of the century, the real gold of the West, the railroads, came to the region, as the presence of ample water attracted Las Vegas railroad entrepreneurs who were already engaged in developing Los Angeles.

A Montana copper baron turned senator and real-estate speculator, William Clark, arrived on the scene in 1902. By then it was widely recognized that the most cost-efficient route between Los Angeles and Salt Lake City was through Las Vegas (Moehring 1989: 3). Clark built the San Pedro, Los Angeles and Salt Lake Railroad, that connected the Union Pacific main line in Utah with southern California. Like other venture capitalists who built railroads, he also speculated in real estate, building homesites in the Las Vegas area alongside the new railroad (Gottdiener 1994a). Huge fortunes were made as these enterprises worked successfully in tandem, attracting large numbers of people to settlements in sparsely populated areas of the western United States.

On May 15, 1905, Clark's townsite officially became the city of Las Vegas. The dusty main drag was named "Fremont Street" after the famous "pathfinder," explorer John C. Fremont, who popularized the area, not Antonio Armijo, the Spanish trader whose party first discovered it. Clark's railroad auctioned off 1,200 town lots plotted by the company, many to wealthy businessmen from Los Angeles who were active at the auction. Corner lots in the town went for $150 to $750 and inside lots for $100 to $500, both considerable sums at the time (Paher 1971). The early town was nothing more than a tent city, a dusty desert depot housing trading companies and the railroad office, but in 1909 Las Vegas became the county seat, giving the site an important government connection. The state legislature named the new county after Clark.

Las Vegas grew slowly during its first decades, with warehousing and distribution as its main economic functions. Gambling was legal at first, as it was in many towns throughout the West. But the state of Nevada, under intense pressure from reformers, passed a stringent anti-gambling law in 1910. All forms of gambling became illegal, even including the western custom of flipping a coin to see who paid for drinks. Despite the law, however, illegal gambling continued to flourish in the city until new legislation in 1931 made it legal once again.

During this time Las Vegas had become a major provisioning site for traders and merchants traveling to and from California and a transshipment depot for mining operation supplies. A new railroad spur served the mining towns of Tonopah, Rhyolite and Bullfrog and converged with Clark's San Pedro, Los Angeles and Salt Lake line at Fremont Street. The area around the depot also became the city's downtown.

In 1905 Charles P. "Pop" Squires built a tent hotel at the intersection of Main and Stewart streets to house the visitors who came for the auctions. Two other crude hotels followed, the Overland Hotel (presently the site of the Las Vegas Club) and Hotel Nevada (presently the site of the Golden Gate), both located across from the railroad depot. Plentiful artesian wells in the area attracted real-estate speculators, who began to develop the surrounding land for homesteads. City leaders interested in promoting growth adopted a commission style of government, one of the Progressive reforms that would foster an image of Las Vegas as a "good government" city. At the same time, the reality of a wide open, free-wheeling town was already well established, contradicting the prim image of Progressivism. As one observer noted:

> Since 1905, the town's boisterous clubs had played host to thousands of railroad passengers on train layovers. By railroad order, the sale of intoxicating liquors was limited to Blocks 16 and 17, a zone conveniently located on Fremont Street near the railroad station. Within a few years of the town's founding, the area had evolved into a red-light district as well.   (Moehring 1989: 11)

Later, in 1942, Block 16 prostitution was eliminated by the city at the request of the War Department because a military base had been established in the area. The city accomplished this first by raids and then by refusing to approve new business and liquor licenses for the bars, that often doubled as brothels.

## Boom and Bust

The cities of the southwest grew in a manner that contrasts with those on the East Coast or in the Midwest. Created with little population and a limited infrastructure, they had to attract people and resources in order to grow. Great risks have always been part of the equation in southwest development as most business initiatives were of the speculative kind. If they worked, fortunes could be made. If they failed, however, they added to the stock of abandoned dreams that still dot the landscape throughout the arid regions in the southwest.

Las Vegas' development has been typical of this boom and bust cycle. In the early 1900s a boom period came with the discovery of gold nearby, and speculators like William Clark cashed in on real estate and railroad development. By 1919, however, mining activity in the region declined and Las Vegas languished as a lonely way station in the desert.

## The Paradigm Shift in Urban Sociology

Urban sociologists have traditionally analyzed the process of city development by using East Coast or Midwestern cities as examples. In

**Figure 1.1**   The Las Vegas Valley, 1997

the 1930s, scholars at the University of Chicago formulated the "ecological" approach to urban development, based almost exclusively on
the Chicago experience. They saw growth not as the product of powerful actors who influence the flow of investment, but as the aggregate
outcome of many individual decisions by people seeking a variety of
goals, such as making money or raising families. The limits of the ecological perspective, however, are numerous and well known, including its failure to mention the role of government in channeling
resources, the obvious effect of a select group of powerful business-
people in determining important land-use decisions and in influencing the flow of investment, and the conflict between residents
struggling to achieve a satisfactory quality of life and local business or
governmental interests (see Gottdiener 1994b).

A second explanatory model for development is the "growth-
machine" approach, associated with the work of John Logan and
Harvey Molotch (1988). This theory argues that in every city a particular, unified elite of business and political interests controls resources
and defines development patterns. Molotch and Logan claim that a
particular "class" of rentiers lies at the heart of this unified elite and
devotes itself to earning profits solely from real estate. Other business-
people and local politicians support the activities of the rentier class
because they too experience an increase in wealth or power from

growth. Local newspapers and hospitals, along with city merchants, for example, thrive on population growth, as do construction companies. Even city servants, such as the police or teachers, find their ability to raise wages enhanced by the activities of rentiers who expand the real-estate sector and attract more permanent residents.

The growth machine perspective is deficient, however, in explaining the way metropolitan regions develop in the US. First, there has never been a separate group of rentiers devoted exclusively to real-estate investment and who constitute a distinct class in America. More accurately, the existence of a free market in real estate is a prime source of profit for any business interest and large numbers of people from diverse backgrounds invest in it in different ways. Homeowners, for example, invest in real estate as part of the purchase of a home, yet do not belong to a special class. Also, they often oppose unbridled growth because it threatens their lifestyle even while enhancing property values. Hence they are often split over questions of growth and sometimes take to task politicians who give blanket approval to development.

Secondly, while some business interests, such as newspapers and retailers, seek population growth as a way to increase their profits, other equally powerful capitalist interests, such as the owners of factories or global corporations, do not depend on local growth for profits and therefore have no incentive to support a local conspiracy of growth-machine elites. Yet the actions of these powerful economic actors often determine the fate of the local community. This has been the case especially in the 1980s and 1990s as global corporations have remolded the economic terrain of advanced countries like the US according to their own needs. The growth-machine approach is at bottom a rather simplistic view of elite control, as there are, in fact, several factions of capital that pursue profits in any given area. At times these interests may join together and concur in making decisions, but at other times they compete openly and are at odds concerning growth plans.

Finally, while development and the quality of life are correlated at initial stages of growth, these two dimensions ultimately diverge as the environmental costs of population expansion drag down the quality of life through such nuisances as increased traffic and pollution or the disappearance of open space. Thus, there are community interests that may support growth but also equally powerful social groups that oppose growth or seek to manage it to protect the quality of life. In short, both the business community and the public are made up of many factions that often compete over development decisions. Fragmentation is fluid as coalitions constantly emerge, splinter and regroup in new forms. These diverse interests hardly comprise anything like the seamless growth machine hypothesized by Molotch and Logan.

A third, more recent perspective on urban development is the globalization approach (Chase-Dunn 1985; Sassen 1991). As presented in the urban literature it is basically a catchphrase meant to orient analysis of local areas toward larger economic forces operating at the global level. Although conceptually undertheorized, globalization analysis has made a contribution to urban research by identifying the *transnational corporation* (TNC) as the principal actor in the circulation of capital across the globe. According to the globalization thesis, the TNCs dominate economic activity today and search out the best locations around the world for cheap labor to produce their products. For this reason local areas and individual industries must go about their business with one eye peeled to the world-system level as the future prosperity of any given place is now tied to the way that area fits into the structure of global business.

The main problem with the globalization approach is that it ignores history and the political economy of capitalism (Gottdiener and Komninos 1987). Investment on an international scale has been occurring for centuries. While it is certainly true that many cities in advanced societies have lost their major industries since the 1970s, the reasons for this decline are quite complex and have more to do with the crisis tendencies of late capitalist societies (Mandel 1977) than with the actions of transnational corporations alone (see Harvey 1989). Although the local economies of many important cities are increasingly tied to financial and producer services, this trend alone cannot explain the major forms of urban restructuring since World War II. The most significant trends have been the massive shift to the suburbs of both people and economic activity, on the one hand, and the massive shift of both people and economic activity to the Sunbelt area of the United States on the other, and globalization does not deal with either of these important recent trends (Gottdiener 1994b).

A final perspective, derived from the work of Henri Lefebvre (1991b), is called the *socio-spatial approach* (see Gottdiener and Feagin 1988; Gottdiener 1994a, b; Feagin 1998). This analytical perspective views local areas as comprised of various, often competing, growth networks rather than a single coalition, even though all urban areas in the United States remain dominated by business interests. Each network of business leaders and politicians is seen as having its own particular interest in promoting growth. Entrepreneurs have the difficult task of trying to valorize both their location and their businesses to attract capital and people.

Elites usually do run towns, but their interests do not necessarily

conform to the particular needs of a separate class of real-estate speculators. More accurately, the elite is by definition composed of the
most successful business interests – at the time. As investment opportunities change, so too does the ruling coalition of elites. Thus, in the
course of development a city can experience leadership from a succession of elites, each of which rides a particular wave of prosperity
only to decline later in the typical cycle of boom and bust, being
replaced by a competing group with a new vision.

Although real-estate interests are, indeed, central to the growth of
regions, the more general case of city development is explained best
by conceptualizing investment activity in the built environment as a
combination of actors and structural conduits known as the "second
circuit of capital" (Lefebvre 1991b). Real estate is seen not as the exclusive domain of a separate rentier class, but as consisting of a structure
of banks, other financial conduits and diverse modes of agency, such
as business interests, real-estate agents, and public and private
investors, including homeowners, who channel money into the built
environment. Thus, despite changes in the economy, investment in
land is always a way of acquiring wealth under capitalism and the
economy is comprised, in part, of different real-estate factions that at
times compete and at other times cooperate with each other for this
opportunity. This flow of capital is not dependent on the conspirator-
ial activities of a separate class, as the growth-machine perspective
argues, nor is it controlled solely by the transnational corporations
and investment patterns emphasized by the globalization perspective.
Rather, the ebb and flow of investment involves the actions of various
growth networks existing at different spatial scales, some local, some
national, some global, that are often in competition with each other.
Unlike the ecological and globalization perspectives, and in a more
theoretically sophisticated way than the growth-machine approach,
socio-spatial theory is used in this book to describe urban growth in
Las Vegas as a complex, shifting process of conflicting interests
devoted to the accumulation of capital and the protection of the
quality of community life.

Understanding the growth of cities requires an appreciation for the
dynamics of the real-estate market, competing economic interests
within each locality, the role of local government and of community
groups, and the relation of the local area to the larger political
economy of the nation and the globe. In particular, the socio-spatial
perspective suggests that metropolitan development is highly dependent on incentives that are created by the various forms of government policy, in addition to the actions of individual private
entrepreneurs. In fact, business people and public officials often work

closely to promote growth schemes. Thus, urban development is as much a product of state intervention as it is of the activities of a select group of capitalists who invest in land.

In the early period of Las Vegas' development, a succession of elites ruled the town beginning with early Mormon settlers, business owners providing provisions for prospectors, and eventually railroad moguls and real-estate speculators like William Clark. Despite their efforts, however, early Las Vegas' growth was equally dependent on external factors, such as the need for cost-effective travel across the desert to California and the discovery of gold deposits in the area. During the 1920s, however, neither these factors nor the best efforts of the business elite could budge Las Vegas from its post-gold-fever downturn and depression doldrums. Without outside help, the town would not have grown in the Depression years.

## The Federal Trigger

By all historical accounts, Las Vegas would have remained a backwater town if not for the intervention of the federal government. Thus, as the socio-spatial perspective asserts, it was the link to the larger system of political economy that provided the necessary valorization of the Las Vegas location for future expansion, despite the best efforts of local elites and growth boosters. As historian Eugene Moehring suggests, this government intervention was not much different from the spending which also aided the development of other Sunbelt cities:

> Las Vegas' triumph as a world resort was never assured. Virtually no one in the 1920s would have expected the town to blossom into the metropolis that it is today. Lack of water, fertile land, productive mines, and heavy industry made it an unlikely candidate. But the same forces which forged the new west and lured millions of people to the sunbelt, also expanded Las Vegas. Reclamation projects, New Deal programs, defense spending, air conditioning, interstate highways, jet travel, right-to-work laws, low taxes – all of the factors that promoted Atlanta, Houston, Phoenix, Los Angeles, and other sunbelt cities – helped Las Vegas, too. (1989: 13)

In 1928, Congress passed the Boulder Canyon Act, which authorized spending to construct the world's largest dam on the Colorado River at a site just southeast of Las Vegas. The Boulder (later renamed Hoover) Dam project eventually pumped millions of federal dollars into the area at a time when the rest of the nation was suffering in the grip of the Depression. Jobs were advertised nationally, attracting a large influx of people. At the peak of construction, 5,128 laborers were employed at the building site, nearly doubling the Clark County population. In addition, the dam "immediately multiplied Las Vegas' economic assets, awarding the town a substantial water, power, and construction hinterland to the southeast" (Moehring 1989: 14).

Federal dam construction was thus a powerful financial stimulus that counteracted economic depression in the region. The decision to build the dam near Las Vegas was not secured by the local elite, although they had helped lobby the government for the project. Instead it was largely due to the efforts of Nevada's two Senators, Republican Tasker Oddie and Democrat Key Pittman. The federal government supported the region with a payroll of half a million dollars a month, but bypassed Las Vegas proper to construct its own town, Boulder City, adjacent to the construction site to house the workforce of more than 5,000 people. Boulder City was a company town controlled by the federally sponsored construction firm that was building the dam. Strict regulation of the workers, including restrictions against the sale of alcohol as well as union activities, ensured a trouble-free labor force, as did the site's distance from Las Vegas. Because so many laborers were unemployed during the Depression, the company had its pick from a large pool of eager workers who migrated to the construction site.

Although the dam workers were housed twenty miles away, Las Vegas merchants benefited enormously from the project. Downtown warehouses and railroad shipment facilities expanded and, even more significantly, the dam construction site became a major tourist attraction:

> Almost 100,000 came during the first full year of construction in 1932 while double that amount visited Las Vegas. In 1933, the dam drew 132,000 and Las Vegas 230,000. Recognizing the magnetic value of the new "world wonder," the latter's chamber of commerce began to bill Las Vegas as "the gateway to the Hoover Dam."   (Moehring 1989: 18)

By the late 1930s more than a quarter of a million tourists a year visited Las Vegas, a city with only 8,000 residents in 1940, spurring the growth of a nascent hotel and casino industry. Thousands of people arrived each year looking for work at the dam construction site and many remained in Las Vegas. In addition, a significant number of homeless persons also emerged from the population of Depression-weary work seekers. Eventually this problem was addressed by the federal government, which provided funds and relief supplies to the city. Local growth also attracted investors, many of whom took their chances building housing and dabbling in real estate: "In 1930 developers built over $1.2 million worth of new structures. . . . Many were small houses whose rooms could be easily partitioned off to form apartments" (Moehring 1989: 19). The Union Pacific Railroad also invested capital in its Las Vegas yards. This created new construction jobs and a larger handling capacity for the tons of supplies now passing through the city, further stimulating the expansion of the warehousing sector and other businesses in the region.

Gamblers and local business interests successfully petitioned the state legislature to re-legalize gambling in 1931 as purely a business proposition: "The legislature's action did not reflect panic at the depression, frustration at continuing illegal activity, or a desire to collect revenue. Rather, gaming became legal again due to a concerted effort by a business community that saw the economic potential of gambling and the tourism that would come with it" (Green and Elliott 1997: 167). Although tourism was a burgeoning industry due to the dam site, gambling activity was not considered at the time to be a principal Las Vegas attraction, as Moehring observes:

> City fathers did not foresee gaming as the town's economic savior – even the location of gaming clubs was limited. The municipality passed a redlining ordinance confining the industry to Fremont Street between First and Third Streets. Subsequent years saw the district expanded to Fifth Street and beyond, but (except for the Moulin Rouge in 1955) town authorities were careful to prevent casino activity from spilling over into residential neighborhoods. (1989: 20)

These restrictions probably had a lot to do with the fact that the majority of the town's 5,000 residents lived within a few blocks.

During the 1930s, then, a boom period returned to Las Vegas due primarily to federal government spending. After 1933, the presence of two influential Democratic senators, Key Pittman and Pat McCarran, helped Nevada get more New Deal money thanks to their strong support of President Roosevelt (FDR). The city possessed a diverse service sector that included retailing and transshipment of construction supplies, marketing, tourist services, and hotels. The federal government channeled millions into the area for dam construction, also constructing a post office and War Memorial Building in downtown Las Vegas. The municipal government responded by launching an ambitious infrastructure improvement scheme that included urban-style sanitation, a zoning ordinance, and the building of schools and sewers. In short, the town grew because of its diverse services built around the influx of federal funds, a growing population of job seekers and tourists, and municipal support for urban services.

After gaming was again legalized, development took off in the 1930s. Speculators built small casinos along the southwest corridor leading to Boulder City, the only Nevada town where gambling remains illegal to this day. The gambling casinos were successful as dam workers and tourists flocked to them. In 1932, downtown Las Vegas' first "luxury" hotel, the three-story Apache, also contained two other firsts, the city's first elevator and a refrigerator. In 1934, the Coca-Cola Company built a bottling plant to service the local tourist industry. In addition to creating jobs, the plant also anchored a growing food service sector that supplied local restaurants and hotels.

During the 1930s, Las Vegas also introduced another innovation, the swamp cooler, which "revolutionized living in the desert town" (Moehring 1989: 22). While swamp coolers in 1938 were "almost unknown in many parts of the nation, every hotel, auto court, restaurant, business establishment and home in Las Vegas was now cooled" (Jones, cited in Moehring 1989: 22). While unattractive and noisy compared with today's powerful air conditioners, swamp coolers made life in the desert bearable for a wider variety of residents.

The principal infrastructural innovation fueling the Las Vegas expansion, however, was the prevalence of cheap and plentiful electricity. While the city could not exist without water, it could not have grown into a tourist mecca without this relatively inexpensive source of power. More than anything else, Las Vegas is a city of lights. The recently opened pyramid-shaped Luxor features a high megawatt searchlight, which shoots up from its apex into the night sky. Airline pilots can see the beam hundreds of miles away and NASA astronauts circling the globe commented that Las Vegas is by far the brightest spot on the Earth. Access to cheap electricity, however, often was a major source of conflict in local politics, particularly during the 1930s.

## A "Good Government" Town

Before the establishment of its image as a tourist mecca, Las Vegas was, and in many ways remains today, an ordinary town. In fact, as gambling expanded during the 1930s, some local residents expressed concern that the town not be burdened with an unsavory reputation. The majority of the population was not connected directly to casino operations, consisting largely of service people and small businessmen who were making a steady income from retailing, warehousing, and the railroad. At the time of the 1931 municipal election, the same year that gambling was re-legalized, the Democrats put forward a candidate who symbolized the good-government/small-business ethos, Ernie Cragin, an insurance broker and long-time resident. The local paper, which was identified with the Democrats and would play a special role in boosting FDR's Depression recovery administration, was a major supporter of Cragin, who ran as an "Honest Businessman." His campaign was based on an appeal for anti-corruption government and decent community values.

Ernie Cragin thus became the first self-proclaimed "reformist and civic-minded" mayor of Las Vegas, in 1931. The concept of reformism here must be understood within the historical context of the times, however. Cragin's predecessor, Fred Hesse, had been arrested and nearly recalled for violating prohibition laws. Thus, opposing corruption was more lip service than reality. Also, Cragin was a well-connected businessman who equated reformism and civic mindedness with a pro-business approach. He did, however, embark on an ambitious program that brought important infrastructure improvements as the city caught up with developers by putting in miles of paved roads, sidewalks, curbs, gutters, and drainage facilities. Cragin also built city parks and even managed to construct a modest municipal golf course. Again, many of these projects were aided by funding from Washington as Nevada's powerful senators, McCarran and Pittman, secured considerable funds from Depression-era programs, especially the Works Progress Administration (WPA).

In the mayoral election of 1935, however, Cragin ran into trouble. Despite improving the basic infrastructure of Las Vegas, he had not been able to work out a satisfactory arrangement with Boulder Dam officials for cheaper electricity rates. His opponent, Leonard Arnett, won by promising to build a power plant and transmission line to service the town of less than 8,000 residents. Local Las Vegas political life didn't run smoothly under Arnett, however, as he failed in his assault on the power company and suffered from poor health, subsequently moving to California to buy a chicken ranch. His successor, John Russell, became so estranged from the city commission that they resigned and a new commission was appointed, after which the original commissioners rescinded their resignations, which Russell in turn refused to accept, leaving two city commissions in operation. Cragin's re-election in 1943 restored order and a pro-business environment. Cragin served two more terms until being defeated by C. D. Baker, a city surveyor and land developer. His close association with Senator McCarran, and the fact that his insurance company insured most major local businesses, hurt Cragin. Thus, while not directly accused of corruption, Cragin, despite his reformist rhetoric, appears to have been one of the good old boys all along.

During the 1930s, Las Vegas established itself as a tourist destination, averaging a remarkable 300,000 visitors annually, despite its small permanent population. Tourism early on was stimulated using the theme of a western, frontier experience, with "Wild West" signifiers deployed in an organized effort to attract visitors to a town with unpaved streets and wooden sidewalks. The town held a "Helldorado" rodeo, complete with a cowboy parade, and constructed a mock Helldorado village that simulated a frontier western town. Casinos borrowed images from cinematic depiction of Old West saloons and Hollywood used Las Vegas in its western films. The Roy Rogers movie "Heldorado," with one "l" removed to make the title suitable for the movie-going public, featured frontier celebrations of the town, and actor Gabby Hayes was the first to call Las Vegas a "booming metropolis" in the movies.

Las Vegas also established a Hollywood connection thanks to Nevada's six-week residency requirement for uncontested divorce. The process was much easier than the extensive wait and bureaucratic hassle required by California and other states. Film celebrities thus began to travel east from Los Angeles to Nevada when their marriages broke up. The most notable case was the divorce by Ria Langham from Clark Gable in 1939 (see chapter 3). Celebrity divorces brought the aura of Hollywood glamor to Las Vegas, rivaling the town's frontier image and becoming critically important in later development of the region.

## Saved by the War

By the late 1930s the United States had still not fully recovered from the Depression. Despite the influx of tourists, the Las Vegas economy was in recession, and business prospects remained bleak. When the United States entered World War II, however, government spending changed the fortunes of Las Vegas forever, as it did other areas of the Sunbelt. Because of its desert location and excellent year-round flying weather, the Army Air Corps decided to locate a major gunnery school and air force training base in the area. The Las Vegas Army Air Corps Gunnery School was established eight miles north of downtown Las Vegas in the early war years, costing more than $25 million to construct. It's successor was reopened by the Department of Defense in 1949 and renamed Nellis Air Force Base. The base remains a major national training facility to this day, with more than 3 million acres of ground space and more than 5 million acres of air space, the largest of its kind in the world.

As federal coffers overflowed with funds to support the war effort, Nevada's senators, especially Pat McCarran, were cashing their chips with the Roosevelt administration in return for their many years of support. One pet project to establish a magnesium plant was in doubt, however. Magnesium was an essential ingredient in armaments, used for tracer bullets, bombs, flares, and airplane components, and California had the manufacturing labor force, as well as excess plant capacity to accommodate a magnesium-production sector. However, the largest manganese deposit was in Gabbs Valley, in Nye County, Nevada, and after intensive lobbying by the Nevada congressional delegation, the Roosevelt administration sanctioned the establishment of a new facility, the Basic Magnesium (BMI) plant, southeast of Las Vegas. The factory eventually employed more than 10,000 people and spawned a new town, Henderson. During the war, the plant employed approximately 10 percent of the entire Nevada population (Moehring 1989: 35). The air force base and the magnesium plant thus combined to produce a mini-population boom for Las Vegas, as the flood of federal funds boosted the sagging economy. In short, World War II was an economic blessing to Las Vegas, and the Clark County population tripled during the war years from 16,000 to more than 48,000.

During the war, with so much money and active housing development in the region, Las Vegas developed a close relationship with the rapidly growing adjacent state of California. As the latter grew in population and wealth, so did the former. According to Moehring: "As early as 1942, the symbiotic relationship between the two 'martial cities' was evident. Las Vegas provided the electricity and magnesium to feed southern California's aerospace and munitions factories, while Los Angeles provided the defense workers and troops who thronged Las Vegas' casinos throughout the war" (1989: 36).

This symbiotic relationship persists to the present, as the Las Vegas economy is fundamentally dependent on the many people who travel regularly from southern California to gamble. As we shall discuss in chapter 4, despite California's recessionary economy in the 1980s and 1990s, people and money still flow regularly to Las Vegas, helping the area prosper.

## African-Americans come to Las Vegas

Though named by Spanish explorers, Las Vegas remained a city dominated by Anglos. During the construction of Boulder Dam, the federal government and the Six Companies reflected racist attitudes of the time, as few black workers were hired on the project. While the peak workforce on the dam was 5,251 in July 1934, only 11 were African-Americans (Fitzgerald 1997). While blacks and other minorities lived in Las Vegas from early on, World War II increased the number of minorities, with the establishment of the federally funded magnesium-production industry in Henderson. During the war the plant was plagued by persistent labor shortages, so management recruited a large number of African-Americans from the South, principally from Arkansas, Louisiana, and Mississippi.

The influx of black people was accommodated by segregated housing facilities. The Carver Park housing project was built with provisions for single and family apartments and amenities such as a park and grammar school, all separated from the white part of Henderson by Boulder Highway. This segregation of housing facilities set the tone for the future treatment of imported black workers. In Las Vegas, African-Americans settled in the blocks just to the north and west of downtown, which became known as the Westside. Segregation, both formal and informal, continued to be the norm until the early 1970s.

## From Town to City: The Role of Venture Capital and Real Estate

In the period following World War II, Las Vegas' population increased dramatically, tripling in the 1940s and again in the 1950s, remarkable for an isolated desert outpost. While the growth spurts of the 1930s and early 1940s were the direct result of federal spending, from 1945 to 1960 development also was the consequence of money invested in casino gambling by individual entrepreneurs who realized the vision of Las Vegas as a major tourist destination.

Prior to the 1940s, gambling was widespread throughout the southwest. Ironically, in the 1920s Los Angeles had more gambling activities than Las Vegas. In 1938, however, a reformist mayor, Fletcher Bowron, assumed office in Los Angeles and banned the practice, with ample support from the new State Attorney General, Earl Warren. Efforts to clean up the city resulted in the migration of many big-time gaming interests to Las Vegas, where they flourished.

The shift from frontier town to city after World War II thus was fueled by the attraction of investment capital to its gambling operations. Throughout the United States both small and large fortunes were made by businesses as a result of the war effort and the billions spent by the federal government. With plentiful surplus capital, venture capitalists, undaunted by potential risks, sought out opportunities to make even more money in peacetime and some in the West saw Las Vegas as a good place to put their new-found fortunes to work.

One of the earliest visionaries was also the first to introduce the idea of the "resort hotel" to Las Vegas. Thomas Hull became wealthy in California by constructing Spanish-style resort hotels that featured large pools and recreational facilities in a sprawling, garden setting. In 1941 he built the El Rancho Vegas in the same style. Wayne McAllister, a Los Angeles architect, was hired by Hull to design the stucco and shingle resort "with 50 rooms wrapped around a court and a pool area" (Gapp 1992: 36). According to architectural critic Alan Hess, McAllister and other Los Angeles architects, such as Douglas Honnold and Martin Stern, Jr, invented the "Googie Style" of urban strip architecture (Gapp 1992: 36). First used in coffee shops, such as Ships, the style stressed parabolic shapes and long, angular roofs. According to Hess: "Coffee Shop Modern was also at least obliquely connected to the work of Miami Beach kitschmeister Morris Lapidus, whose Fontainbleu, Eden Roc, and Americana Hotels spoke of unbridled luxury and self indulgence" (Gapp 1992: 36). McAllister later designed the Flamingo for mobster Bugsy Siegel.

Hull also is credited with a second innovation. The El Rancho Vegas was deliberately constructed just a few feet south of the city line in order to avoid taxes and government controls. Later others followed his lead, constructing their hotel-casinos outside city limits along the dusty, two-lane highway that led south to California, which is now Las Vegas Boulevard, the famous "Strip." According to Moehring:

> The El Rancho's early success demonstrated the feasibility of combining casino operations with a large resort hotel. Moreover, Hull convinced hotelmen everywhere that the spacious tracts bordering the Los Angeles highway were ideal locations to build the mammoth resorts which eventually made the town famous. (1989: 45)

Yet another innovation of Hull's was hiring singers and comedians to entertain his guests. Thus, the legendary Las Vegas lounge act was born.

Hull, however, was ahead of his time and after suffering financial losses the El Rancho was sold to another investor. Such turnover was a constant feature in early Las Vegas real-estate dealings, where an uncertain terrain of shifting fortunes, bankruptcy, buyouts, and changing ownership lay behind the façade of the world famous hotels. Typically, however, yet another venture capitalist would purchase the existing building, avoiding the headaches of new construction and trying his or her luck at running a casino-resort. If s/he went bust, someone else would step in. In this way, the fortunes of real-estate venture capital were very much like those of the ordinary gambler. Investors were attracted by the dream of riches, they gambled and some lost, while still others were waiting to take their places.

Entrepreneur R. E. Griffith made a fortune during the war as a theater operator. He visited Las Vegas in the early 1940s and became convinced of the city's growth potential. With his nephew he built a casino-resort on a parcel of land further south on the Los Angeles highway outside the city boundary. They chose a Western motif and designed a huge building with elaborate interior furnishings. Their Last Frontier resort, with a large bar and restaurant, epitomized the grand Western, cowboy style of the old southwest and became an overnight success:

> The decor was deliberately extravagant awarding the resort instant notoriety. The main building contained a trophy room lined with large stuffed animals. . . . The Horn Room and Gay Nineties Bar were illuminated by lighting fixtures shaped in the form of wagon wheels suspended by chains hanging from the ceiling. The main banquet facility, the Ramona Room, seated 600 guests and was supported by expensive flagstones and large wooden beams. . . . In the guest rooms cow horns adorned every bed. . . . the hotel provided guests with horseback and stage coach rides, pack trips, a showroom seating 600 and parking for 400 cars.    (Moehring 1989:46)

The developers also built a mock frontier village next to the resort, complete with hundreds of Western artifacts. This feature attracted many tourists and was the first "themed resort" in Las Vegas.

The Frontier was eventually sold to other investors although, unlike the El Rancho, this turnover took a full nine years because of the Frontier's healthy profit margin. Following a series of owners, the hotel-casino complex was eventually torn down and replaced by a much larger building in 1965. A few years later, Howard Hughes purchased the property during his Las Vegas buying spree.

While these pioneering resort-casino complexes changed the face of Las Vegas, a third entrepreneur added another element to the regional growth miracle. Benjamin "Bugsy" Siegel, a mobster associated with the East Coast mafia, became obsessed with building a world-class resort, though the idea for the Flamingo came from Billy Wilkerson, publisher of the *Hollywood Reporter*, who himself lacked access to funding and supplies during the war. Siegel's significance for Las Vegas lay not only in his mob connections, the source of funding for the Flamingo's construction, but also in his close links with the Hollywood community. Las Vegas had already achieved some notoriety as a place offering quickie divorces to celebrities, but Siegel recruited Hollywood stars as a glamorous attraction. His vision of a lavish resort complex, unparalleled in Las Vegas, was realized when the Flamingo opened, after several delays, in December 1946. The resort had more than 100 rooms appointed with luxurious details, including marble bathrooms with expensive fixtures. Excessive construction cost overruns led to Siegel's murder by mob bosses, who reopened the Flamingo, after a brief period of closure, in March 1947. Moehring sums up Siegel's contribution to Las Vegas:

> While elegant in a western sense, the El Rancho and Last Frontier were little more than opulent dude ranches. The crucial event, which transformed Las Vegas from a recreational to a full-fledged resort city, was Bugsy Siegel's Flamingo Hotel. In a sense, the Flamingo was the turning point because it combined the sophisticated ambiance of a Monte Carlo casino with the exotic luxury of a Miami Beach–Caribbean resort. The Flamingo liberated Las Vegas from the confines of its western heritage and established the pattern for a "diversity of images" embodied in future resorts like the Desert Inn, Thunderbird, Dunes, Tropicana, and Stardust.  (1989: 49)

In short, by attracting movie star glamor to the desert, Siegel merged earlier Las Vegas venture visions with those of Hollywood fantasies.

Soon thereafter a fourth hotel, the Thunderbird, opened in 1948 on what was to be the Strip, with Siegel's old friend Meyer Lansky as the hidden owner. By then, distinctive symbols and themes were beginning to define individual casinos as hotel owners vied with one another to provide unique thematic or symbolic environments to attract tourist dollars. For example, the Thunderbird resort-casino featured a Native-American theme. The thunderbird is an ancient Navajo symbol and the hotel's Navajo-style decor included the "Wigwam" and "Navajo" rooms that functioned as restaurants.

During the postwar period a second prominent aspect of Las Vegas' development also emerged. Hotel openings on the Strip were viewed with alarm by the city's established gaming interests so they struck back with development schemes of their own to maintain the downtown Glitter Gulch's status as the focal point of tourism and gambling. In 1945, the Golden Nugget casino opened, and three years later sported the largest neon sign in Las Vegas, one that could easily be seen from the Los Angeles highway, establishing a pattern of competition between downtown and the Strip that continues to be a factor in Las Vegas' development. Also, in contrast to the monolithic view of development hypothesized by the "growth machine" perspective, Las Vegas provides a clear example of growth factions and the way real-

estate investors compete with each other for profits using the properties of location and differences in state regulation.

## Venture Capital and the 1950s Growth Spurt

Development in Las Vegas prior to the 1950s was largely a result of
extensive federal spending, first on the dam and then on the war
effort, a pattern typical of other Sunbelt cities as well. As a tourist
town, however, Las Vegas also has experienced a unique version of
the boom and bust cycles afflicting real-estate investment across the
nation. During certain years, such as the late 1940s, things were relatively quiet and only a few casino projects were announced. Then, as
if by magic, the area was inundated with real-estate investments.

The socio-spatial perspective argues that the explanation for these
cycles lies in the workings of a national economy that is split between
a sector for investments in industry and a "second circuit of capital"
that channels investor money into real estate (Lefebvre 1974). While
the industrial sector historically has been the main circuit for the accumulation of wealth in the United States, real estate has always been an
alternative way of acquiring wealth owing to the free market in land.
According to Lefebvre, both the primary and the secondary circuit go
through periods of capital investment expansion and contraction,
although the two circuits follow different cycles. Thus, at times, when
the opportunities for profits in the industrial sector are attractive,
capital will be siphoned through banks and other financial conduits to
that sector and real-estate investment will suffer, leading to a slowdown in development. In contrast, when the primary sector experiences recession and opportunities for profits from investment dry up
in industry, capital switches to investment in real estate as a means of
making money. During this period, housing, hotel, resort, mall, and
recreational businesses experience a rapid influx of new capital,
funding expansion in these areas.

Focusing on the second circuit of capital in real estate and its related
cycles in the primary circuit of industrial growth is critical to understanding the case of Las Vegas. While the area has some manufacturing, largely derived from federal spending in the 1940s, the
overwhelming source of profits has come from investments in real
estate, more specifically, from the construction and operation of casino
resorts.

Since the 1940s, the two most outstanding periods of investment in,
and construction of, casinos took place in the 1950s and again in the
current period, from 1988 to the present (1999). In between, more

subdued building periods were seen in the middle 1960s and again in the early 1970s. Each time, huge amounts of money were poured into the construction of massive casino projects and, as the socio-spatial approach suggests, each expansionary phase came as a result of a downturn in primary-circuit investment activity in industry. The 1950s real-estate boom, for example, occurred following the acquisition of huge fortunes during World War II, but at a time of recession when the high pitch of wartime industrial production was winding down. Similarly, during the famous recession under the Eisenhower Administration in the late 1950s, casino construction in Las Vegas also increased dramatically.

Later expansion in the desert community was also dependent upon another crucial factor, finding a way to deliver water allocated from the Colorado River to the valley, as ground water was becoming seriously depleted. To resolve the water delivery issue, McCarran's protégé, Senator Alan Bible, along with Senator Howard Cannon, secured an $81-million public works project from President Lyndon Johnson. The Southern Nevada Water Project provided construction, maintenance, and operation of a water delivery system that included six pumping plants, a regulatory reservoir, a four-mile tunnel, and more than thirty miles of pipeline to valley users. According to one observer: "The Southern Nevada Water Project was the key factor in triggering the growth and development of the Las Vegas Valley in the 1970s and beyond" (Elliott 1997: 166).

Once the infrastructure was in place to provide the necessary water for additional growth, the present casino-resort expansion period began. This was also helped by an unprecedented increase in wealth resulting from the deregulation of banking and industry during the Reagan years. In both cases government policies were at least indirectly responsible for the enormous profits generated, but large sums of money also were made in real terms due to industrial and commercial expansion. With each cycle of expansion in the primary circuit, however, diminishing returns to capital created crisis conditions for subsequent investment there, stimulating capital flows to the second circuit of real estate, which promised higher returns. In all these cases, then, the cyclical flow of immense sums of money into real-estate speculation spawned spectacular periods of growth in Las Vegas.

From the late 1940s into the 1950s Las Vegas' four major Strip casino-resorts, the El Rancho, the Last Frontier, the Flamingo, and the Thunderbird, prospered as Californian tourists came for quick and relatively inexpensive vacations. According to John Findlay: "Upward mobility teamed with rising affluence, southern California's car culture, and new patterns of leisure to boost Nevada tourism in the decades following World War II" (Findlay 1990: 13). But money flowing into the region found the downtown area impractical for further investment because the market demanded resort-casinos, not old-fashioned gambling joints. The more established downtown casinos made more money on gambling than the four resorts outside the city limits, but the Strip region south of Las Vegas contained large expanses of undeveloped desert land not owned by the federal government, necessary for golf courses, swimming pools, riding trails and tennis courts. The newer planned developments thus could offer comparative luxury, upscale accommodations and active leisure pursuits in addition to twenty-four-hour gambling.

The 1950s thus saw extensive real-estate development along the Strip. In 1950, the Desert Inn was constructed on Las Vegas Boulevard near the Frontier. Famous at the time for having the largest golf course in Las Vegas, the Desert Inn hotel-casino was built in the Miami Beach/Havana pastel style. Fronted by Wilbur Clark, part-owner of the El Rancho, with investors from the Cleveland underworld (Moe Dalitz, Sam Tucker, and Morris Kleinman) actually in charge, it was an upscale resort with an image of luxury and glamor. The "DI" attracted some of the most visible personalities of the time.

Four more world-class resort-casinos opened between 1955 and 1958. The Riviera opened in April and the Dunes in May, 1955. A year later the Hacienda hotel-casino anchored the southernmost end of the Strip and the high-rise Fremont Hotel opened downtown, while the following year the Tropicana opened as a deluxe resort with a tropical/Caribbean motif, rivaling the Flamingo as *the* luxury Las Vegas resort. The 1950s resort-building boom came to an end in 1958 when the Stardust hotel-casino opened as "the largest hotel in the world" with more than 1,000 rooms.

Collectively, these resorts boasted several firsts. The nine-story Riviera was the first high-rise hotel on the Strip, in marked contrast to the low-rise motel or bungalow style of other establishments (Moehring 1989). It also had a decidedly European flair. The Dunes, with an Ali Baba/Arabian Nights theme, lost money during its first years of operation but added a burlesque review, the "Minsky's Follies" strip-tease dance show, the first of its kind in Las Vegas, and immediately turned a profit. The Hacienda was the first casino-hotel to cater specifically to a family crowd, with several swimming pools and a go-cart track. The Stardust was not only the largest hotel in the world, but also replaced the downtown Golden Nugget as the casino with the largest neon sign, containing "over 6 miles of wiring, 7,100 feet of neon tubing and 11,000 lamps. On a clear night it served as a great beacon for approaching cars sixty or more miles out on the dark desert roads" (Moehring 1989: 83).

The Stardust also distinguished itself from other resorts by introducing the first spectacular stage show, the "Lido de Paris" production, imported from Paris, and featuring topless dancers. "The success of the Lido encouraged other resorts to adopt the production show policy. The Dunes engaged 'Casino de Paris' and the Tropicana brought the American rights to the 'Folies Bergères'" (*Review-Journal* 1989: 27AA). The glitz of classy Parisian stage shows, large neon signs, themed environments, and the creation of a resort ambiance thus established the stylistic and competitive differentiation of the Strip from the city's downtown, which retained its traditional Wild West theme and its primary emphasis on casino gambling.

Accessibility to the area was enhanced in the 1950s and 1960s by the development of interstate highways, while government housing programs stimulated suburbanization, making Las Vegas a viable market for the development of single family homes. Though residential home construction was a risky venture in the desert (see chapter 5), home construction flourished in the suburban regions outside the Las Vegas city boundaries in unincorporated townships such as Winchester, Sunrise Manor, and Paradise. By 1970 Clark County boasted a population of 273,288, sufficient to be classified as a Standard Metropolitan Statistical Area by the Census Bureau and making Las Vegas, along with Phoenix, Tucson, and San Antonio, a prime example of rapid Sunbelt city growth.

In the mid-1960s, another mini-boom in Las Vegas' casino construction took place. Jay Sarno, the owner of Circus Circus, a successful family-oriented casino, opened Caesars Palace in 1965. Sarno's massive property featured a Romanesque theme complete with faux-marble statues. Four years later Sarno sold it for $60 million, at three times its cost. A year later, in 1966, the Aladdin Hotel opened with an Arabian theme similar to that at the Dunes. Its Baghdad Showroom offered three different theme shows twice a night, featuring "big name" entertainers. Construction of both properties was financed largely by loans from the Teamsters Union's pension funds.

One of the most spectacular players among Las Vegas venture capitalists was Howard Hughes, who began investing in the area in the 1960s. In a short period of time, he purchased the Frontier, the Sands, the Castaways, the Silver Slipper and the Landmark, becoming the largest owner of casino property in the area. Hughes also initiated an influx of global investment funds, financing his purchases with defense-related profits and Hollywood money, a trend that became more prominent in Las Vegas during the 1980s (see chapter 2). Hughes also transformed the nature of Las Vegas casino ownership. Prior to his arrival, many casinos were owned or controlled by the mob and were built with Teamsters Union funds. By supplying his own corporate financing, Hughes introduced "legitimate" corporate control of casinos to Las Vegas, another feature that was to become more significant in the 1980s and 1990s, though not without controversies of its own.

Another prominent Las Vegas investor with Hollywood connections was Kirk Kerkorian, who bought controlling interests in the Flamingo and Bonanza casinos. In 1969, he financed construction of the International Hotel, later renamed the Las Vegas Hilton, which became the world's largest resort. With more than 1,500 rooms, the resort featured a 30,000-square-foot casino. After selling his major properties in the early 1970s, Kerkorian bought MGM studios in Hollywood and then returned to Las Vegas in 1973, bankrolling the construction of a resort-hotel that also became Las Vegas' largest. His 2,100 room "MGM Grand" (now Bally's) was named for the Hollywood film *Grand Hotel*.

An equally important development in Las Vegas was the growth of the city's convention industry. Most large casinos had their own convention facilities, but in 1959 a separate convention center opened east of the Strip on Paradise Road. By 1970 the area hosted 269 conventions annually with 269,000 delegates who spent an estimated $63.6 million, and by 1980, that figure had jumped to 449 conventions with 656,000 delegates and an estimated income of $227 million (Moehring 1989: 122), providing a significant boost to the burgeoning tourism industry (see chapter 4).

## Las Vegas' Growth, Like Every Place Else

Because of the prominence of casino gambling and tourism, Las Vegas' patterns of development are clearly unusual when compared with other cities. In other ways, however, Las Vegas is very much like any other Sunbelt town as the importance to the town of the railroads, government spending, and the World War II shift of national resources to the south and west also were major factors in the growth of other cities in the region. Historically, urban sociologists have utilized the ecological paradigm to explain growth trends (see Hawley 1981), stressing the role of "demand-side" factors such as the desire to locate housing and industry in areas with mild climates, open space, and cheap taxes. Today, however, the ecological approach has been replaced by a new paradigm, the socio-spatial approach (see Gottdiener and Feagin 1988; Gottdiener 1994a; Feagin 1998), which balances the demand-side view with "supply-side" considerations. The latter include the important role of government spending in channeling growth towards specific patterns, the role of real estate as a leading edge of development, and the actions of businesses to locate where labor costs and class conflict are reduced. These and other supply-side factors, such as military spending, government programs, federal highway construction, and the mortgage interest tax deduction for homeowners, clearly were major factors in the development of Las Vegas as well as of other Sunbelt cities.

In 1956, for example, Congress passed the National System of Defense Highways Act, more commonly known as the Interstate Highway Act. Using federal funds and a gasoline tax, this measure was single-handedly responsible for the construction of an immense system of divided and limited-access highways stretching across the United States. Construction of these superhighways also proved to be a gold-mine for real-estate speculators. By carving up the interior of the nation and allowing for high-speed commuting between city centers and surrounding areas, the Interstate Highway Act facilitated the massive movement of people and industry to the suburbs and to the southwest region of the country (see Gottdiener 1994a).

The Interstate Highway Act had an especially profound effect on Las Vegas, as the old Los Angeles highway was replaced by Interstate Highway 15, allowing rapid auto travel between Las Vegas and both Los Angeles and Salt Lake City. Also, speculators and developers moved in to construct moderately priced single family homes, drawing a steady population influx of permanent residents from around the country. During the 1950s, Clark County grew from 48,289 to 127,016 people, and to 273,288 by 1970, a five-fold increase in twenty years. In the late 1960s, more than 1,000 new residents a month moved to Las Vegas, while more than 2.5 million tourists visited each year. Easy access to the region via the interstate highway thus figured prominently in the growth and prosperity of the area.

Another supply-side factor enhancing Las Vegas' growth was military spending. As we saw, the introduction of Nellis Air Force Base to the region during World War II proved to be a major boon to Las Vegas, as did government support of the Basic Magnesium Plant in Henderson. Also, during the 1950s the federal government designated Nevada as the nation's nuclear test-site facility. The federal government knew, or at least acknowledged, far less about the dangers of nuclear testing back then and local boosters welcomed the presence of the Atomic Energy Commission. Its spending provided a significant boost to the area's economy and was seen by locals as a patriotic contribution to national defense and the Cold War at a time when Estes Kefauver's Senate hearings were attacking the city. Some residents even held backyard parties to view the blasts and a local bar was named "The Atomic Cafe."

A third factor common to Las Vegas and other Sunbelt cities is their multi-centered pattern of metropolitan growth. In the past, urban sociologists viewed metropolitan development in terms of population and resources concentrated in large central cities with active and growing suburban rings of low density. Today, one finds a different picture of the patterns of growth, as almost all metropolitan areas are now polynucleated (see Gottdiener 1994a). Both population and economic activities are dispersed throughout the expanding metro region, with many centers, interspersing suburbs, mixes of industry, commercial and retail malls, public facilities, airports, and an expanding network of highways and roads.

As in so many other ways, Las Vegas was a trendsetter in this regard, as the region began to decentralize and regroup as a multi-centered area early in its history. The magnesium plant built during World War II helped found the city of Henderson and earlier construction of the Hoover Dam was responsible for the establishment of Boulder City, both southeast of Las Vegas. Even earlier, in 1917, North Las Vegas began as a residential subdivision, with bootleggers using the area's artesian wells in the 1920s and lower-income workers settling there in the 1930s.

Perhaps the most significant event, however, was the failure of Las Vegas to annex Strip resort development. The boundary between the city and Clark County was fixed at what is now Sahara Boulevard, so entrepreneurs like Tommy Hull and Bugsy Siegel avoided city taxes by developing resort-casinos on the Strip south of the city line. The early success of Strip hotels prompted the city in 1946 to attempt an annexation of the area but in a referendum this was opposed by 90 percent of Clark County's voters. Strip casino owners resisted all attempts at consolidation to maintain the lowest possible taxes and a minimal municipal burden, as there was no incentive to join the city once it was discovered that a Strip location, the first stop for California travelers, had no dampening effect on tourist dollars. Eventually the Strip casinos formed their own unincorporated area, Paradise Township, legally establishing by the 1960s a pattern of multi-centered growth.

## State Politics and Change in the 1960s

Our discussion of regional development so far has neglected to high-light the role played by local political interests in expansion. In addition to technological innovations in transportation and communication, the role of real-estate development, changes in the national economy, and the stimulation of federal government pro-grams, the activities of the local government also are essential for understanding metropolitan development patterns. In the case of Las Vegas in particular, regulation by the state of Nevada has been directly responsible for the special character of its development. This is so because it has explicitly legitimated activities that other areas of the nation considered illegal, such as gambling and prostitution, though the latter is legal only in rural counties. Nevada law also permits easy uncontested divorce and marriage, attracting millions of people over the years, including many Hollywood celebrities. State government, in short, has helped make "sin" profitable for Las Vegas.

In the 1940s and 1950s great concern was expressed at the national level over alleged mob influence in Las Vegas, often placing local and state leaders in conflict with the federal government. In the 1950s, Tennessee Senator Estes Kefauver used his committee investigating organized crime to train a glaring spotlight on mob activities in the region. The powerful influence of the Mormon Church also outwardly added to the pressure to clean up the town, although many Mormons served in high-ranking casino executive positions.

As a result, Nevada's state government was moved to try to chase the mob out of the state. Under the guidance of Governor Grant Sawyer's "hang tough" gaming policy, the groundwork was laid to clean up the industry. In 1959, Sawyer replaced the Tax Commission with a State Gaming Commission to oversee the industry. He appointed commissioners with high profiles in law enforcement, including former FBI agents, and created the List of Excluded Persons, the infamous "Black Book." However, the most far-reaching transfor-mation of the state's principal industry came in 1969 when the Nevada Legislature passed the Corporate Gaming Act. For the first time, publicly traded corporations were permitted to own casinos. As a result, hotel chains such as Hyatt, Hilton, and Ramada in-vested in Las Vegas. The Corporate Gaming Act also prompted local casino operators, such as Sam Boyd, to incorporate and invest in gam-bling enterprises elsewhere. Boyd Gaming is now a national corpora-tion with twelve casinos in five states. Corporate control soon overtook individuals as the principal form of ownership and forever changed the operating environment of Las Vegas, greatly diminishing the free-wheeling influence of the mob and its Wild West predecessors.

Another important feature of local politics mentioned above was the failure of Las Vegas to annex its surrounding suburbs, which resulted in an inefficient fragmentation of political jurisdictions and services. According to Moehring:

> The city's relative failure to expand its borders created a political vacuum, which the suburbs ultimately filled. Instead of one city government for the entire metro area, four cities and one county government have administered police, fire, planning, and other government functions. This political fragmentation, in turn, has led to needless duplication of services and inefficiency. (1989: 140)

In this sense, then, Las Vegas is different from other Sunbelt cities, which grew by annexation and were able to establish metro area governments that could pool scarce resources in support of services. While excessive costs of duplicated services and governmental inefficiency continue to be problematic, steps were taken to make amends and in 1973 the Las Vegas and Clark County Police Departments were merged. The community has since also implemented a Regional Flood Control District and Regional Transportation Commission for public transit. Nevertheless, Las Vegas is still hampered by the redundancies of a large county bureaucracy and four city governments (Henderson, North Las Vegas, Las Vegas, and Boulder City).

Another aspect of urban development in Las Vegas and elsewhere, emphasized by the socio-spatial perspective, is the relationship between phases of growth and the dynamics of change in the national and global political economy. A mid-1990s *TIME Magazine* cover story periodized the phases of Las Vegas' growth differently, however, highlighting the cultural aspects of change. It suggested that the first period came in the 1930s and 1940s when Las Vegas was an "ersatz Old West outpost," becoming a "gangsters-meet-Hollywood high-life oasis in the 50s and 60s," and finally, "an uncool polyester dump in the 70s and 80s" (Anderson 1994: 43). While amusing, this point of view ignores the profound economic growth of the region and the ways transformations in Las Vegas are linked to changes in the national and international economy. Focusing on these crucial factors, the history of Las Vegas can be more adequately periodized in the following fashion:

Phase one, which lasted from 1861, when Nevada became a territory of the United States, to 1931. The local economy was dominated by mining, railroad, and commercial interests from Los Angeles who developed warehousing, as well as the first hotels. Phase two lasted from 1931, when gambling was legalized, to 1954, just before the local economy was transformed by casino gambling. During the Depression, the federal government was the principal actor, providing funds for the construction of Boulder Dam, for manufacturing, and for the creation of an air base during World War II, bringing people and substantial resources to the area. This "federal trigger" (Moehring 1989) made Las Vegas into an urban center in the middle of the arid, dusty desert.

Phase three, between 1954 and 1969, saw the rise to dominance of gambling and casino interests in the region. Mob involvement contributed to Las Vegas' racy image as a town of wheeler-dealers, though it also contributed to the bankruptcy of many casino-resorts. A steady flow of new construction filled in the spaces along the Strip and added to the stock of downtown casinos. Big-name entertainment created a strong association between Las Vegas and show business. Growth was moderate, however, as was the annual increase in tourists.

During phase four, lasting from 1969 to 1987, mob influence on casinos was legally addressed to improve the city's image and Howard Hughes introduced a less unsavory, corporate image to casino ownership. The Nevada state legislature's passage of the Corporate Gaming Act in 1969 allowed public corporations to purchase casinos for the first time, changing the face of Las Vegas forever.

Also during the fourth phase, the annual influx of tourists intent on a gambling vacation reached into the tens of millions and, by 1977, gambling profits in Clark County surpassed $1 billion. Las Vegas enhanced its reputation as the home of celebrity acts as casinos added spectacular floor shows, many of them imported from Europe. The split between downtown and the Strip, however, remained an active conflict zone in southern Nevada politics.

The fifth phase, from the late 1980s to the present (1999), is characterized by the dominance of corporate control and the advent of megaresorts, and is the subject of the next chapter.

# 2 Corporations and the Advent of Megaresorts

## The Fifth Phase of Growth: From the 1980s to the Present

Up until the 1970s, the United States economy was a robust growth engine, with cities like Pittsburgh, Detroit, and Buffalo producing manufactured goods of every conceivable kind. In contrast, Las Vegas, with its emphasis on casino gambling, was an anomaly, a "sin city" among an otherwise honest, hardworking nation of industrial cities. Profound changes transformed the American economy during the 1970s, however, as manufacturing activity declined precipitously and millions of factory workers lost their jobs. By 1980, the manufacturing sector employed fewer workers than the service component of the economy. With the onset of deindustrialization (Bluestone and Harrison 1982; Harvey 1989), major consumer durable goods, such as cars, tires, and appliances, were increasingly produced overseas. Unions lost their clout and many workers were forced to switch from factory jobs that provided a relatively comfortable standard of living to lower-wage, service jobs. Pittsburgh was no longer a steel town, Detroit saw its manufacturing base erode, and the industrial towns of the Northeast and Midwest assumed a new collective name, the Rust Belt.

Large American conglomerates divested themselves of manufacturing concerns that were being decimated by foreign competition. US Steel, for example, became USX, and electronics companies like RCA shifted their production facilities outside the US. Many of these same companies also transferred investments from other sectors of the global economy to casino gambling following passage of Nevada's Corporate Gaming Act. Large hotel chains like Hilton and Ramada purchased casino-hotels in Las Vegas and introduced corporate-style management. At the same time, Nevada casino operators began building gaming resorts outside the state and many became publicly held corporations themselves.

The introduction of corporations significantly changed the face of Las Vegas gaming. Loss leader buffets, inexpensive shows, and under-priced room rates were phased out as a corporate mentality, concerned with bottom-line reports to stockholders, replaced the more personal, informal atmosphere that had characterized Las Vegas' resorts for decades. Suddenly the Las Vegas tradition of "comps" (complimentary tickets) for free rooms, meals and shows were given only to those customers a computer determined would play, or "drop," sufficient dollars at the host casino's machine and table games. One writer summed up this shift as follows:

> Today many of the hotels are owned by squeaky-clean, image obsessed companies like Hilton and Holiday Inn. They are staffed by bean counters and micro-managers who live in the same suburbs and sport the same dress-for-success suits as ... the stockbroker from Iowa. ... The hottest ticket in town is no longer a revue of bare-breasted showgirls, but the Siegfried and Roy magic act starring white tigers.   (Gabriel 1991: 68)

Legalized gambling thus became popular as a means of making money when the large conglomerates developed "leisure" components and transformed the image of casino gambling into vacation entertainment. Legal gambling, including casinos, lotteries, and video games, grew to become a multi-billion-dollar industry. In 1987 alone, Americans wagered $210 billion (Holmstrom 1993). According to one account:

> Consumer experts and academics who follow gambling say its explosive growth has been sparked by three key factors: cash hungry governments turning to gambling to raise revenue, leisure company promotion of gambling as entertainment, and the appeal of new, high tech video gambling. Decades of church-sponsored gambling has also tended to lend approval to games of chance.   (Holmstrom 1993: 8)

Also, as US industry slumped in economic recession, the Reagan Administration de-regulated the banking industry, making it possible for entrepreneurs of all kinds to develop creative investment strategies that previously were prohibited. As the industrial segment of the corporate economy struggled against highly competitive foreign businesses and frantically restructured to deal with the new realities of international investing and manufacturing, finance capitalists made superprofits from speculation. Among the latter were "junk bond" investors such as Michael Milken, who created new financial incentives to attract capital from millions of people shying away from corporate stocks during a period of industrial uncertainty. At the same time, new players entered the Las Vegas scene and established connections with Milken and other junk bond kings.

As the success of casino gambling in Las Vegas contrasted greatly with the declining fortunes of cities based on manufacturing, several areas of the country explored the possibility of legalizing gambling to offset the effects of deindustrialization. In 1976 casino gambling was legalized in Atlantic City, and its first venture, Resorts International, opened in 1978. Also, in 1977, the first year Clark County gaming revenues surpassed the $1-billion mark, the Nevada legislature passed a Foreign Gaming Law, allowing Nevada-based operators to run casinos outside state borders. Several Nevada casino operations, including Caesars, Bally's, the Sands, the Golden Nugget, and Harrah's, rushed to open New Jersey resorts by 1980. This was soon followed by the spread of state lotteries; riverboat gambling was launched, and a decade later, previously isolated Bingo games operated by Native American tribes exploded into a full-fledged gaming industry. For the first time, Las Vegas felt competition from legal gambling sites outside of Nevada.

One Las Vegas casino operator who invested in Atlantic City is notable, not for the scope of his project, but for developing a new form of financing. Perhaps no one better exemplifies the transition from shady Teamsters Union Pension Fund financing of casinos to the world of junk bonds, corporate-stock investments and joint ventures than Mirage Resorts chairman, Steve Wynn. The transition was effected through Wynn's relationship with two financial powerhouses, E. Parry Thomas and Michael Milken. Wynn had inherited part of his father's Bingo operation in Wayson Corner, Maryland, and arrived on the Las Vegas scene in 1967, when he purchased 3 percent of the Frontier Hotel for the deeply discounted price of $45,000. Following that quick and profitable deal, Wynn spent the next few years producing lounge shows and running an unsuccessful liquor distributorship. All the while he benefited from excellent connections provided by his mentor, E. Parry Thomas, through whose Valley Bank had flowed nearly $230 million in Teamsters' Central States Pension Funds, much of it used to finance Las Vegas casinos (J. L. Smith 1995). Thomas brokered Hughes' purchase of the Frontier and used his Hughes connection to help Wynn purchase 1.1 acres of land in a Caesars Palace parking lot for half its value. Like Wynn's Frontier investment, it was financed by borrowed money, a no-interest loan from Thomas, and was quickly sold at a profit, in this case $1 million. In 1973, again aided by Thomas, Wynn became the majority stockholder in the Golden Nugget, a 1940s grind joint with no hotel rooms. With millions in financing provided by Thomas's Valley Bank, an extensive remodeling and expansion of the Golden Nugget was completed in 1977, adding 579 rooms (J. L. Smith 1995).

The Golden Nugget was making money so Wynn wanted to expand to Atlantic City, a move he estimated would cost $120 million. Seeking the necessary financing, Wynn made another fateful contact when he was introduced to Michael Milken, from the Investment Company of Drexel Burnham Lambert, who raised $160 million to build the New Jersey resort. Milken saw casino gaming as a sound business built on mathematical laws: "In the late seventies I'd take money managers and pension fund people into the casinos and show them that it wasn't a gambling business, it was a business that was built on the laws of probability and statistics" (cited in J. L. Smith 1995: 194). While Milken's junk bond house of cards would later lead to the demise of more than fifty savings and loan associations across the nation, it was a major funding factor in the construction of the Golden Nugget in Atlantic City and later the Mirage, Las Vegas' first megaresort.

Thus, when the Golden Nugget opened in Atlantic City in 1980, it represented a major shift in casino financing that also would forever change the face of Las Vegas. The smallest resort in New Jersey, the Nugget made $80 million to $90 million a year and "establishing himself as a presence in Atlantic City with less than $15 million in cash, Wynn was rapidly emerging as the new face of legalized gambling" (J. L. Smith 1995: 114).

In 1986, as Atlantic City casinos were experiencing their first bankruptcies, Wynn sold the profitable Atlantic City casino for $450 million to help finance his dream resort. After transforming the Golden Nugget into the only four-star casino-hotel in downtown Las Vegas, Wynn wanted the brass ring, a luxury resort on the Las Vegas Strip. Although his corporate debt surpassed the billion-dollar mark in the process, Wynn purchased the Strip property for the Mirage from the Hughes Corporation, again turning to Milken to help raise construction financing. Wynn has been quoted as saying, "No Milken, no Mirage," on several occasions, a sentiment shared by a local journalist: "If Jimmy Hoffa's pension fund bankrolled the old Las Vegas, Michael Milken's black magic constructed the new one" (J. L. Smith 1995: 192).

Equally significantly, the nationwide competition for gambling dollars brought on by the proliferation of gaming in Atlantic City, state lotteries, riverboats, and Indian gaming forced Las Vegas' resorts to create more elaborate themed attractions. A Western, Arabian, or Polynesian themed resort was no longer enough. The Mirage, which opened its doors in November 1989, was the first of these new "megaresorts," costing more than $700 million.

As Teamsters Union funds had ceased to be a viable option for casino construction, the Mirage was the first new Strip property to be built in fifteen years, since Kirk Kerkorian's original MGM Grand, now Bally's Las Vegas, opened. The new, junk-bond-financed megaresort was not cheap. The Mirage had to take in $1 million a day just to service its interest payments and cover its operating costs. This was hardly an obstacle, however, as the megaresort reported $50-million monthly revenues, nearly $2 million per day, in its first year of operation. There were no loss leaders at the Mirage or at the other megaresorts that soon followed. Shortly after opening, the resort reported making $25,000 per day in tee-shirt sales alone in its gift shops.

The Mirage's tropical theme was not new in Las Vegas; the Tropicana for years had been called the "Island of Las Vegas," but it lost a lawsuit to prevent the Mirage from copying its motif. The Mirage took the theme to a new level, however. Visitors enter a high-domed lobby and dense tropical rain forest, while the hotel registration desk is backgrounded by a gigantic 53-foot-long tropical fish tank. Featuring more than 3,000 rooms in three 29-story structures, the Mirage charged nightly prices that were higher than most Las Vegas hotels, from $89 to $450, in 1990, although not unprecedented at resorts like Caesars Palace. Outside, the *pièce de résistance* is a 55-foot simulated tropical volcano set amidst a lush forest with waterfalls in a four-acre lagoon. After dusk, every fifteen minutes, the volcano erupts, spewing hot flames and piña-colada-scented gases high into the air. This spectacle of simulation became the first of several such attractions that converted the sidewalks along the Strip casinos into an outdoor sideshow for strolling tourists.

Wynn's flamboyance did not end with the erupting volcano in front of the Mirage. A dolphin enthusiast, he built a $14-million habitat behind the hotel, in the hot Las Vegas desert, to house his "pets." In a move to attract "whales," or high rollers, several cabana suites, each costing $3 million, also were added. The Mirage Villas feature inlaid marble floors, antique furniture, a private pool, and a putting green. Wynn also hired the popular Siegfried and Roy, whose magic show was a long-time Las Vegas institution at the Tropicana, Stardust, and Frontier. The illusionists signed a five-year, $57-million contract to perform in a $20-million showroom specially designed to accommodate their act. Ticket prices more than doubled to $70 per person (now $90), a Las Vegas record at the time. Building upon the popularity of the show, an exotic white tiger habitat was created near the registration desk where hotel visitors and others could observe the big cats sleeping and playing in their customized pool environment when they weren't performing with Siegfried and Roy.

With its 3,094 rooms, 2,251 slot machines, and 119 table games, the Mirage thus provides a spectacular fantasy environment. As Wynn himself pointed out: "What keeps Las Vegas powerful is every few years it becomes more fabulous, more outrageous. ... I'm more of a Disney person than a casino guy" (Gabriel 1991: 68).

Six months after the Mirage opened, the much larger Circus Circus Enterprises castle project, the Excalibur, became Las Vegas' second megaresort. Opening in June 1990, the more than 4,000-room resort property lowered its medieval castle drawbridge over a moat at the intersection of the Strip and Tropicana Boulevard. For three years it would hold the title of world's largest hotel. Excalibur was the magical sword freed by King Arthur in the legend of Camelot and the Knights of the Round Table. The resort's medieval theme is reflected in restaurants with names such as Lance-a-Lotta Pasta and the Robin Hood Snack Bar. Costumed employees, jesters, serving wenches, and jugglers roam the cobblestone foyer, the Royal Village Shopping area, and the Fantasy Faire booths. The showroom features King Arthur's Tournament, a jousting match with mounted knights battling in full armor. The dinner feast is a medieval equivalent of ye olde boxed lunch – *sans* cutlery. The pageantry includes thundering steeds, bloodless hand-to-hand combat, lasers, fiber optics, Andalusian horses, Merlin, Guineviere and King Arthur, as well as good and evil knights. The 117-acre site also features four massive stone turrets and 265-foot-high castle spires topped by red, gold, and blue cones. With a relatively low construction price tag of $290 million for four 28-story hotel towers and medieval castle decor, the Excalibur is judged wondrously tacky by some. Being tacky, however, never stopped anything from being successful in Las Vegas and the resort attracted 11 million visitors in its first year, with a healthy operating-profit margin of 25 to 30 percent.

The opening of the Excalibur launched a room-rate war in 1990. Other Las Vegas resorts advertised hotel room rates in the *Los Angeles Times* Calendar section for less than $20 per night, including a meal and show-tickets. Within six months, the opening of the Mirage and the Excalibur added more than 7,000 hotel rooms to the Las Vegas Strip inventory, which was supplemented with another 4,000 rooms in the off-Strip Rio Hotel and Casino and expansions at the Flamingo Hilton and Holiday Inn Casino. The latest Las Vegas building boom was on. Over the next decade the Las Vegas hotel room-count would skyrocket from less than 60,000 to more than 100,000. The ten-year building boom made construction cranes a permanent part of the Las Vegas skyline.

A major financing glitch struck Las Vegas' casino expansion plans when Michael Milken pleaded guilty to insider trading in late 1990. Junk bonds had rapidly become crucial to Las Vegas' resort construction, as many companies accumulated junk-bond debts with the intention of refinancing them with more junk bonds when the first ones came due. Several resorts, most notably the Riviera, were threatened with bankruptcy due to the junk bond collapse. The method of financing construction of the Excalibur shifted away from this pattern and capitalized on the profit-making success of megaresorts. Eschewing debt altogether, the publicly traded Circus Circus Enterprises built the Excalibur almost exclusively with cash-on-hand, as it also later did its Egyptian-themed Luxor pyramid.

Even more so than Steve Wynn, financier Kirk Kerkorian brought the grand scale to Las Vegas by dramatically increasing the scale of Las Vegas resorts in three different decades, building the largest hotels in the world in the 1960s, 1970s, and 1990s. In the 1960s, he built the International, which became the Las Vegas Hilton, and in the early 1970s Kerkorian built the first MGM Grand, later renamed Bally's after the new MGM Grand opened in 1993. In 1988, Kerkorian demonstrated his acumen as a wheeler-dealer when he purchased the Desert Inn, its golf course, and the Sands for $167 million, turning around two months later and selling the Sands for $100 million. In the 1990s, he built the MGM Grand Hotel and Theme Park from his own pocket when outside financing prospects were slim. Kerkorian owned 80 percent of the new MGM Grand through his Tracinda Corporation. Tracinda put up the first $140 million, then Kerkorian sold the Desert Inn for $160 million and issued additional shares of common stock. At the time, Kerkorian also owned 10 percent of Chrysler and was making a move on Trans World Airlines. Financing for the world's biggest megaresort, the new MGM Grand, was thus assured at a time when investment dollars were scarce. Due to high profit margins for casino gambling and tourism, self-financing on an unprecedented scale thus added three of the largest hotels in the world to the Strip – the Excalibur and the Luxor, both built by Circus Circus Enterprises, and Kerkorian's MGM Grand.

In 1993 the next phase of Strip casinos was launched. Within a two-week period, the Luxor and Treasure Island resorts opened, followed two months later by the MGM Grand, the world's largest hotel. Thus, in the last three months of 1993, these three resorts added more than ten thousand hotel rooms to the Las Vegas inventory.

The Luxor, a $375-million Egyptian-themed pyramid, welcomed visitors to its 2,526-room resort in October 1993. Luxor is the site of Thebes, the capital of ancient Egypt, but in Las Vegas it is nestled alongside the Excalibur's storybook medieval castle. The simulated 47-acre domain mixes several ancient Middle Eastern themes, including a 10-story-high Sphinx with laser beam eyes aimed towards the obelisk, the hanging gardens of Babylon, and a 30-story dark reflective glass pyramid. Although ancient Babylon is located on a different continent from Egypt, this geographic dyslexia is not uncommon in the fantasy world of Las Vegas. The pyramid's massive 29-million-cubic-foot atrium, the world's largest, is reportedly large enough to stack nine Boeing 747s. Initially, the lobby also sported a Nile River barge cruise, but it was later replaced by more profitable attractions. Inclining elevators ascend at a 39-degree tilt up each corner of the pyramid; the light-beam projected from its peak has forty times the candlepower of a strong searchlight and is visible from Los Angeles, at airplane cruising altitude, on a clear night.

In 1993, Circus Circus continued its effort to attract the low-roller, family market by adding a five-acre, $90-million, pink-domed, water-themed amusement park, Grand Slam Canyon, to its original casino. The park features roller coasters, dinosaurs, and waterfalls in a climate-controlled environment. The next year Grand Slam Canyon was further upgraded, providing entertainment options for local children as well as tourists, and was later renamed Adventuredome at Circus Circus.

The Circus Circus casino was built in 1968, with the hotel added in 1972. The big-top resort pioneered the "plate-o-plenty" buffet dining style, feeding ten thousand customers a day. When the buffet was remodeled in 1997, it wasn't completely shut down because of customer demand. In regard to the resort, the notorious Hunter Thompson caustically commented that:

> Circus Circus is what the whole hep world would be doing on a Saturday night if the Nazis had won the war. This is the sixth reich. The ground floor is full of gambling tables, like all the other casinos ... but the place is about four stories high, in the style of a circus tent, and all manner of strange County Fair/Polish Carnival madness is going on up in space. (1971: 88)

Thompson's wisecrack notwithstanding, Circus Circus Enterprises Inc. has been incredibly profitable, repeating its plebeian formula at the Luxor and the Excalibur with equal success.

In October 1993, Steve Wynn opened his second Strip property, the Caribbean-themed Treasure Island, adjacent to the Mirage. With the two properties, Mirage Resorts had more than 6,000 rooms, two casinos, a volcano and a pirate battle on a 100-acre Strip site. With a significantly lower construction cost than the Mirage, the $430-million Treasure Island was referred to disparagingly by some locals as "Motel Six." Slightly smaller than the Mirage, Treasure Island contains 2,900 rooms, 2,169 slots, 83 table games, and its revenues are about half those of the Mirage.

The resort's defining feature is a mock pirate battle, waged several times daily in front of the casino directly on the Strip, with the British

Navy in a voyage of perpetual defeat. The HMS *Britannia* sails around the corner of Spring Mountain Road and Las Vegas Boulevard to engage the pirate ship, *Hispaniola*, in a battle to the death, or more accurately, to a simulated sinking to "Davey Jones' locker." Cannon balls fly, pyrotechnics abound, the sound system blasts in excess of 100 decibels, and wounded combatants tumble from the decks and masts into the waters of Buccaneer Bay. The mock battle brings pedestrian and vehicular traffic on the Strip to a virtual standstill every ninety minutes from late afternoon until midnight. In a phoenix like resurrection, the British frigate after each performance backs up on an underwater track around the corner of Spring Mountain Road to prepare for its next doomed voyage.

According to one observer: "for all its Disneyesque innocence, the battle scene at Treasure Island is actually a hook to bring pedestrians into the casino, a ploy underscored by the blatant commercial issued by the victorious pirate captain at the end of the show. 'It's time to enter our village and share in our victory celebration,' he says. 'So come to Treasure Island'" (Kamin 1994: 10). Does this kind of attraction work? "A security guard who patrols the pier claims that between 4,000 and 8,000 people attend each naval battle outside the hotel-casino. 'Three thousand of them walk away,' the guard says, 'but the rest – it's a steady flow; they go right in'" (Kamin 1994: 10).

Treasure Island also introduced a major marketing change to Las Vegas. Previously, many major resorts lost money on their hotel operations, entertainment, merchandising, and dining. In the late 1980s, revenue from businesses other than gaming on the Strip accounted for only 30 percent of total revenues, according to the *Nevada Gaming Almanac*. By 1994 that number had climbed to 45 percent. The metamorphosis of hotel operations from loss leaders to profit centers was a result of the corporatization of Las Vegas, along with expansion of the number of tourists and growth of the family market. Also, recent Las Vegas tourists are a more diverse lot than their predecessors the single-minded gamblers, wanting attractions, shopping, and entertainment options. Along with this came merchandising that exploited the popular names of the resorts, generating unprecedented sales of tee-shirts, hats, jackets, whiskey tumblers, and other knick-knacks, all emblazoned with a megaresort logo. Mirage officials contend that Treasure Island was the first Las Vegas resort intentionally designed to generate a minority of its revenue (40 percent) from gaming. This shift in the source of profits by playing to a mixed tourist market constitutes a diversification of the Las Vegas casino economy, (see chapter 4) and is part of the normalization process.

In December 1993, Kerkorian's new MGM Grand, the Strip's first billion-dollar baby, opened across from the Excalibur at the intersection of Tropicana and the Strip. Located on the 133-acre site of the former 18-hole Tropicana golf course and the Marina Hotel, the 5,000-room MGM Grand featured a theme park, health spa, and 9,000-space parking structure. As mentioned earlier, it is also the largest hotel in the world, with four 30-story towers and a 275,000-square-foot exhibition hall that doubles as a 15,200-seat arena for sporting events. The massive lobby boasts numerous large-screen video displays and a casino larger than the playing field at Yankee Stadium, with four separately themed casino areas. The Grand Garden Arena debuted on New Year's Eve, hosting Barbra Streisand's first live concert in more than a decade, with fans paying up to $1,000 for seats. The singer had also opened the International Hotel showroom for Kerkorian in the 1960s. The 33-acre theme park, touted as a cross between Disneyland and the Universal Studios tour, never captured public favor, however. Visitors balked at the $20 admission fee to ride the Grand Canyon Rapids and the MGM Backlot River tour, so pricing and attraction adjustments were made.

Other problems also plagued the giant resort. A cultural *faux pas* was created when Oriental visitors were offended by walking into the massive, 88-foot-high lion's head entrance from the Strip since they considered it "bad luck." In response, the resort underwent a $40-million renovation in 1997, removing the fiberglass lion's head with glowing green eyes to make way for a full-bodied lion statue on a 25-foot-high pedestal surrounded by water fountains and dramatic night-time lighting. In deference to Asian visitors, a Feng Shui blessing ceremony was conducted when the project was completed. At fifty tons, the 45-foot statue is the largest in the United States made of polished gold-bronze.

Although only three years old, the MGM Grand also announced a $700-million interior renovation and expansion to replace its Land of Oz theme and Emerald City motif with a "city of entertainment" and Hollywood-sound stage theme. A Studio 54 nightclub, modeled after the 1970s icon, opened in 1998, officially dedicated with a performance by Elton John. Also, fifteen acres of the unsuccessful theme park were converted to a plush conference center, a pool and spa. Additional attractions were added to the remaining eighteen acres of the theme park, best known for its highly advertised Sky Screamer thrill ride. These changes at the MGM demonstrate that resort owners never hesitate to rework their properties to conform to market demands, or to blow them up, for that matter (see below). In Las Vegas no lasting sentiment is attached to ideas when their realization fails to turn a profit.

The MGM Grand, Luxor, and Excalibur brought the room total near the intersection of the Strip and Tropicana to more than the entire hotel room-count in San Francisco or San Diego. In 1994, four pedestrian elevated walkways were built so that the 100,000 vehicles and even greater number of pedestrians could be more easily and safely moved through the busy intersection each day. More than any other project so far, the opening of the MGM Grand punctuated the megaresort trend now dominating the Strip. In the 1970s a typical new hotel had 500 rooms or less, but since the opening of the Mirage, roomcounts at the new Strip resorts average more than 3,000.

## Out with the Old

Las Vegas began yet another new trend in 1994. As progress dictated the replacement of smaller 30-year-old properties to make way for the construction of themed megaresorts, highly publicized hotel demolition's were added to the Las Vegas entertainment experience. Famous Strip landmarks were blown up, or "imploded" in the local vernacular, for entertainment – again reflecting the fragile attachment to tradition when profits are involved.

The first spectacular implosion was that of the Dunes on October 27, 1994. A Strip landmark for decades, the Dunes Hotel was demolished as little more than a warm-up act for the opening festivities of Treasure Island. Mirage-owner Steve Wynn stood on the bridge at Treasure Island to signal the implosion and an accompanying $1.5-million fireworks spectacular. The hotel, a block south on Las Vegas Boulevard, was blown to dust to make way for Wynn's next Strip resort, the Bellagio. Most of the crowd cheered while some silently watched as the place where they had worked, or that they had enjoyed as part of the Las Vegas experience, disappeared into a pile of rubble. The implosion was also filmed as part of a made-for-television movie. Three months after Treasure Island opened, an hour-long commercial, thinly disguised as entertainment, was aired on a major network. Mirage Resorts paid NBC $1.7 million to air the program on a Sunday evening, maintaining total control of the $1.5 million infomercial. More than three million dollars was spent to produce and air one of the lowest-rated programs of the week, featuring Wynn in a cameo role. While the brilliant and volatile casino mogul demonstrated that the size of his ego matched that of his empire, his foresight was also evident, as the same night that Wynn opened his second Strip property, land was cleared for a third, the Bellagio.

The next implosion was far less spectacular. The Landmark was erased from the Las Vegas skyline on November 7, 1995, to make way for additional parking for the Las Vegas Convention and Visitors Authority. The odd-shaped space needle had been once a proud symbol towering above Las Vegas, where locals and tourists dined and danced with a panoramic view of the city. In its decline, however, the earth beneath the property became more valuable for convention parking than as a fading hotel-casino. The Landmark demolition lives on in media history, however, as part of the movie *Mars Attacks*.

The third Las Vegas resort implosion came on November 26, 1996, when the Sands was demolished to make way for construction of a new property, the Venetian. The "great lady of the Strip" had opened in 1952, built by Houston hotelier and prodigious gambler Jake Friedman, along with Copacabana producer Jack Entratter. The Sands' 17-story round tower was the tallest on the Strip when it opened in 1952. The postwar glamor resort had a mystique that attracted high rollers, the infamous "Rat Pack" (Frank Sinatra, Dean Martin, Sammy Davis Jr, Peter Lawford, and Joey Bishop), and even heads of state. In the late 1960s, Howard Hughes bought the resort for $14.6 million and severely curtailed most of the Rat Pack's more outrageous activities.

The seven-second demise of the Sands was a no-frills event, lacking the fiery pyrotechnics of the other casino implosions. The grand dame of the Strip paused like a faded star taking a last bow, then collapsed into a thirty-foot pile of rubble, disappearing in the middle of the night at 2 a.m., to the cheers of the mostly local pre-Thanksgiving holiday crowd. Its image also lives on, however, as a movie set for the film *Con Air*, which held its national premier in Las Vegas.

The eleven-story Hacienda Hotel became the fourth Strip hotel to be imploded. The event, on December 31, 1996, at 9 p.m. local time, was aired live on the East Coast as part of a nationally televised New Year's Eve celebration. The six-lane Las Vegas Strip was turned into a pedestrian mall for eight hours, from 6 p.m. to 2 a.m., as a crowd of 200,000 gathered at the south end of Las Vegas Boulevard, along with another 100,000 revelers down the street at the Mirage block party. A fireworks display lit up the skies both before and after the forty-second implosion. The size of the crowd and the hotel implosion/fireworks served formal notice to New York's Times Square that there was competition for the New Year's Eve party crown – reinforced three days later when the New York-New York resort opened on the Strip. The mayors of Las Vegas and New York City engaged in a friendly argument over which event attracted the largest New Year's Eve crowd in 1996–7. However one measures the competition, Las Vegas did very well, boasting near total occupancy of its 98,000 hotel rooms and taking in $56 million in non-gaming revenues alone.

On April 27, 1998, the 1,100 room Aladdin Hotel and Casino, judged too small by megaresort standards, was demolished in the fifth implosion on the Strip. The venerable casino will be replaced by a new 2,600 room Aladdin that will be part of a projected $1-billion resort complex scheduled to open in early 2000.

## Financing Las Vegas' Development

According to the socio-spatial perspective (Gottdiener 1994b), the constant reworking of real estate alters the terrain of any metropolis and is the leading edge of growth. Important to this "second circuit" of capital are the diverse forms of financing that feed the framework of investment in property, often in ways that differ from those of the primary circuit of industrial capital. Individuals or groups assemble money in these diverse ways and often take existing property owners by surprise as they buy them out or build new, competitive projects next door. Venture capital thus finds opportunities, where none were thought to exist, in the second circuit. At other times, major investors in the primary circuit sell lucrative properties, as Howard Hughes did with Trans World Airlines, and use their capital to buy real estate in a big way, thereby altering the existing landscape and creating new competitive forces through novel location decisions.

Nowhere was this process more evident than in the development of Las Vegas. Initiated by Howard Hughes' buying spree, the trend continued into the 1990s megaresort era, changing both the face and the nature of the Las Vegas experience once again. Each of these giant hotels was financed through novel means; Wynn's projects used junk bonds, Circus Circus its own profits, and the large multinationals, such as Hilton and Sheraton, used corporate stock to claim Las Vegas properties.

### Joint Ventures

In the late 1990s, however, yet another Las Vegas casino financing trend has emerged in the form of joint ventures, through which competitors combine forces to create new resorts. The first joint venture resort casino on the Las Vegas Strip was the French Riviera-themed Monte Carlo, which opened in June 1996. Mirage Resorts provided the land from the old Dunes property, and Circus Circus Enterprises supplied the capital for the project. The $344-million, 3,014-room resort, designed and operated by Circus Circus, reflects that company's tried and true formula of budget rooms and inexpensive food. The resort includes a 700-seat buffet and a showroom for magician Lance Burton, who has a 13-year contract with the resort to fill a 1,200-seat replica of a Victorian-style vaudeville theater.

Unlike most Circus Circus properties, the Monte Carlo provides credit and "comps" to rated casino customers. Circus Circus had planned to incorporate credit play at the Luxor but lacked the upscale suites, meeting rooms, service elevators, and other amenities needed to cater to the high end of the gambling market. The corporation did, however, add 2,000 rooms with suites and other amenities to the Luxor in an attempt to attract the 10 percent of casino revenues that come from the premium-player niche of $10 thousand to $50 thousand gamblers.

The second joint venture Strip resort was New York-New York, which opened on January 3, 1997, in a ceremony marked by a fireworks display and the piped-in strains of a classic rendition of the song "New York, New York." The $460-million, 2,034-room hotel-casino features scaled-down replicas of the Statue of Liberty and the Brooklyn Bridge, providing the ambiance of Gotham City, including teeming crowds and massive traffic jams, to the Las Vegas Strip. It also features the Manhattan Express roller coaster, that does an inverted flip near the Statue of Liberty, roars past the Harbor and through the New York $lot Exchange casino. The New York Stock Exchange filed a federal court lawsuit against the resort within months of its opening, charging that the columned façade and letters NY$E suggested Wall Street sponsorship. The lawsuit charged that the casino was "bastardizing" NYSE trademarks and diluting their value by "tending to make them generic, the subject of ridicule, [and by] associating gambling, its speculative nature and risks, and its reputation with the [NYSE] and its marks" (J. L. Smith 1997).

A "must see" attraction, New York-New York was a 50–50 joint venture of MGM Grand Inc., noted for catering to the mid- to high-level customer, and Primadonna Resorts, which has a low-end customer orientation. Primadonna started in 1977 with a twelve-room motel and gas station located forty miles south of Las Vegas on Interstate 15 at the California border. In less than two decades, the company has grown into a publicly traded corporation with three hotels at Stateline, which has since been renamed Primm, Nevada.

The opening of New York-New York also finalized the crowning of the intersection of Tropicana Avenue and Las Vegas Boulevard as the hub of the Strip in terms of total room-count, as well as a traffic-count total at more than 100,000 vehicles per day. The intersection of Flamingo Road and Las Vegas Boulevard, which included Caesars Palace, Bally's, the Dunes (now replaced by the Bellagio), and the Barbary Coast, had long held that title.

## Corporate Collateral Financing

The most recent multi-billion-dollar wave of Strip casino development was launched in October 1998 with Mirage Resort's $1.6-billion, 3,000-room, 35-story Italian-style resort, the Bellagio, built on the 126-acre former home of the Dunes Hotel and Golf Course. Financing of the Bellagio, as well as other projects presently under construction, suggests that the biggest players in Las Vegas are now leveraging their assets and taking on massive debt in order to continue expanding. Their hope, of course, is that their debts will be paid off quickly by increased profits, but the scale of the new projects and their billion-dollar indebtedness is unprecedented. The Bellagio will be, for a while, the world's most expensive building, even though the land under it was purchased at the bargain price of $70 million (well under 10 percent of its present value). Named for a resort town on the shores of Lake Como in northern Italy, the upscale resort, with room rates topping $500 on busy weekends, is situated on an eight-acre artificial lake. Bellagio, like other Mirage Resort properties, with the volcano at the Mirage and the pirate-ship battle at Treasure Island, features a major public entertainment attraction. A $40-million dancing fountain features 1,200 nozzles, highlighted by 4,500 colored lights choreographed to shoot water as high as 250 feet into the air and orchestrated to match the booming musical accompaniment. The Bellagio also introduced a $92-million *Cirque du Soleil* aquatic production show, "O." The spectacle is the most expensive show ever on the Strip, surpassing Siegfried and Roy (Mirage) and the EFX (MGM Grand) production shows, both of which topped $50 million. A customized, 1,800-seat oval showroom overlooks a 1.5-million-gallon pool and stages rise from the depths with acrobats, synchronized swimmers, and world-class divers in waterproof costumes and make-up. Another record was set as ticket prices broke the $100 barrier.

   Shopping and dining are central features at Bellagio. Lakeside restaurants are operated by world-renowned chefs from New York's Le Cirque, San Francisco's Aqua and Boston's Olives. High-end retail shops include Tiffany's, Hermes, Armani, and Chanel. The lobby ceiling features a $10-million, hand blown, multi-colored glass chandelier designed by artist Dale Chilhuly that contains more than 2,000 separate pieces. The 9,000-square-foot conservatory is an aromatic retreat with a 50-foot-high glass ceiling and contains thousands of plants that are replaced monthly and change with the seasons. A $300-million art collection includes paintings by Renoir, Monet, Matisse, and Van Gogh. Following the recent megaresort trend, it is projected that a larger percentage of its income will derive from hotel operations than from the casino. In effect, Bellagio is marketed as a resort with a casino.

Several other megaresort properties, totaling nearly $7 billion and involving debt financing on this immense scale, are nearing completion. Furthest along among these is Las Vegas Sands' Inc.'s massive Venetian. Ground was broken in April 1997 for the first phase of the $2.5-billion resort, with 3,036 suites and a 35-story tower due to open in April 1999. A second phase with another 3,036-room tower is scheduled to open the following year. The two phases together will include one million square feet of shopping space, the size of a large regional mall, on the grounds of the imploded Sands. The resort will also include Venice-style statues and artwork, as well as full-scale canals with gondola rides running through the property. Financing for the $1.2-billion first phase came from bank loans, bonded debt, and the personal wealth of owner Sheldon Adelson, which according to *Forbes Magazine* is approximately $500 million. Unfortunately, portions of the loan interest rate range as high as 14.25%, the same high rate that led the Stratosphere into bankruptcy, and much higher than the debt financing of the Bellagio, as well as of the other projects nearing completion, Hilton's Paris and Circus Circus's Mandalay Bay.

Circus Circus Enterprises Inc., owners of the Luxor, Excalibur, and Circus Circus resorts and co-owners of the Monte Carlo, plan a massive 13,800-room hotel-casino complex at the far south end of Las Vegas Boulevard. The company-owned land covers 121 acres west of the Strip and 15 acres east, from the Luxor south to Russell Road. A pedestrian bridge is planned to span Las Vegas Boulevard connecting the Luxor with the projected Luxor East, a 2,000-room time-share hotel that will also house a quarter-million square-foot shopping mall.

The planned complex includes several resorts, with the first, the $1-billion, 43-story Mandalay Bay, due for completion in March 1999. The 3,700-room resort, being built on the site of the old Hacienda south of the Luxor, features waterfalls, terraced gardens, and mythical statuary reflecting an ancient South Seas odyssey. A ten-acre tropical lagoon includes a sand-and-surfing beach, snorkeling reef, and a swim-up shark exhibit. The $1-billion tropical-themed resort would bring Circus Circus properties to a total of 20,000 hotel rooms by the year 2003, by far the most for any one corporation on the Strip.

**Figure 2.1**   The Venetian Hotel Tower

Financing comes from a combination of Circus Circus Enterprises' cash flow and corporate bank lines of credit.

A unique aspect of Mandalay Bay is the combination of two different resort hotels under one roof. A more intimate 417-room Four Seasons Hotel will occupy the 35th to 39th floors of Mandalay Bay. Designed as a five-star luxury resort, the Four Seasons at Mandalay Bay will have its own entrance off the Strip and its own lobby and express elevators. The Circus Circus "miracle mile" of megaresorts, which company officials propose as a self-contained "gateway to Las Vegas," will be designed to serve every segment of the gaming and tourism market. It is projected to be completed with a proposed third resort, tentatively titled Project Z, planned to contain five hotel towers ranging from 31 to 43 stories with a total of 8,000 rooms and 750,000 square feet of casinos, shops, and restaurants.

Plans for the resort complex became less solid in mid-1998, however, when it was discovered nine months before opening that Mandalay Bay was sinking, up to 16 inches, an amount that significantly exceeds the expected settling of 2 to 8 inches for resorts that size (McKinnon 1998g). The foundation of the already constructed resort was subsequently supported by the addition of 500 steel pipes. The resort is on track for its projected opening in early 1999 and will employ 5,000.

Hilton Hotel Corporation also is constructing another Strip megaresort on a 24-acre site adjacent to Bally's. The company broke ground in April 1997 for Paris, a self-financed French-themed resort featuring a 50-story replica of the Eiffel Tower. Due to open in fall 1999, the $760-million, 34-story X-shaped tower will contain 2,900 rooms, including 300 suites. Paris will also feature replicas of the Arc de Triomphe, the Paris Opera House, the Louvre art gallery, a health spa, convention space, and a French-themed retail-shopping complex.

## Renovations

For decades the Las Vegas Hilton, built by Kirk Kerkorian, reigned as the world's largest hotel and benefited greatly by its location adjacent to the Convention Center. Since it catered to business conventioneers with expense accounts, the Hilton charged higher prices for rooms and beverages to offset its off-Strip location. Elvis and Liberace once held court in its showroom, which underwent a multi-million-dollar remodeling in a move away from big-name entertainment. The new showroom hosted Andrew Lloyd Webber's *Starlight Express*, a musical with an entire cast on roller blades, though it, too, has since been replaced by a return to headliner entertainment.

In the midst of renovation of the three-year-old MGM Grand, plans were announced for a 1,500-room Marriott Grand Hotel and a 500-room Ritz-Carlton on its property at Tropicana and the Strip. MGM also plans to build thirty luxurious high-roller residences with a Tuscan theme. The Mansion at MGM Grand features private suites and villas ranging in size from 3,000 to 14,000 square feet, eleven of which will have private indoor swimming pools.

Another extensive renovation designed to appeal to upscale travelers took place at the sprawling Desert Inn resort, which was built in the 1950s and was later featured on national television as the home of the TV series *Vega$* (see chapter 3). With the demise of the Dunes and

Tropicana courses, the Desert Inn has the only remaining golf course on the Las Vegas Strip. ITT Corporation bought the property in 1993 from Kerkorian's Tracinda Corporation for $160 million and spent $200 million in 1997 to turn it into the first five-star resort on the Strip.

In sum, following a brief and highly publicized fling at attracting a "family crowd" (more hype than real), the most recent Las Vegas projects are decidedly upscale and now aim for affluent tourists who also like to gamble. The new megaresorts seek to attract these big spenders with five-star resorts featuring simulations of high-status European environments, such as Lake Como, Paris or Venice, or of exotic Mediterranean and South Seas locales.

## Real Estate Investment Trusts

Real Estate Investment Trusts (REITs) were created in 1960 to encourage real-estate investment by people of modest means. They avoid corporate income taxes by paying out 95 percent of their taxable income as dividends. In 1997 REITs emerged as yet another potential ownership trend in Las Vegas, further revealing the increasingly corporate nature of gaming, when Hilton Hotels initiated a $10.5-billion hostile takeover bid of ITT. As part of its defense, ITT divested itself of properties worldwide, but retained its Caesars World Casinos and Sheraton Hotels (427 in mid-1997) and reinvested the proceeds in those businesses. ITT also put the Desert Inn, with its expansion well underway, up for sale in the $320 million to $340-million range to obtain cash to battle Hilton's bid. Though the year-long, widely publicized attempt failed, it introduced the new financial players to the Las Vegas scene, as ITT was bought by the Starwood Lodging Trust, a Phoenix-based REIT, for $13.7 billion in a deal that included Caesars Palace and the refurbished Desert Inn.

Also, in January 1998, the pending purchase of Station Casinos for $1.7 billion by another REIT, Crescent Real Estate Equities, headed by billionaire financier Richard Rainwater, was announced. Station Casinos operates four Las Vegas-area casinos geared towards local gamblers, as well as two Missouri casinos. The Station Casino deal was canceled in August 1998, as REITs were losing their luster to investors following recent tax-court rulings. Potential investors also became fearful of the volatility in room and casino revenues that began plaguing Strip operators, despite the fact that Station Casinos, with its appeal to local residents, was largely insulated from such problems.

## New Forms of Competition

The Las Vegas gaming mecca surpassed the 100,000-room level in 1997, hosting more than 30 million tourists. However, for the first time in recent memory, both Las Vegas and Nevada gaming revenues flattened in 1996. The relentless march to increase the tourist count and gaming revenues had stumbled only once previously, in 1981. That year Atlantic City added five new casinos, while the negative publicity of the MGM and Hilton fires limited Las Vegas' gaming revenues to a 1 percent increase. No major Strip resorts were built in the 1980s as a result of these and other factors, such as the 1983 recession, devaluation of the Mexican peso, rising airfares, and a 20 percent yearly increase in Atlantic City revenues.

Since 1989, more than 40,000 hotel rooms have been added to the Las Vegas inventory and 20,000 more are nearing completion. While more tourists are coming for longer stays, potential gains in gaming revenues have been offset by the fact that there are so many other entertainment options. Thus, Nevada's leading industry must adjust to the indisputable fact that the increasing numbers of tourists are spending less on gambling. In fiscal year 1997–98, Clark County resorts reported only a modest 4.7 percent gain in gaming revenues (Berns 1998b), a particularly worrisome figure given the 12.5 percent increase in the number of hotel rooms.

Gloomy projections that Las Vegas is overbuilt and over-themed are not new, however. In 1991, the wisdom of building the planned MGM megaresort project was questioned. In 1993, after ITT Sheraton purchased the Desert Inn, former chairman John Kapioltas proclaimed that, "Las Vegas may be themed out" (Berns 1997a). This statement was made before New York-New York, Monte Carlo, the Bellagio, and the Venetian were built. Yet, despite such cautionary warnings, a 1997 poll of Chief Executive Officers by *Fortune Magazine* named Mirage Resorts Inc. the second most respected company in the country.

High-tech spectacles make Las Vegas' attractions larger-than-life events that tourists can't experience anywhere else in the world. The Las Vegas Hilton's "Star Trek: The Experience" beams visitors to the bridge of the *Starship Enterprise* in the 24th century, where they experience an action-packed 23-minute simulation. The $70-million attraction premiered in 1998 as a "must see" event – and will undoubtedly be replaced eventually by a more spectacular attraction. The Mirage volcano drew tourists and locals in droves when it first began its noisy and fiery eruptions. Within a few years, however, the fickle public raced past the exploding volcano, hardly paying attention, in their

rush to view the Treasure Island's mock pirate battle. Even new properties are constantly being upgraded, as in 1996, when the three-year-
old Treasure Island received a $3.5-million upgrade of its lobby area.

## High Rollers

Competition for gaming and entertainment dollars is fierce and is
escalating in intensity. In this competition, baccarat, a card game
similar to blackjack, plays a particularly prominent role as the *crème de
la crème* of casino games, drawing large-stakes gamblers or "high
rollers." It even has its own separate space in the casino environment,
as high-limit games are held in plush private salons where players are
served by tuxedo-clad dealers. Baccarat revenues are so large that
severe fluctuations can make or break quarterly earnings at individual
resorts. Accordingly, "whales," industry parlance for the world's top
one hundred to two hundred players, who are capable of betting
$250,000 per hand at baccarat, are aggressively pursued. Whales, who
often have credit lines of 5 million to 10 million dollars, mostly came
from the Middle East in the early 1970s, and later that decade, from
Mexico. When the Mexican economy collapsed in the early 1980s,
efforts shifted to attract players from the Far East. One of these high
rollers was reported to have lost $70 million over a three-year period,
although the house doesn't always win. Resorts sometimes put up
whales in million-dollar suites, wine and dine them, only to see them
walk away with a million dollars in winnings. Losses of that magni-
tude at one large resort can negatively impact overall quarterly
gaming revenues for the Strip, and ultimately for the entire state.
Thus, while volume has become the primary focus in the era of
megaresorts, intense competition to attract high rollers also continues.

## Conventions

In 1959, the Las Vegas Convention Center (LVCC) opened one block
east of the Strip on Paradise Road. The silver-domed rotunda seated
6,300 and the adjoining hall contained 90,000 square feet of exhibit
space, but its off-strip location prompted newspaper publisher Hank
Greenspun to dismiss it as a "white elephant."

Since that time, however, the Convention Center has undergone
repeated expansion and is now one of the nation's premier convention
sites as well as its second largest center. It is the largest single-level
convention facility in the country, an important asset for moving

massive exhibit materials in and out. The Las Vegas Convention and Visitors Authority (LVCVA), operator of the Convention Center, is financed by room taxes and convention-center revenues. Convention and trade-show attendees in the mid-1990s accounted for approximately 10 percent of annual visitor volume.

In 1990, a $50-million modernization and upgrade of the thirty-year-old facility added an additional 200,000 square feet of meeting and exhibit space. In the process, one of Las Vegas' most recognizable landmarks, the center's flying-saucer like rotunda, was demolished along with its Gold Wing, another previously prominent feature of the facility.

In 1997, yet another multi-million-dollar expansion added 280,000 more square feet of exhibit space to North Hall, bringing the overall total to 1.9 million square feet. The Convention Authority plans to have more than 2.5 million square feet of exhibit and meeting space available within fifteen years, with the capacity to expand over the top of Desert Inn Road. In anticipation, eastern access to the major cross-town arterial was lowered below ground level to prevent gridlock between the pedestrian and vehicular traffic generated by conventions, and local traffic.

The number of conventioneers rose from 1.7 million attendees in 1990 to 3.5 million in 1997, when the city hosted 3,700 conventions, generating a non-gaming economic impact estimated at $4.4 billion by the LVCVA. Las Vegas hosted 32 of the top 200 conventions that year, placing it in the top spot for large shows and total trade-show attendance, ahead of Chicago, Atlanta, and New York (H. Smith 1998b). Although convention attendance slowed somewhat in 1998, convention business overall has been so good for Las Vegas that in 1998 the LVCVA declined invitations to bid for both the Republican and Democratic national conventions. An official for a national exhibition company that wants to subsidize the addition of more space commented: "You're a tough ticket to get into. A lot of shows want to come to Las Vegas but can't get dates" (H. Smith 1998b). Unlike most other cities that cater to conventions, Las Vegas has more than double the amount of convention-center space in its resorts, giving the city a total of 4.2 million square feet of meeting and exhibit space, and predicted to surpass 6 million square feet by the year 2000.

Less than a mile southwest of the Las Vegas Convention Center, at Spring Mountain Road and the Strip, sits the privately owned and operated Sands Expo and Convention Center. When the Sands Expo opened in November 1990, it was perceived by the LVCVA as a competitor. Since then, however, the growing number and size of conventions in Las Vegas has allowed both facilities to operate at full capacity.

Sands' owner Sheldon Adelson is the former board chairman and CEO of Interface Group, which annually produced the city's large Comdex computer convention. In 1983, Adelson, on behalf of Comdex, joined with executives of the Consumer Electronics Show (CES) to build the West Hall of the LVCC and then sold it to the LVCVA for one dollar. Occupancy at the Sands Expo Center is demand driven because the rates are higher, nearly double those of the LVCC, as it is not subsidized by tax dollars. Its prices are still competitive by national standards, however. By 1993, the Sands Expo Center had one million square feet of convention space, and a room total of 1,800 before the Sands' implosion. The opening of the first phase of the Venetian in early 1999 on the former site of the Sands Hotel, adjacent to the Expo Center, will replace that with 3,000 rooms.

Many Las Vegas hotels have publicly stated their lack of enthusiasm for conventioneers, who, they claim, don't gamble enough because they are busy in meetings all day and dine on freebies at night. However, room rates triple when the massive Comdex convention, with more than 200,000 attendees, is in town. Also, "girlie shows" on and off the Strip do a resounding business, as it seems that computer enthusiasts would rather stuff dollar bills into G-strings than slot machines.

Conventions originally filled in the gaps during otherwise slow tourism times. The enormous growth of Las Vegas' resorts, however, in terms of both total room-count and convention facilities, has allowed the convention and tourism industries to co-exist year-round. A tourism-related organization, Las Vegas Events, is a private corporation that exists on a $3-million annual budget of public funds provided by the convention authority. Las Vegas Events produces the National Finals Rodeo that brings big-spending cowboys and rodeo fans to Las Vegas after the Thanksgiving holiday, traditionally a slow time for tourism.

## Downtown Fights Back – The Fremont Street Experience

Competition between the Las Vegas Strip resorts and the downtown casinos has been a major factor in the dynamic growth of the region since the 1950s. Before the advent of the megaresorts on the Strip, the downtown properties had several advantages. Their old-style casinos, many of them family-run operations, had a reputation for looser (higher paying) slots and friendlier table games with lower betting minimums. Also, because the casinos were much closer together, they provided an atmosphere where gamblers could easily move among several establishments. For years, visitors looking for inexpensive steak dinners, loose slots, friendly dealers, and a more forgiving environment felt no need for such frills as sphinxes or tropical forests

However, in the 1990s, the Strip's themed megaresorts gained the upper hand and gaming revenues at downtown resorts declined steadily. In November 1995, downtown casino businesses, in cooperation with city government, responded with a spectacular project of their own, the Fremont Street Experience, in an attempt to boost their revenues.

Fremont Street was the original heart of Las Vegas, being the first street to be paved, in 1925, having the first elevator (in the Apache Hotel in 1932), and the first high-rise building (the Fremont Hotel in 1956). Also, when gambling was re-legalized in 1931, the first Nevada gaming license was issued to the Northern Club at 15 E. Fremont Street, and the Horseshoe was the first casino to install carpeting, while the Golden Nugget was the first structure designed from the ground up to be a casino. In the 1940s the introduction of neon transformed drab Fremont Street, with its wood-planked sidewalks, into Glitter Gulch, and in 1947 the multi-story-high neon cowboy, Vegas Vic, arrived to welcome visitors with a wave and a "Howdy Partner" greeting. In short, Fremont Street *was* Las Vegas until the upstart, county-based Strip began to develop.

A major factor contributing to Glitter Gulch's more recent competitive disadvantage is the stereotypical seediness of its downtown location, which has largely offset its comfortable, old-time feeling. The core of downtown is comprised of some of the oldest casinos in the region; the Pioneer Club (now a souvenir shop), the Fremont, the Four Queens, Fitzgerald's, the Golden Nugget, the Las Vegas Club, Binion's Horseshoe, Sassy Sally's Slots, the Golden Gate (established in 1906), and the (Union) Plaza. For nearly a century these establishments' combined themes of the Wild West and California Gold Rush days dominated the downtown area and the overall Las Vegas image. Intermingled with the older casinos today, however, is a motley array of bail-bonds, storefronts, motels advertising adult movie channels, gun shops, liquor stores, temporary day-labor businesses, blood banks, pawn shops, tacky gift shops, and fast-food outlets. The homeless and the derelict wander the side streets, mixing with the gamblers and other tourists, creating a less than glamorous image of a scruffy, hand-to-mouth Las Vegas, the Vegas of people who are down on their luck, looking for their last big chance.

The Fremont Street Experience was designed to overcome Glitter Gulch's tarnished image and to stem the financial hemorrhaging as tourists and gamblers were lost to the pirate battles, pyramids, and

**Figure 2.2**   Fremont Street Experience at night time

volcanoes on the Strip. The idea for renovation came from Golden Nugget owner Steve Wynn, who originally proposed building canals to be traversed by gondolas delivering patrons to the casinos. In 1991, Wynn brought in renowned architect Jon Jerde, designer of Horton Plaza in San Diego and the City Walk in Universal City, California.

Jerde proposed construction of a canopy of light over Glitter Gulch, and the city of Las Vegas, along with a collective of ten casino owners, chipped in to build the attraction.

The $70-million Fremont Street Experience features a pedestrian mall with misting systems to cool the air and a 90-foot-high, four-block-long canopy that boasts a unique computer-generated animated light-and-sound show. Even Vegas Vic found a place under the canopy after part of his hat was lopped off. The animated lighting includes more than 2 million lamps and the 208-speaker sound system boasts 540,000 watts. A 1,400-space parking plaza was built by the city for $23 million, although land for the garage was secured only after controversial eminent-domain (or compulsory purchase) proceedings by the city.

A second phase of the Fremont Street Experience was approved by the city council in 1998. The $100-million "Neonopolis @ Fremont Street Experience" will be a 254,000-square-foot retail and entertainment center. The city will contribute up to $30 million on property acquisition and for construction of a 630-space underground-parking garage. The non-gaming complex will be modeled after Cocowalk, an urban entertainment center in Miami's Coconut Grove district. If the developer, World Entertainment Centers of Atlanta, secures funding, the project will be built at the corner of Las Vegas Boulevard and Fremont Street, directly north of the red Fremont Street Experience parking garage. The Neonopolis project is significant because it represents a departure for the downtown area from casino-oriented enterprises towards a more diversified mix of commercial businesses. Thus, as the Strip has diversified after its own fashion by building upscale resorts that are less dependent on gambling revenues, the downtown is trying to achieve the same goal by attracting commercial businesses and producer services.

Another project designed to boost downtown gaming revenues was built in the netherland between Glitter Gulch and the Strip, within city boundaries. When the press conference announcing the project that would become the Stratosphere Tower was held, owner Bob Stupak only had permission from city officials to build an 800-foot-high, concrete and steel, three-legged base for the structure. However, Stupak, a maverick entrepreneur, soon announced more ambitious plans to build the world's tallest free-standing structure at 1,800 feet. Though it was not at first considered a serious proposal by the Las Vegas city council, Stupak hired a well connected development attorney, son of the then-sheriff, to handle the legal and political details. A coalition of McCarran Airport and FAA officials contended that the tower would constitute a hazard to aviation, yet construction began in February

1992. The project went through several incarnations and a series of setbacks that included battles with contractors, disagreements with the city council and the FAA, a spectacular late-night fire, and a steady stream of financial troubles. One of the mammoth concrete legs was bowed to such a degree that the defect was visible from most of the Las Vegas Valley, causing local residents to speculate that the structure might not be safe. After an electrical fire 500-feet up in August 1993 lit up the night skies and delayed construction, rumors spread locally that the tower, nicknamed Stupak's Stump, was cursed. Construction that was planned for two years, ended up taking more than four.

In April 1996 the $550-million Stratosphere Resort, with its 1,149-foot tower, opened as the tallest building west of Mississippi and with the tallest free-standing observation tower in the nation. The first hotel phase contained 1,500 rooms but cash flow problems, exacerbated by high-interest-rate debt payments, delayed the crucial second phase to add 1,000 additional rooms. While tourists and locals crowded onto elevators to get to the observation decks in the 12-story pod atop the tower, the "Let It Ride" roller coaster was a disappointment, as its record-setting height above ground didn't make up for its slow ride that lacked a spectacular drop. The "Big Shot" attraction, billed as a reverse bungee-jump, launching passengers by pulling 4 Gs, proved to be more successful. A proposed 48-passenger, animatronic-ape ride up the outside of the tower was never built, yet the tower quickly became a defining symbol of the Las Vegas skyline and airline passengers had no trouble picking it out from their window seats.

While people came to see the tower and take the rides, however, few of them stayed to gamble, shop, or dine. Grand Casinos Inc., the Minnesota-based company that owned 44 percent of the property, took operational control of the Stratosphere less than six months after it opened and began an extensive gaming marketing program, advertising that they had loosened the slots to increase payoffs. Additional changes also were made, including closing the "Top of the World" restaurant for lunch to focus on the more popular dinner service. Revenues picked up somewhat and the high-cost debt was refinanced, but the reduced annual rate was still a high 14.25%, making it difficult to cover the payments. The resort thus filed for Chapter 11 Bankruptcy reorganization within its first year, although it has remained open and was purchased by corporate investor Carl Icahn for approximately 50 cents on the dollar. When the Nevada Gaming Commission approved Icahn to take control in August 1998, the financier pledged to invest $100 million to finish the hotel tower and add a swimming pool and spa.

Location was perhaps the biggest obstacle to the Stratosphere's becoming a successful operation. The casino-hotel is situated next to a low-income, drug infested area known as the Naked City. Once a desirable place to live, Naked City received its name from the large number of showgirls who once lounged around the area's apartment-complex pools, *au naturel*, to obtain even tans. The neighborhood has since declined, however, into a hovel of run-down apartments rented by the day or week, populated by low-income residents. Efforts by city leaders to rename the area Meadows Village, and increased police patrols, have only slightly changed its slum-like ambiance and the presence of drug dealers, addicts, and prostitutes.

## A World-Class Airport

It can truly be said that without McCarran International Airport and the volume of traffic it handles, the Las Vegas economy would never have attained its current multi-billion-dollar status. However, the story of the airport's success is not a simple case of the landing field keeping in lock step with growth. Vision and innovative entrepreneurship were involved. In this sense, the rise of McCarran Airport was as much a risk-taking adventure as the construction of the more heralded casino environment.

During World War II the federal government constructed Nellis Air Force Base, one of the largest military air bases in the country, eight miles north of Glitter Gulch. In addition to the base, which was originally used as a gunnery range to train bomber and fighter crews, a second, smaller base was created through the lobbying efforts of powerful Nevada Senator Pat McCarran. In 1942, the Civil Aeronautics Administration commissioned the first air traffic control tower at the new joint-use military and civilian McCarran Airfield. Before then, commercial and mail planes landed on the present site of the Sahara Hotel. In 1947 the base was decommissioned and McCarran Airfield became the main commercial airport for Las Vegas. The following year, the airport was moved to a larger site on Las Vegas Boulevard South. The renamed Clark County Public Airport served four airlines: Bonanza, Western, United, and Howard Hughes' Trans World Airlines. In the first year of operation 35,000 passengers passed through its gates and the field averaged twelve flights per day.

Senator McCarran continued to lobby the federal government for support for the fledgling airport, including its re-classification to handle large aircraft, and in recognition of his efforts the field was rededicated as McCarran Airport in 1949. With the building boom on the Strip in the 1950s the volume of air traffic increased significantly, with average daily flights increasing to 45. In 1955, voters approved a $2-million bond issue to expand facilities at the two-runway-field, and by 1959, McCarran had a record 686,268 passengers, a more than ten-fold increase since the beginning of the decade. The airport also began construction on a new $5-million terminal building that same year. During the 1960s passenger-jet traffic was introduced, bringing the total passenger count to more than one million a year. In 1963 the airport moved to its present site and in 1966 a $30-million expansion doubled the size of the terminal, created a third, general-aviation runway, and lengthened the two existing runways. In that same year the facility became McCarran International Airport and was taken off the tax rolls. In 1969, the first Boeing 747 landed at McCarran, ushering in the age of jumbo jets and greatly accelerating the number of people that could be handled by the field. Additional construction took place throughout the 1970s and annual passenger traffic increased from 4 million to more than 6 million during the decade.

Most of the tourists who visited Las Vegas in the 1960s continued to come by car. In 1971, however, the airport received an official "port-of-entry" designation that allowed it to land international flights. International air traffic primarily came from Mexico, but the change in status also enabled the field to later promote direct flights to other lucrative foreign links, such as Japan and Europe.

During the 1970s, Las Vegas came into its own as a major tourist destination, as airlines worked together with local hotels to promote the town as a vacation spot. In 1977, John Solomon was hired as airport director, and the next year, airline de-regulation expanded the number of airlines landing in Las Vegas from 7 to 21. Then, following a year-long study, a $1-billion, three-stage, twenty-year, McCarran 2000 expansion project was announced. In August 1982 the Airport Authority issued more than $300 million in revenue bonds, which represented "the largest airport bond sale in history" (Airport Authority pamphlet, undated). Construction began to reshape every aspect of the airport, from the air traffic control tower to the central terminal building. The massive expansion and remodeling project was complicated by the fact that it took place in a working facility with more than 10 million passengers passing through the airport during each year of the construction process. One of the unique characteristics of Las Vegas air travel at the time was that only 10 percent of McCarran's air travelers were local residents. Because of that, a relatively small parking structure was built, though a much larger public transportation area was required (Collins 1986).

In 1985, completion of Phase One of the expansion included a

$93-million terminal and parking facility. A high-rise parking garage comprised the third through sixth floors of the terminal, with baggage claim on the ground floor and an esplanade with shopping concessions on the second. A $7.5-million Automated Transit System (ATS), or people mover, linked the C-Gate satellite building to the central terminal. The airport was designed by Seattle-based TRA, who also designed the Seattle and Salt Lake City airports and remodeled the Dulles Airport. As the entry point to the resort destination for millions of tourists and convention delegates, McCarran Airport is intended to convey an upscale image for the Las Vegas community. Airport designers opted for an all-encompassing central terminal that would include mall shopping and gambling, rather than several small unit terminal buildings. The next year an average of more than a million passengers a month passed through the airport, which handled an average of 444 daily flights, making it the 22nd busiest airport in the nation and the 30th in the world in 1987.

As noted above, however, this continued expansion over the years did not proceed without problems. Prior to the 1980s, most airport capital improvements were funded largely by the tax-paying public living in the community served by the airport. In contrast, expansion of McCarran Airport over the years was funded by a combination of bond issues, federal funding, airline fees, and non-airline general revenues derived from gaming, parking, transportation, and concession sales fees. Although McCarran had passenger traffic in the mid-1980s equivalent to airports in Houston, Philadelphia, and Boston, its 600,000 Clark County residents provided a much smaller tax base to support an airport. In the mid- 1980s, Las Vegas, like cities undergoing major airport-construction projects such as Chicago, Orlando and Phoenix, began channeling user fees into capital improvements. Although landing fees at McCarran nearly tripled in 1985, they were not out of line with fees charged at other similarly sized airports, especially those with recent construction additions. The airlines using McCarran viewed this as a dangerous precedent, however, and thirteen of them filed a lawsuit against the airport the day the new facility opened for public use in October 1985, alleging "capricious rates and charges." High airport fees had become a fighting matter and McCarran was selected by the airline industry as the one to challenge in court.

At that crucial time, Airport Director John Solomon, who had overseen the construction and opening of McCarran 2000, was replaced. Robert Broadbent, who served on the Clark County commission from 1968 to 1981, returned from Washington where he had served as Assistant Secretary of the Interior, to take over as Airport Director in March 1986.

Broadbent and his staff sat down with the airlines and negotiated a settlement of the issues underlying the legal complaint, lowering rates and charges from about $123 a square foot to about $83. As Broadbent (1997) observed, the airport "had 50 or 60 million dollars worth of construction planned, so the suit had to be settled." The authority agreed to lower their fees with the knowledge that the destination would be attracting more tourists each year. It also realized that future growth of the airport would be a direct function of that of the tourist industry. According to Broadbent, "for every hotel room built, 320 new passengers a year pass through the airport." In its compromise with the airlines, the airport authority also made another concession. Though the airport sported a major terminal facility, the field had one east–west and one north–south runway, and, according to Broadbent, the runways were deteriorating: "they were in bad shape and the ramps were in bad shape and when we settled our agreement with the airlines, they got what they wanted, which was the rehabilitation of our runways and taxiways and a new runway, a new east–west runway" (Broadbent 1997). The settlement thus also benefited the airport, which now had an excuse to further expand its capacity.

Airport passenger volume continued to expand along with development of the megaresorts. At that time, "it became apparent that the biggest restriction to the growth of the airport was the surface roads and our inability to bring people in and out of the airport" (Broadbent 1997). The authority commissioned a study of its ground-transportation requirements and identified the need for a new access road from McCarran to Interstate 15, the highway connecting Las Vegas with Los Angeles and Salt Lake City. At the same time, the county had done an assessment of ground-transportation needs in relation to the rapid increase in residential community development, especially in the Henderson area's Green Valley master-planned community (see chapter 5). As a result, the county planned a beltway that would eventually encircle the Las Vegas Valley, with the airport linked to the southern leg of the county project.

The main obstacle to approving the beltway was the need for an environmental impact assessment. Broadbent's long-time connections in county government were invaluable here, as the unofficial "eighth county commissioner" successfully linked the airport's need for access with those of the county public-works agency to provide money for the environmental impact assessment. By the end of the 1980s, construction began on this major addition to the highway network in the Las Vegas Valley. The first phase of the beltway was the Airport Connector, which included construction of a tunnel under the airport.

An added benefit to having McCarran overseen by the county involved gaining advance notice of new construction, which aided its ability to make realistic plans to meet future demand, something that not all airports are able to do. Given that all proposed resort projects must get air-space approval from the county and that it is well recognized that expansion of tourism depends heavily on adequate functioning of the McCarran facility, it remains strongly in the interests of private casino developers to maintain clear channels of communication with the county and airport operators.

In the 1990s, the airlines suffered heavy financial losses. Most cut back on the number of planes they flew in order to fly at full capacity, reducing the number of flights in and out of airports around the nation. The Las Vegas area, however, needed not only to sustain its passenger volume, but also to expand it in order to sustain economic growth. The Las Vegas Convention and Visitors Authority joined the airport and resort industry to make a special appeal to national carriers to consider Las Vegas as an important stop in their daily flying schedules, since most aircraft in and out of McCarran fly at full capacity.

The airport also sought increased international traffic, as a 13,600-foot runway, one of the longest civilian runways in the United States, was added to accommodate the 747 jumbo jets and also because long runways are needed so that fully loaded aircraft can take off in the heat of the summer. In 1990, the port of entry customs and immigration facilities also were expanded to accommodate federal agencies involved in overseeing international flights. According to Broadbent: "We have a facility now that will comfortably handle two wide bodies in thirty-five or forty minutes. That's 700 or 800 people [going through customs]." However, the major carriers who fly overseas do so from their own hubs, not from Las Vegas: "They all want to fly out of a hub where they can fly a lot of people in on their own planes and then put them on a plane to go overseas" (Broadbent 1997).

As a result, the airport has aggressively pursued international charter business to pick up the slack and expand passenger volume. Charter flights from Germany, England, Switzerland, Canada, and Mexico already fly into McCarran and a bilateral agreement between the United States and Japan signed in 1998 led to nonstop service between Tokyo and Las Vegas:

> We are trying very hard to get charters or regularly scheduled transportation out of the Pacific Rim Asian countries. In order to get a carrier to fly in from another country, however, there has to be an agreement between the two countries to let you do that. We are very active in that

bilateral process or trying to get what they call "open skies" which
means any air carrier can fly into the United States and any US carrier
can fly into that other country.   (Broadbent 1997)

Another airport arena targeted for growth is warehousing facilities:
"The large planes, like the 767s, that come in here from Germany and
England have a lot of room and you could fill it with freight coming
and going out. They are more likely to land here if they can make
money from freight" (Broadbent 1997). Las Vegas thus has become a
major warehousing and distribution point for several western states
and is the hub for overnight mail for the US Post Office in 14 western
states.

The air cargo business also plays an important role in attempts to
diversify the southern Nevada economy. More than 25 air freight companies provide service through McCarran and in 1996, 125 million
tons of cargo were shipped or received at the airport. Air cargo is
handled at the 160-acre Foreign Trade Zone in the Las Vegas
International Air Cargo Center and the race is on to jet even more
packages into Clark County so that regional businesses can cash in on
the international boom in air cargo traffic. They also want to capitalize on the central location of Las Vegas in the region, as competition
with other southwestern states is fierce. Additionally, 6,000 acres in
the Ivanpah Valley, near the California state line, has been dedicated
for an air cargo facility, and long-range planners predict that the facility could become the next southern Nevada airport once McCarran
reaches its maximum passenger capacity of 60 million.

The airport has aggressively purchased surrounding land to miti-
gate noise complaints and any roadblocks to further expansion.
Mobile home parks north of Tropicana Boulevard were purchased and
relocated southeast of town, replaced by a golf driving range. Office
and warehousing facilities such as the McCarran Business Park, with
more than 1.4 million square feet located between the airport and
Interstate Highway 215, are also moving into the airport buffer zone.

Another potentially serious issue that was resolved favorably by the
airport involved complications created by the growth of private, small
plane traffic. To resolve the issue, Clark County acquired the general
aviation facility at the North Las Vegas airport in October 1987 for the
express purpose of transferring small plane traffic to that location, and
another private-plane facility is being constructed for the Henderson
area to the southeast. As Broadbent (1997) observed, "There are more
and more people in small planes and you don't want them at
McCarran because it just jams the airspace." While far-sighted airport
planners have been able to meet the needs of an expanding tourist

industry, the facility has also been fortunate in being able to generate funds through its own operations and bonding authority. For example, the airport receives over $20 million a year in gambling revenue from leases for slot machines that are conveniently placed near arrival and departure gates. After all, this is Las Vegas.

The airport continues to expand its facilities. In November 1996, an additional covered parking structure opened with 6,000 square feet of space and a $200-million, 26-gate, state-of-the-art extension, the "D-Gate" terminal, opened in June 1998, bringing the airport's total number of gates to 93 and its total passenger capacity to 45 million per year. The new terminal is connected to the main terminal by an $80-million people mover. The debut of the D-Gates was not without political controversy, however. For months the State Ethics Commission had been investigating charges of political favoritism in the awarding of lucrative concession contracts. One D-Gate concession was awarded to the daughter of former airport director Broadbent and most other successful bidders had close personal relationships with several county commissioners. The same week the D-Gate terminal opened, two county commissioners, including the commission Chair, were found guilty of violating ethics laws by the State Ethics Commission. The violations included using public positions to benefit friends, failing to disclose the relationships, and failing to abstain from voting in the profitable contract-award process (see chapter 8).

Despite its overall impressive growth, there are potential problems for the airport looming on the horizon. In late 1997, as D-Gate construction was in its final stage, passenger counts at McCarran began dropping. The number of airline passengers in 1997 declined 0.5% from 1996, a year with aggressive airline advertising and promotional low fares. Even more ominous, in the first nine months of 1998 passenger traffic was down 1.5%, although a continuing increase in motoring tourists helped produce an overall gain in visitor volume of 2.9% in 1997. Since airlines get higher fares for non-tourist routes because business travelers typically pay higher fares, more planes are being diverted from tourist destinations as major aircraft builders struggle to keep up with demand. Airport expansion continues unabated, however, as work was completed recently on an additional north–south runway, bringing the total number of runways to four.

In addition to the crucial economic impact the airport has on the tourism economy, it is also a major factor in the local employment community, as more than 10,000 employees work at McCarran, with nearly 800 employed by the Clark County Department of Aviation. McCarran Airport is now the tenth busiest in the nation and the fifteenth busiest in the world.

## The New Face of Las Vegas

The third boom in venture capital has now lasted more than a decade, although it has undergone a series of transformations in terms of how resort development is financed. Gaming and tourism, however, remain the major industries in southern Nevada. Many Las Vegans have become jaded as each new resort is proclaimed the world's largest, most exotic, most expensive, or most entertaining, but the resorts continue to attract tourists and their money. As a result, legalized gaming has made it into the upper echelons of American entertainment earnings, with the hotel–casino industry approaching annual revenues of $30 billion, prompting Glenn Schaeffer, president of Circus Circus Enterprises, to proclaim in a keynote address to the American Gaming Summit in December 1996: "That's the sum of the other major location-based entertainment industries combined – theme parks, box office cinema, cruise ships and professional spectator sports." Resorts on the four-mile-long Strip alone generate total revenues that outpace the revenues of all the theme parks in America put together.

One example of the growth of revenues in southern Nevada can be seen in the fiscal 1998 annual budgets. Clark County had a $601-million operating budget and a total budget of $2.6 billion. The city of Las Vegas had a $240.6-million operating budget, a 9% increase over the prior year, while Henderson had a $164-million budget, a 10% increase, and North Las Vegas had a $118-million budget, a 6% increase. The Clark County School District budget alone totaled more than $2 billion for more than 190,000 students.

The phenomenal growth in resort revenues, however, has attracted hordes of new residents who have in turn jammed roads, crowded schools, overburdened a dwindling water supply, and adversely affected air quality and sewage treatment. The Las Vegas community may be as far as ten years behind in infrastructure construction, even though approximately $25,000 to $35,000 of the price of a new home reflects the cost of building government-mandated infrastructure plus taxes, transfer fees, and licenses. Low taxes have so far been a leading factor in business and population growth but much depends on how long this third boom in venture or second-circuit capital lasts (see chapter 9).

No less lamentable in the eyes of some observers are changes in both the Strip and downtown brought about by the megaresorts since the opening of the Mirage in 1989. According to Blair Kamin: "The old Sin City . . . has traded in its G-string for a G-rating. So much for the garish neon signs, topless showgirls and smoke-filled casinos. Las

Vegas has become Disneyland in the Desert, a family resort instead of an adult playground. Or, at least, that's the impression left by a flood of recent newspaper and magazine articles" (1994: 10).

As some casinos shifted their marketing strategies to emphasize "family vacations," gambling activity seemed to be shoved to the background in an attempt to portray Las Vegas as an attractive resort destination for the entire family, or as one observer noted, as shifting from "sin city to fun city." One major motivating factor for this change was the growing popularity of gambling across the nation. By 1994, some form of legalized gambling could be found in 48 of the 50 states, with only Utah and Hawaii holding out. Legalized casino operations were established in 25 states and 35 states ran their own lotteries, largely removing the stigma of gambling in American culture. While Las Vegas' casinos profited in some ways from this change, they also experienced greater competition and were pushed to expand their appeal. "Why travel to Las Vegas" some asked, "if people could gamble at local churches or Indian gaming casinos in their immediate area?" One solution to this dilemma was to capitalize on the social acceptance of gambling by redefining casinos as family vacation resorts, especially for affluent baby boomers.

In the early 1990s over $3.1 billion was invested in "hybrid amusement-park casinos" by two of the biggest names in Las Vegas. The MGM Grand and Circus Circus developed amusement parks adjacent to their casinos to entertain families. Typical of the new mentality, Larry Wolf, then manager of the giant, 5,005-room MGM Grand, stated that the hotel-casino complex wasn't competing with other casino resorts in the area but with Disneyland. He described the resort's theme park in the following fashion: "The rides are unspectacular and the park is one tenth the size of Disneyland, but it is central to the hotel's family image. It appears on page two of the brochure, while 'gaming' is tucked coyly at the back" (Longman 1994). In addition to amusement parks, casino-resorts also added glitzy, high-priced, "effects-driven" shows, electronic arcades featuring virtual-reality games, and health spas, to create an all-purpose tourist destination that could compete with places like Orlando, Florida (Longman 1994).

In addition to virtual-reality arcades to keep the kids busy, the MGM Grand also provided a day-care facility that accommodated children aged from 3 to 12, with rules that assured patronage of their establishment: "If you want to leave your child there while you gamble, certain conditions must be met: Your kid has to be potty-trained, you have to be a registered guest of the hotel and you have to sign a form promising to stay on the premises. Which means, of course, that you stand to leave your gambling money at the MGM rather than at a competing casino" (Kamin 1994: 10).

Most casino operators did not buy into family-oriented marketing because, although families with children visiting Las Vegas have almost doubled in twenty years, the average visitor's gambling budget did not increase proportionally. Also, the amusement parks failed to generate profits necessary to justify their space. As the average stay of tourists increased from 3.1 to 3.5 days from 1994 to 1997, visitors spent less time in the casinos. The newest properties, such as the Monte Carlo, the Bellagio, and the Venetian, have maintained an emphasis on the resort concept with a focus on upscale adult entertainment. Uncharacteristically expensive rooms and more on-site services such as health spas, dining, and shopping represent the current mix of features that are designed to attract upscale visitors, with or without children, who are more interested in resort vacations than family-oriented theme-park holidays.

While the shift to family-oriented resorts was overrated, the new "mega" scale of casino construction continues to transform the ambiance of the city. Today, almost as much goes on outside the casinos as inside them. "Archi-tainment" attractions, or entertainment derived from architecture, have produced an urban street culture of gawkers. Egyptian pyramids, Fairyland castles, Roman Forums, Alpine resorts, and European-themed environments have replaced Wild West saloons and semi-naked showgirls as the symbols of Las Vegas. The vibrant street life on the Strip and downtown created by these Fantasyland attractions thus constitutes a significant departure from the old days when "the approach from the casinos' point of view was to bring people in, and then lock the front door so they couldn't get out" (Warner 1995: 4).

Some commentators on the new milieu cite the declining importance of neon as one indicator of the transformation. In the past, hotels such as the Flamingo or the Stardust were lit up at night by neon tubing covering their façades. None of the megaresorts built in the 1990s, however, the Mirage, New York-New York, the MGM Grand, the Bellagio, or the Venetian, use neon on their buildings, although the MGM and Treasure Island have two of the largest free-standing neon signs in the world. According to Veldon Simpson, architect of the Luxor and Excalibur: "You don't need neon any longer. When you have something as powerful and dynamic as that architecture is [meaning his two hotels], you don't need a sign. It would be an insult to the architecture to sign it" (Gabriel 1991: 68).

According to architectural critic Alan Hess, however, abandoning neon also eliminates the most enduring symbol associated with Las

Vegas. Hess is particularly upset at the changes the vaulted Fremont Street Experience brought to Glitter Gulch:

> They've completely destroyed Fremont St. The play of neon, buildings and sky is completely gone. It's a big loss. The neon signs of downtown Las Vegas are one of those primary American icons everyone knows all over the world. ... Las Vegas has always trashed its past in order to move into the future – that's the tradition. ... I think we are losing a lot of the character of Las Vegas.   (in Warner 1995: 4)

Another change lamented by some observers is the disappearance of the Las Vegas lounge act. Today megaresorts feature big-name celebrities or expensive, effects-driven production shows. While the lounge acts were free, tickets to the big shows that have replaced them are costly. According to Dave Hoekstra:

> Lounge culture has crumbled into a cloud of desert dust. During the 1950s and 60s, Las Vegas lounges used to swing to the rhythms of Louis Prima and Keely Smith. Lots of cats went to school with Mr. Prima, who died in 1978. ... There aren't many left of the Las Vegas showrooms that a 16-year-old Wayne Newton used to sneak into. Big stars don't play the showrooms anymore. Now they only headline at the large arenas, such as the Thomas and Mack arena at UNLV, or at the biggest casinos. (1996: 36)

However one views these changes, they continue unabated as Las Vegas' interests relentlessly pursue their goal of becoming the world's premier tourist destination, recycling building and spaces regardless of their value as historical landmarks.

# 3 Media Vegas: Hype, Boosterism, and the Image of the City

## The Image of the City

The image of Las Vegas is complex and multi-layered, with associations ranging from cowboys to gangsters, from streetwalkers to *Folies Bergères* showgirls, from high rollers to compulsive gamblers, and from instant riches to economic ruin. In a miracle of sanitization, cutthroat sociopaths such as Bugsy Siegel and Tony "the Ant" Spilotro are romanticized as bringing vision and colorful character to the city, itself pitched simultaneously as both an Adult Disneyland and a family vacation destination. Hyperbole and contradiction are not simply products of different readings of the historical record, however, as in postmodern conflicts that give us contrasting interpretations of Christopher Columbus or Thomas Jefferson. They are instead the direct result of decades of media and advertising hype that have characterized Las Vegas since its founding.

In the fledgling days of the town, the notorious Block 16 was set aside for card games and prostitution. Sin and commerce have marched hand-in-hand ever since, but this alliance made Las Vegas no more atypical than any other American city of the time. The difference is that Las Vegas extolled with pride what other places sought to hide. To the commonplace culture of heavily populated cities and industrial towns that made up the urban fabric of the country, Las Vegas alone stood as the behavioral "Other," a land where the "victimless" crimes of sex, drink, and gambling were not only condoned, but celebrated.

Equally significant, Las Vegas has always advertised its tourist attractions with a heavy dose of hype (as the "Gateway to Hoover Dam" among other things). When city after city today tries to market itself as an attractive location to offset the relocation of traditional businesses and industries south of the border and overseas, they are simply doing what Las Vegas has done since its founding as a lonely desert outpost. A lively, if somewhat off-color, image of Las Vegas pervades Western culture today, because the city has hyped itself, in order to survive and prosper, for almost a century.

In short, Las Vegas' prominent place in contemporary American popular culture has been produced by two interrelated processes. On the one hand, it has flourished as the unique cultural "Other" to the puritanical, provincial, and hardworking industrial ethos of the American heartland. On the other, the dusty desert town has also prospered because it sells itself as a tourist mecca and entertainment capital. As a place of entertainment, Las Vegas has helped spin its own myths, with headliners like Elvis Presley, Liberace, Frank Sinatra, Wayne Newton, Don Rickles, and Ann Margaret, who in turn helped make or sustain their entertainment careers through their gigs at flamboyant Las Vegas resorts.

## Hollywood Vegas

Nowhere has Las Vegas' ability to market itself, to a degree rivaling older towns such as New York and Chicago, been more evident than in its recent emergence as a *mise en scène,* a backdrop, for movies and television dramas. In the 1990s, numerous films such as *Bugsy, Honeymoon in Vegas, Indecent Proposal, Casino, Vegas Vacation, Leaving Las Vegas, ConAir* and *Mars Attacks* all have used Las Vegas the way an earlier generation of film makers set their stories on the streets of Brooklyn or Los Angeles. Countless other films have depicted Las Vegas as a unique destination that brings about a magical transformation or, at the very least, a second-act climax, as in such memorable films as *Rain Man* and *The Godfather.* With help from Hollywood, the city has thus established its image in the American consciousness, as Las Vegas associations – brilliant neon displays, leggy showgirls, roulette wheels, high-stakes poker games, and the flash of cash – have become seminal signs in the basic vocabulary of our popular culture.

The earliest cinematic examples provided the fundamental elements that later became standard referents for Las Vegas' glitzy image. While Nevada served as a location for several early Hollywood films, the first film focusing on Las Vegas as a city was *Las Vegas Nights*, released in 1941. Lacking any real plot, the low-budget movie showcased the Tommy Dorsey Band and its crooner, Frank Sinatra.

When entrepreneur Howard Hughes assumed control of RKO pictures during the red-scare days of Hollywood, he produced the first picture explicitly devoted to the town. *The Las Vegas Story* (1952) starred his franchise sex symbol, Jane Russell, "Hollywood Hunk" Victor Mature, Vincent Price, later to become a malevolent presence in many B-movies, and songsmith Hoagy Carmichael on piano. The film featured Russell as a femme fatale who once had a torrid affair with Mature while she was a singer at the Last Chance Casino and he was a sergeant stationed at Nellis Air Force Base during the war. She later returns to Las Vegas, married to Price, a sharpster businessman on the road to economic ruin. The Last Chance Casino is just that for the characters, as Price's quest for easy riches is doomed to fail, while Russell reconnects with her old flame. Wealth, greed, romance, sin, and gambling are thus interwoven as central themes for subsequent film depictions of Las Vegas.

Having established himself in Hollywood, Howard Hughes was already measuring the lay of the desert land when he made the film. He had his eye on several Las Vegas properties during this embryonic stage of the town's rise to resort status and *The Las Vegas Story* starts off much like a real-estate advertisement. The first shot features a map of Nevada with Clark County in outline, and Carmichael's voice-over is more a didactic sales speech than a cinematic monologue: "Yes, its Clark County, Nevada. Excepting for folks around here, most people never heard of Clark County." Then a second map duplicates the first, with a shaded area signifying the city of Las Vegas. Carmichael continues, "But just you say, Las Vegas, and folks pick up their ears, and the lucky ones some money too, or drop some, along with last year's wife. But you can't say Las Vegas without including Clark County because they go together." In this way, Hughes neatly valorized Clark County land, where new casino-resorts were being built along the Strip, in a seemingly innocent, homespun introduction. This was particularly ironic given that Hughes justified his move into studio ownership during the infamous McCarthy period by claiming that Hollywood was a hotbed of radical ideologists secreting their own subversive politics into seemingly innocuous film scripts.

The Las Vegas depicted in Hughes' film is one that reflects the bare-bones milieu of casino gambling characteristic of Bugsy Siegel's time, when the Hollywood–Las Vegas connection was first being forged. A classic photo montage of casino exteriors featuring the large neon signs of the El Rancho, the Desert Inn, the Thunderbird, and the Flamingo establishes the setting for the film. Against this backdrop sit two fictitious venues, the Last Chance Casino and the Fabulous. The former is depicted in the low-budget film as little more than a large bar with a few craps and poker gambling tables. In a scene reminiscent of *Casablanca*, Carmichael sings at an upright piano, amidst young women in hoop skirts who seem to have been abandoned by their gambling-obsessed mates. Price pursues his fate at the more upscale Fabulous, located on the Strip. Yet, it too is nothing more than a large room divided into a bar and hotel-registration area on one side and on the other a sunken, carpeted space containing a small assortment of gaming tables, where Price gambles himself into oblivion.

While this 1950s scale is quaint and intimate compared with the immensity of present-day casino structures and movie settings, an even more striking feature of the film is the absence of slot machines. Russell, Mature, and Price romp through a 1950s Las Vegas devoid of glazed-eyed slot players transfixed in front of one-armed bandits. The doomed trio seems to want just one more chance to roll the dice of their ill-fated lives. Here, as in real life, Las Vegas is portrayed as a place that offers visitors the promise of a quick fix, both romantically and financially.

In the 1960s, two films helped establish Las Vegas as a playground for the rich and famous, an entertainment fantasyland where anything goes. *Ocean's 11* (1960) featured the "Rat Pack," Frank Sinatra, Sammy Davis, Jr, Dean Martin, Joey Bishop, and Peter Lawford, romping through the "no-holds-barred" resort mecca. The entertainers are portrayed as ex-army buddies scheming to "get rich quick" by robbing casinos. *Ocean's 11* thus functioned as a celebrity travelogue that provided Las Vegas with the cachet and glamor of Hollywood as a playground for the rich and famous, focusing primarily on the aura of Frank Sinatra and his cronies. The entertainers played two shows a night at Strip resorts while shooting the film during the day in their own 24-hour party environment. The first Las Vegas skyline view is a long shot of Fremont Street and its Vegas Vic sign, a major Glitter Gulch signifier of the town's image. Robbery targets are Strip casinos, the Flamingo, Sands, Desert Inn, Riviera, and Sahara, also the real-life playgrounds for Sinatra and his associates. In contrast to later films, and more reflective of the times, the interiors of these Strip casinos are depicted as small scale, with only a limited number of slot machines and gambling tables near the bars and lounges. The wartime buddies pull off a $5-million heist, hiding the loot in a coffin that is then inadvertently cremated, ending the film somewhat anticlimactically as the group exchanges perplexed looks after learning of the fiéry demise of their loot.

*Ocean's 11* did prove, however, that stars and Las Vegas Strip ambiance could overcome a bad script. The glittering Las Vegas backdrop and partying entertainers showed a good-time, anything-goes Las Vegas: "For millions of movie goers, that good time helped make Las Vegas not just the entertainment capital of the world but the swingin'-est place in the universe" (Cling 1997).

The Las Vegas mystique was enhanced further in another 1960s film that combined images of freedom, romance, coolness, and excitement in a musical extravaganza. Starring two Las Vegas icons, Elvis Presley and Ann Margaret, *Viva Las Vegas* (1964) became a signature film and provided an unofficial anthem for the town. The high-octane mix of beautiful women, gambling, poolside hi-jinks, romance, and fast cars produced an even more potent image of Las Vegas as the premier adult vacation destination in the country. With *Viva Las Vegas*, the Sin City and Lost Wages associations were joined in a Hollywood sign system that expressed the idea of "Vegas" as a spectacle of consumer indulgence.

In 1972, fictional Mafia boss Michael Corleone expands the family's operation from New York to Las Vegas in Francis Ford Coppola's epic, *The Godfather*. The opening montage highlights famous resort marquees featuring celebrity entertainers, Patti Page at the Desert Inn, Joe E. Lewis at the El Rancho, and Dean Martin and Jerry Lewis at the Sands. Las Vegas is depicted as a mecca of headline entertainment rivaling Hollywood and New York City. Elsewhere in the country, Patti Page could only be heard on records and Dean Martin and Jerry Lewis were seen on television and in the movies, but only in Las Vegas did they appear live onstage. Corleone and his mob entourage pull up to the porte cochere of Moe Green's casino, with Michael wearing a homburg hat and black three-piece business suit, looking like a visiting Brooklyn rabbi. In contrast, his more "Vegas"-style brother, Fredo, wears a cream-colored sport jacket, a black silk shirt, and dark sunglasses. Fredo ushers Michael into a room filled with high-priced callgirls and offers him "anything that you desire, anything" but the future Don refuses this stereotypical form of Las Vegas entertainment. The ill-fated Moe Green attempts to welcome Michael and his entourage by arranging for them to have stacks of chips "on the house." As Green soon finds out, however, the Brooklyn Corleones didn't come to gamble.

The Corleone operation moves into Las Vegas, depicted as the land of gambling and pimps, as a logical extension of the mob enterprise; it's better business than the old, "olive oil" rackets in New York City. Ironically, the movie was made as mob involvement in Las Vegas casino operations was declining as efforts were underway to exorcise it by a combination of federal, state and local public officials, and "legitimate" entrepreneurs like Howard Hughes.

The 1990s ushered in a rash of movies set in the city that also featured traditional Las Vegas themes of romance, gangsters, gambling, and greed. The 1992 film *Honeymoon in Vegas* starred James Caan as a mafioso gambler, Nicholas Cage as a lumpen proletarian loser, and Sarah Jessica Parker as a ditzy blond. The movie displayed megaresort Las Vegas in all its cartoon glory, as clichés from decades of media representations of Las Vegas were depicted within the Strip's

immense casino spaces. Gangsters had become like part of the furniture, as merely local color. Sociopathic killers resembling Bugsy Siegel
and the fictional Michael Corleone had mellowed into *gangster*-types,
as semiotic signs of "gangster-ness," acted out by Hollywood tough
guys like Caan, who had earlier played the volatile, hot-headed "bad
Don," Sonny Corleone. In *Honeymoon in Vegas* he portrays a suave,
well-dressed mobster with power-trip romance, not Moe Green's
casino empire, on his mind. Cage plays a marginal, hand-to-mouth
New York private detective who proposes a quickie Las Vegas marriage ceremony and honeymoon to his girlfriend Parker, a school
teacher. "If I had just said 'City Hall'," he states, "the story would
have ended here. But I didn't."

As the film begins, Las Vegas is approached from the air with the
camera zooming in on a night scene that is a riot of neon colors. The
slowly descending sky-shot settles on the Strip, near the Mirage
resort's gigantic animated sign, while the soundtrack blares out the
Elvis song "Viva Las Vegas." The Strip is glitzier and more animated,
but it remains the setting of *The Las Vegas Story* the backdrop to a
clichéd, but twisted, "boy loves girl" tale. The soon-to-be-married
couple stay at Bally's, where an Elvis impersonator convention is
being held. By the 1990s, Las Vegas had merged with Elvis into a
double sign, with the entertainer posthumously multiplied as the
definitive Las Vegas entertainer by hundreds of impersonators.

The camera repeatedly pans across a cavernous interior space that
is the now familiar hyper-domain of the Las Vegas megaresorts. As a
travelogue, the film documents the robust progress of the Las Vegas
resort industry, revealing a champion boxing training ring, video
arcades, lounge acts, chorus-line shows, Elvis impersonators, slot
machines, and a sea of gambling tables. Any sense of intimacy has
been lost within these immense interiors, with their endless banks of
one-armed bandits and giant halls filled with gambling tables and
sportsbook TV screens.

The young couple are separated when Caan's character wins the
bride-to-be in a poker game. Women have always been objectified in
the Las Vegas image of fun, but a new level of "lover as commodity"
is reached here as the fiancée is no different than a stack of poker chips
to be won or lost. The couple ultimately are reunited, but not before
Cage joins a skydiving club of Elvis impersonators and literally leaps
from the air to rescue his bride. Everything and everyone can be
wagered or is for sale in this media-created Las Vegas, including a
fiancée, a theme that is continued in *Indecent Proposal*.

In other 1990s films set in Las Vegas the city itself becomes a main
character, in a postmodern reversal where it switches from being the

background of the setting to the foreground as the subject of action. For example, in the 1995 film *Leaving Las Vegas*, the city itself becomes a dark metaphor for the terminal trip of a lost soul, again portrayed by Nicholas Cage, this time as a self-pitying, alcoholic who finds last-chance love on the way to his obsessive demise. He links up with a prostitute who falls in love and nurtures him, though she fails to prevent his slide into suicide. Local tourism officials were not pleased with the way Las Vegas was used to frame this decidedly downbeat story, and the local film commission was less than cooperative during production of the award-winning film, as it provided an unpleasant, but not totally inaccurate, portrayal of an aspect of the town not advertised in tourist brochures.

More consistent with the preferred version of Las Vegas media hype was the glorified and romanticized story of the life of mobster Bugsy Siegel and his Las Vegas venture depicted in the 1991 film *Bugsy*. As a fantasy rendition of Las Vegas' history, this whitewashed saga attempted to turn a tale about a demented killer, Siegel, and his pros-titute girlfriend, Virginia Hill, into a love story with likeable charac-ters. Siegel here is portrayed as a founding father of the Strip, a visionary who realized the idea of a glamorous casino-resort mecca in the desert, while Hill is depicted as an attractive femme fatale who dallies with Siegel until his bloody demise in her Los Angeles living room. Starring an aging Warren Beatty, this film plays the same chords of greed, romance, and hapless characters found in other Las Vegas-set films. Mob connections are presented as part of business as usual and casino building is portrayed as a glamorous activity with an aura that downplays the brutal reality of Siegel's activities, which ulti-mately cost him his life.

*Casino*, directed by Martin Scorcese, is a grittier exercise in mafia nostalgia, spotlighting the 1970s days of active mob influence in Las Vegas by colorful characters such as Chicago-mob frontman Anthony "Tony the Ant" Spilotro, portrayed in the film by Joe Pesci as a fic-tional mob character, Nicky Santoro. The film's central theme of greed inextricably linked with power, romance, betrayal, and vengeance, focuses on the marriage of mob-related gambling oddsmaker and casino operator "Lefty" Rosenthal, played by Robert DeNiro, and his showgirl wife, played by Sharon Stone. In *Casino*, Scorcese does not glorify the mob and its sociopathic gangsters, however. On the con-trary, the seamy side of Las Vegas is depicted in a realistic fashion not found in other films as the movie exposes the real-life skimming and financial raiding of casino operations, depicting gangsters, such as Santoro, as idiotic thugs obsessed by greed.

Almost all of these films shot in Las Vegas involve some twist on the "boy-loves-girl" theme, sometimes with an added "boy-gambles-away-girl" twist, often intertwined with greed and the glamorization of casino gambling. A similar representation of the Las Vegas experience, under the guise of comedy, was depicted in a 1997 film, *Vegas Vacation*, that manages to exploit for laughs almost every social problem associated with the town. Featuring the Griswold family, with the bumbling Chevy Chase and actress Beverly D'Angelo as his wife, this film portrays Las Vegas in its latest metamorphosis as the "Disneyland of the Desert," a family-oriented vacation destination.

As the Griswolds drive up to their hotel in a limousine, viewers are again subjected to the conventional montage of resort exteriors. Spliced together along with the family's gawking, wide-mouthed stares, this shot provides moviegoers with a surreptitious commercial for Las Vegas' latest themed attractions, as the Griswolds are driven past a Sphinx, a medieval castle, an exploding volcano, and a pirate battle.

As soon as the family arrives at their hotel, the hapless Clark Griswold rushes to the poker tables to lose hundreds of dollars within a few minutes. While the rapidity of his loss is not atypical for many, the implacable Griswold keeps coming back for more, eventually losing thousands of dollars and placing his family on the brink of financial ruin, transforming the personal tragedy of compulsive gambling into a form of light entertainment. Meanwhile, Griswold's son acquires a fake ID and proceeds to win thousands of dollars, along with the friendship of an avuncular gangster figure, spoofing both teenage gambling and the mob. The boy's sister joins a cousin who works as a topless dancer, making light of the sexual experiences of teenage girls. Mrs Griswold catches the eye of Las Vegas icon and shlockmeister Wayne Newton, who wines and dines her. Here, one popular culture fantasy is veneered over another for the boys and girls and mothers and fathers of America in the newly remodeled, themed tourist mecca. In the end, the elder Griswold avoids financial ruin with the assistance of his son's newly acquired bankroll, while the women experience the titillation of Las Vegas-style sex and romance, ultimately bringing the family closer together through their mega-casino experience. The image of Las Vegas as a transformative, magical space is thus reinforced via yet another cinematic vehicle, this time the family comedy.

Just as Las Vegas became a recognizable backdrop for Hollywood movies by the 1970s, a strong sense of the city's image was also constructed on television at the same time, when in 1978 Aaron Spelling's weekly TV series *VEGA$* premiered on a national network (ABC). For three years, Robert Urich starred as detective Dan Tanna. Each week a glitzy episode of Glitter Gulch adventure was introduced into millions of American homes during prime time. Set in and around the Desert Inn, the program emphasized the standard Las Vegas signifiers; bright neon signs, leggy showgirls, casino lounges, bars, and flashy cars. All this glitz and glamor were made even more exciting by mixing in the seamy underbelly of murder, betrayal, desperation, mobsterism, and other sleazy activities also associated with the town in American popular culture. The flashy backdrop of *VEGA$* functioned similarly to that of other TV detective series, such as *Hawaii-Five-O* and *Magnum, PI*, both of which used lush Hawaiian settings and recognizable tourist locations to offset the sordid details of crime. At the beginning of each *VEGA$* episode a pre-megaresort montage flashed images of major Las Vegas casinos of the time, with their signs featuring big-name Las Vegas regulars like Wayne Newton at the Desert Inn, Tom Jones at Caesars Palace, and Dean Martin at the old MGM. As the show unfolded, the focus of action shifted back and forth from downtown to the Strip as Dan Tanna dispatched criminals while rubbing shoulders with gamblers, showgirls, and other Las Vegas mainstays.

Locals watching the program, however, no doubt suffered from a kind of disorientation, as Dan Tanna would turn right out of the Desert Inn onto the Strip and head to the airport (south) via Glitter Gulch (north). Nonetheless, they enjoyed the fame and exposure *VEGA$* brought, and loved having the film crew and stars based in their town. Some residents, like Desert Inn president Burton Cohen, even achieved national prominence through the program, and in a running inside joke, the hotel paging system broadcast the names of locals with connections to the program during each episode. Tourism officials loved the program, not only because of the positive weekly national publicity generated every time Tanna's '57 T-Bird rolled down the neon-lit Strip, but also because an estimated $60 million was spent locally producing its 72 episodes (Collins 1982).

## Hype, Boosterism, and Advertising

While most cities have for some time employed advertising agencies or staff members to coordinate media images of their particular locales, the increase in competitiveness around the globe for manufacturing, commercial, and service investment has made the promotion of tourism through locational boosterism a vital activity for virtually every metropolitan area. Las Vegas, on the other hand, began as a small town with limited infrastructure development, located in one of the most inhospitable desert regions of the United States. Its municipal interests thus have been devoted to hyping the city since its founding in 1905 through a real-estate tent sale. Any event that has profit-making potential is approached by local business and political leaders with one eye peeled toward local needs and the other no less keenly focused on the national media. As the local press observed in the 1950s: "Las Vegas has learned in the space of a few short years how to get its picture on the nation's front pages every day without benefit of gambling or atomic explosions, though both help" (Best and Hillyer 1995: 119). One common form of attention has been the promotion of extreme forms of behavior or grand events. This spectacular hype itself has become virtually synonymous with the Las Vegas image.

## Spectacular Hype

Since early on, each major casino has had a publicity director who tried to outdo colleagues to attract media attention in the competition for tourist dollars. The incredible variety of stunts performed in this quest include parading showgirls on the street in sequined costumes and head-dresses, floating craps games in resort swimming pools, photos of Hollywood and television entertainers, huge buffets, giant wedding and birthday cakes, hotel pools filled with cocktail drinks or jello, and stuntmen performing death-defying tricks.

During the 1950s casinos began spending thousands on advertising in the nation's major population centers: "The Dunes for instance, installed an enormous electric sign on top of the Capitol Theater at Fiftieth St. and Broadway in New York City. The sign cost the hotel $56,000 annually [in 1955 dollars!] for location, lease, and maintenance" (Best and Hillyer 1995: 119). In a similar vein, the Sahara paid to construct a replica of its swimming pool at the intersection of Sunset Boulevard and Doheny Drive in Los Angeles, filled with water and female swimmers "whose jobs were to leap and cavort around the pool for eight hours a day in two shifts" (Best and Hillyer 1995: 121). Extreme wealth also became a part of the image portrayed in advertising. The Golden Nugget housed the "largest nugget in the world," and the social director of the El Rancho was known as the Golden Girl because she worked at a gold desk, used a gold telephone, had a golden Cadillac, and dressed in gold lamé outfits. Finally, by being identified with notorious personalities, extremes of behavior were also incorporated into the Las Vegas image. The notorious daredevil Eivel Knievel, for example, chose Las Vegas as the location for several of his stunts, and the already mentioned escapades of the "Rat Pack," especially Dean Martin and Frank Sinatra, were highly publicized around the country.

## Sex Sells

For many years the term, "the Las Vegas total," used by tourists and local residents alike, has referred to the treatment of gambling visitors to a hotel room, food, gambling, lounge acts, and "commercial sex" (Castleman 1996: 39). Despite the fact that prostitution is illegal in Clark County and in all but a few rural areas of Nevada, its origins go back a long way: "Las Vegas' original sex market, known as Block 16 (downtown between First and Second, Ogden and Stewart Streets) was typical. A mere block from the staid and proper First State Bank, the Block was established in 1905 by staid and proper conservative town planners working for the San Pedro, Los Angeles, and Salt Lake Railroad, as the predictable byproduct of the company's liquor-containment policy" (Castleman 1996: 171).

Years later, when Bugsy Siegel opened the Flamingo Hotel and Casino, he filled the place with attractive young women who did everything from checking hats and coats, to selling cocktails, to entertaining male guests after hours. His long-time associate Moe Dalitz followed Siegel's policy in the other casinos that he operated:

> Dalitz knew that all the conflicting realities boiled down to two basic truths. First, gamblers needed sex: the suggestion of it, with girls parading around on stage and decorating the floor; the mysterious myth of its ready availability with gorgeous and expensive pros; and the eventual consummation – proscribed, safe, hidden – that gets the guy to sleep or wakes him up, makes him feel lucky when he wins or consoles him when he loses, keeps him around the tables a little longer, and sends him home having experienced what has been called the "Las Vegas total." But second, the sex trade had to be directly and carefully choreographed, from start to finish, in order to avoid any chance of offending the millions of straights that filled the hotels, of becoming so obvious or vulgar or hazardous that it menaced in any way the smooth and consistent workings of . . . casinos.   (Castleman 1996: 178)

In short, during the postwar period, when Las Vegas came into its own as a tourist destination, casino operators built on, rather than retreated from, the early reputation of the city as a place for the enjoyment of sex. In no other American city is there a more erotically charged association, or greater sexual mystique, than the one linked to

Las Vegas. Sex is formidably tied to the representation of the city in all its dimensions, from the old days of sleazy sidewalk hookers and low-life men handing out suggestive literature pitching "escort" services to tourists on the street, to the ultra-glamor and sophistication of topless revues and nude extravaganzas imported to Las Vegas show-rooms from Europe. While some of that activity has faded over the years, especially since the megaresorts took control of the sidewalks in the 1990s, taxis still sport large signs advertising sexual enticements such as "Gentleman's choice" with a telephone number for strippers and escorts who "come right to your room." Thus sex, or at least the promise of it, remains a powerful signifier of the Las Vegas image.

## Atomic Vegas

Even more remarkable than Las Vegas' association with some of the seamier aspects of tourism was the city's public-relations' love affair with the atomic bomb. During the 1950s and 1960s, while the con-sciousness of many Americans was haunted by the threat of nuclear annihilation, some local boosters promoted the explosion of nuclear devices outside of town as an entertainment event. Above-ground blasts were conducted regularly at the Atomic Energy Commission's proving grounds at Yucca Flats, about 75 miles north of downtown Las Vegas, and one enterprising promoter, Desert Inn developer Wilbur Clark, timed the gala opening of his new casino, the Colonial Inn, with that of an atomic bomb blast in March 1953.

Clark certainly was not alone in tying the blasts to casino publicity. Shortly after the federal government first announced plans to test atomic weapons at Yucca Flats, "the Las Vegas Chamber of Commerce printed several publicity releases intending to allay the qualms of future visitors. One showed a girl sporting an Atomic Hairdo, the product of a Las Vegas beauty parlor. Another heralded the Atomic Cocktail, invented by a bartender in one of the hotels" (Best and Hillyer 1995: 119). Also, "out along the Strip, the gamblers, and divorcees took to throwing what became known as dawn parties – drinking and singing sessions that began after midnight and ended, if there was a shot that morning, with the sight of the flash" (O'Reilly 1995: 32).

Today, local residents are much less sanguine about the atomic con-nection, having mobilized against the transport of atomic materials on their highways and against the proposed building of a national nuclear-waste dump in the nearby desert. The earlier flirtation with atomic parties, however, illustrates Las Vegas' penchant for hyping any unusual local occurrence in order to gain national publicity.

*Weddings and Romance*

During the postwar years, when returning GIs and their sweethearts began to piece their domestic lives back together, Las Vegas became famous for its fast-marriage franchises, small, shlocky wedding chapels that offered instant weddings. According to one account: "An increasing number of couples from Southern California, too impatient to bother with the blood tests required by their own state, were eloping to Las Vegas to be married in such chapels as the Hitching Post, Gretna Green, and the Wee Kirk o' the Heather" (O'Reilly 1995: 27). By the 1960s, more than 30,000 weddings were performed in the city each year.

The aura of romance attached to this commercialized practice of marrying people with glitzy efficiency rather than traditional ritual was amplified by a number of celebrity weddings that took place in Las Vegas. One of the most nationally visible affairs was the wedding of Elvis and Priscilla on May 1, 1967, in a publicized ceremony at the Aladdin Hotel that melded Hollywood-style romance with a Las Vegas location to help cement the city's glamorous reputation. Even failed marriages added a sense of excitement and revenues as "quicky" divorces were established as a Las Vegas tradition in the 1930s, again helped along by big-name celebrities, in this case Clark Gable and Ria Langham in 1939:

> While Gable cavorted in Hollywood with Carole Lombard, Ria played the gay divorcee role in Las Vegas, dealing craps, roulette and blackjack at Frank Houskey's Apache Club on Fremont Street and cruising Lake Mead on his yacht. She also took horseback rides into the surrounding deserts, hosted big names from Hollywood at her home and boosted Las Vegas in interviews with the national press.   (Moehring 1989: 29)

Over the years other highly visible Hollywood stars took advantage of similar arrangements in well-publicized break-ups. Amazingly, the city's image makers promoted this kind of divorce as another exciting dimension of the Las Vegas experience. If you lose at love or at the gaming tables, ante your bets and try again.

*From Mob Influence to Gangster Hype*

During the immediate postwar years mob influence threatened to tarnish the image of Las Vegas, even as it helped enhance the city's "anything goes" mystique. So pervasive was the infiltration of organized crime in the ownership and running of casinos that the federal government finally stepped in. In 1950, a Senate Sub-Committee to Investigate Organized Crime, led by Tennessee Senator Estes Kefauver, held special hearings in Las Vegas. Their inquiry uncovered extensive mob links to casino operations, but even more damaging were accusations of active participation by Nevada politicians in the operation of gambling, prostitution, and casino skimming activities. One observer noted that the Kefauver hearings "created a media hysteria that flooded the rackets divisions of police departments around the country" (Castleman 1996: 58), making the presence of organized crime a high-profile issue for the entire nation. Senate investigators alleged that mobsters across the country had divided Las Vegas, casinos among themselves, as Meyer Lansky and the New York City mob, Cleveland mobster Moe Dalitz, and Chicago mobsters Sam Giancanna and Tony Accardo all were prominent figures on the local casino scene.

Rather than this discouraging tourism, however, as Bugsy Siegel had predicted, people were attracted to the possibility of rubbing elbows with notorious mobsters as well as Hollywood movie stars at the gambling tables. The gangster atmosphere thus became valorized as yet another sign of Las Vegas excitement, adding to the already existing spectacle of commercial sex and legalized gambling. Although the Kefauver commission and, years later, the McClellan Senate hearings turned a national spotlight on the city: "the publicity was priceless, even if it was of an infamous sort" (Castleman 1996: 59).

The last major holdout in mob influence in Las Vegas was the Chicago crime family, whose activities were depicted in *Casino*. After mob insiders brutally murdered Chicago pointman Tony Spilotro, however, organized crime activity in the city disintegrated. Although Chicago, Buffalo, and Los Angeles crime families have made unsuccessful attempts to regain a foothold since Spilotro's demise, they are now up against the "corporate gangs" of Hilton, ITT Sheraton, and Ramada. In February 1998 the FBI released a report on its Organized Crime Strike Force investigations following the execution in 1997 of a former Spilotro associate, loan shark "Fat Herbie" Blitztein. Twenty-five men were charged with a total of 101 counts of criminal activity "ranging from the Blitzstein murder-for-hire case to the selling of phony diamonds" (J. L. Smith 1998a). The investigation found that the primary players were members of the deteriorating, Los Angeles-based, Milano crime family, along with some Buffalo gangsters who had repeatedly failed to gain a foothold in Las Vegas. Ironically, the arrests were announced during the same week that a worldwide convention of organized-crime experts were meeting in Las Vegas: "With a bus load of hoodlums headed to court on charges that could generate sentences from five years to death," the FBI agents involved "are in the spotlight for generating a mob case the size of which this city hasn't seen in years" (J. L. Smith 1998a).

Overall, however, in the 1990s the Las Vegas gangster heritage was re-cast and bathed in a fond nostalgic light by several star-studded Hollywood films. The sordid, sociopathic nature of people like Bugsy Siegel and Tony Spilotro fell away and was replaced by a nostalgically sanitized, vicariously titillating "mobster chic," glorified by the Hollywood dream machine.

## Professional Sports Hype

Yet another area affected by Las Vegas media hype is professional sports. Although sport already approaches the status of American civil religion on its own, Las Vegas promoters have successfully managed to add their own spectacular Hollywood-première-type twist to professional sporting events such as boxing, golf, rodeo, and stock car racing, further enhancing the reputation of the city as the entertainment capital of the world.

Championship boxing came to Nevada more than 100 years ago in 1897, when the Jim Corbett/Jack Fitzsimmons fight was held in Carson City, in the northern part of the state. Since then, however, Las Vegas has been the primary scene of big-time championship boxing matches in Nevada as the major casinos can rapidly transform their indoor arenas and outdoor venues into boxing rings with thousands of seats. Fighters with their entourages come to Las Vegas weeks before the scheduled bout amidst much media fanfare. The hoopla surrounding each match is milked for all it is worth, with endless interviews and the ritualized weigh-in complemented by a staged confrontation between the combatants. As one local commentator noted in 1997, when a World Boxing Council welterweight championship fight between Pernell Whitaker and Oscar De La Hoya was held in Las Vegas: "This is one event that needs no hype at all," said Rich Rose, president of sports for Caesars World, "but there still will be a mega amount of hype for a megafight. And the setting should be spectacular, with the fight taking place directly in front of Caesars Palace" (Feour 1997).

Thus, despite the brutal nature of the sport, champion boxing matches bring glamor and excitement to Las Vegas, enhanced by the presence of show business celebrities who attend courtesy of "comp" (complimentary) tickets provided by promoters in order to add more glitz and notoriety to the events.

Since the Desert Inn opened in 1949 with the first golf course available to Las Vegas visitors, tourism promoters also have used celebrity golf tournaments to boost the city's image. In 1997, for example, the Las Vegas Convention and Visitors Authority made extensive use of Tiger Woods' popularity in advertisements to promote tourism after the young golf sensation won the Las Vegas Invitational Tournament. Several area golf courses are of championship caliber and host numerous celebrity and professional tournaments, including the Tournament Players Club (TPC) courses in Summerlin. Each time a local golf tournament is broadcast on national television, Las Vegas receives millions of dollars in free publicity.

Another major sporting event that has become a Las Vegas spectacular is the National Finals Rodeo, the nationally televised highlight of the annual rodeo circuit. For a brief time each year, the city reverts to its old Wild West image, with the major casinos catering to the cowboy crowd by featuring country and western stars in its showrooms.

Tennis is another sport seen occasionally in Las Vegas, as the town recently hosted a minor tournament on the professional players' tour at the local university, featuring hometown boy Andre Agassi. The city has also hosted occasional exhibition matches, including a "battle of the sexes" match modeled after the famous Bobby Riggs/Billy Jean King contest held in Houston. Although dismissed by purists as a gimmick, the event generated more free publicity for the city.

Even college basketball has been touched by the Las Vegas showbiz image. Although technically not a professional sport (though millions of dollars are made in its operations), the University of Nevada, Las Vegas (UNLV) basketball program was among the first in the nation to feature a flashy laser-light show as part of its pre-game introductions during the reign of UNLV coach Jerry Tarkanian, himself a local Las Vegas legend.

The most recent event to be added as a Las Vegas sports spectacular is an annual Winston Cup NASCAR automobile race held at the newly constructed Las Vegas Motor Speedway. Las Vegas had previously been the site of high-powered racing on the international Formula One circuit when races were run in the 1980s on a track constructed on the site of the Caesars Palace parking lot and a nearby desert area that now houses the Mirage and the Caesars Palace Forum Shops. Also, for years the off-road Mint 400, memorialized in Hunter Thompson's *Fear and Loathing in Las Vegas* (1971), was run in the desert outside of town. The popular downtown celebrations for the Mint 400 were the predecessors of the celebration along Fremont Street held in

1998, sponsored by the Las Vegas Convention and Visitors Authority, to announce the NASCAR event:

> It had all the trappings of a distinctly "only-in-Las Vegas" experience. There was Richard Petty. There was an Elvis impersonator. There were Rio Rita and a couple dozen feather-cloaked showgirls. There was famed boxing announcer Michael Buffer, loudly imploring the throng to get ready to rumble. . . . The splashy festival at the Fremont Street Experience was to make official an announcement that had been expected for three months: The Las Vegas Motor Speedway, the 107,000-seat shrine. . . . will hold a Winston Cup race Sunday, March 1, 1998.    (Katsilometes 1997)

The first running of the race was sold out and brought an estimated $35 million to the economy, exclusive of gaming revenue, from tens of thousands of out-of-state race fans. It also brought massive traffic jams on Interstate 15, north of the city. The race was televised nationally, giving Las Vegas invaluable exposure in the southeastern United States, a hot spot for racing fans and a difficult area for Las Vegas' advertising to reach. Several casinos participated in the event, now a common occurrence with new attractions: "Along with the showgirls, mascots and full-costumed show room performers from numerous hotels . . . medieval royalty from Excalibur, clowns from Circus Circus . . . and statues of liberty from New York-New York, . . . milled about Fremont Street" (Steinhauer 1997b).

## Las Vegas as a Pop Culture Icon

As a recent newspaper account mentions, the Las Vegas locale has achieved such notoriety on its own that a situation in reverse has emerged, where publicity-hungry celebrities seek out Las Vegas connections in order to promote themselves or their pet projects: "These days, it takes far less than a super-hyped boxing match to bring celebrities to town – and the free publicity worth millions to Las Vegas that come with them. Not since the days when the Rat Pack partied at the Sands have so many highly recognizable people hung around Las Vegas, looking to be seen in front of the city's distinctive backdrop" (Steinhauer 1997a).

For example, actor Bruce Willis hyped his financial interest in the Las Vegas Planet Hollywood Café by performing a free concert with his blues band outside the Caesars Palace Forum Shops for the benefit of national media as well as pedestrian onlookers. This show business "event" also was carried by the Entertainment cable network and reported by CNN. Actor Nicolas Cage did three films in three consecutive years in Las Vegas, prompting a local official to comment, "He's definitely mined that concept. People like to be identified with Las Vegas" (Steinhauer 1997a).

More recently, the music industry and some of the biggest headline entertainers in rock music have showcased Las Vegas. The pop band U2, for example, chose Las Vegas as the place to launch their 1997 US tour. A year earlier, in 1996, the nationally televised Billboard Music Awards chose the Aladdin Hotel and Casino theater to hold its annual event: "The popular music awards are estimated to have attracted a television audience of 13 million and media exposure for Las Vegas that would have cost $1.5 million to buy through advertising" (Steinhauer 1997a). And in February 1998, Elton John officially christened the Studio 54 dance club at the MGM while on the same night the Rolling Stones played down the road at the Hard Rock Hotel and Casino.

## The Physical Transformation of Las Vegas into a Cultural Icon: Neon Signs and Fantasy Themes

### Neon and Signs

During the postwar boom of the late 1940s, Las Vegas casinos began advertising their establishments in a novel fashion. Capitalizing on the availability of cheap electricity from the Hoover Dam, they hyped their locations to motorists traveling along the old Los Angeles highway, now Las Vegas Boulevard (the Strip), using immense neon signs. Because almost all visitors arrived by car at that time, neon signs were an extremely effective way to attract attention. Although these signs have since undergone decades of refinement and enhancement, they remain defining features of the Las Vegas image.

In the 1930s, Thomas Young migrated southwest from Utah to Las Vegas and began a business selling neon signs. By the mid-1940s several downtown casinos ordered and installed large signs from his company, now known as the Young Electric Sign Company (YesCo). The Golden Nugget, then a gambling joint with no hotel rooms, had the largest sign early on, a 100-footer outside the casino. But the Pioneer Club created the first real neon landmark for Las Vegas by installing the giant cowboy, "Vegas Vic," alongside its building on Fremont Street. Vegas Vic was later complemented by the construction of Vegas Vickie, an immense cowgirl sign that sat atop a topless dance club across Fremont Street from the old Pioneer Building. When Bugsy Siegel opened the Flamingo on the Strip in 1946, he rejected the frontier motif of Glitter Gulch in favor of Miami-inspired designs of tropical splendor, but his hotel soon thereafter was framed on both sides by two YesCo fixtures, identical 80-foot-tall highball glasses fizzing with neon pink champagne. Starbursts of neon ran across the entrance of the casino and lighting tubes swirled in the design of pink flamingos and palm trees. By the 1950s, Las Vegas had clearly established itself as the world's showcase for neon signage.

The signs were conceived through competition for auto-borne tourists, but casinos fought each other fiercely for the privilege of boasting the biggest or tallest. In the 1950s, the Golden Nugget had the largest neon sign, and during the 1960s, the Stardust on the Strip boasted the highest sign, at 200 feet. In the 1970s Circus Circus claimed the title, then was displaced by the Sahara Hotel and Casino in 1985. In the 1990s, the immense MGM Grand possesses both the biggest and tallest sign in Las Vegas, along with the largest hotel in the world with more than 5,000 rooms. Other impressive lighting fixtures include a 75-foot-high guitar attached to the side of the Hard Rock Café (which suffered a *simulated* destruction by a planeload of desperate convicts in the movie *ConAir*); the electronic sign/image monitors outside Treasure Island, Caesars Palace, and the Excalibur; and the Fremont Street Experience, a four-block-long canopy over Fremont Street, featuring more than 2 million light bulbs set in a computerized image and sound display. YesCo's neon signs thus continue to be a defining feature of the Las Vegas experience, as one observer notes:

> The five-mile-long stretch of neon art against the black desert sky along the Strip is, of course, the famous cliché. Long neon tubing, in brilliant reds, whites, blues, and pinks, borders the edges of shopping centers, car washes, apartments, and restaurants. And it's not just their designs and colors and size and intensity. In addition, they're all moving – flickering, twitching, blinking; turning on and off; running up and down and across; shooting across space and back again; starting at the bottom, speeding to the top, and exploding.   (Castleman 1996: 76)

The incredibly photogenic display of neon creates a phantasmagoria, a fantasy environment that envelops and overwhelms the pedestrian. Las Vegas is arguably the most easily recognizable city, no small feat among the thousands of contenders with famous landmarks, thanks to its crazy quilt of night-time neon. Signs and displays, however, have been taken to previously unimagined heights during the megaresort explosion of the 1980s and 1990s, as new construction on the Strip has created an even more outrageous fantasy world with the introduction of more elaborately themed casinos. Curiously, however, beginning with the Mirage, these casinos no longer had the need to envelop buildings in neon because of their ability to project fantasy through the very structure of their architectural design, even though they carried on the Las Vegas tradition of being fronted by a large neon sign (see chapter 7).

## Themed Casinos and the Production of Fantasy Environments

The design of the earliest downtown casinos on Fremont Street simply reflected Las Vegas' Wild West traditions. Later Glitter Gulch Casinos like the Golden Nugget, Binion's Horseshoe, the Four Queens, and the Pioneer, along with the giant neon Vegas Vic and Vickie signs, each adorned with cowboy hats, outfits, and boots, created a Fremont Street tableau that continued to resonate with the symbols of western history. The first of the 1940s resorts on the Strip, the El Rancho, was only a slight departure, introducing a Mexican/southern California motif to what was a glorified motel. Bugsy Siegel's Flamingo brought the first major shift, with its tropical-paradise motif. This style continues today in the decor of the Tropicana, the Mirage, Treasure Island and the Rio, while European elegance and Côte D'Azure ambiance are reflected in the themes of the Riviera, Bally's, and the Monte Carlo.

At one time on the Strip an Arabian Nights motif also was popular. The Sahara, the Dunes, the Sands, the Aladdin, and the Desert Inn all exemplified this theme. The Dunes, Aladdin, and the Sands were blown up to make way for more elaborate projects, however, while the other two have been remodeled. Another popular theme is the classical motif exemplified by Caesars Palace and the Egyptian-style Luxor pyramid. Other styles include the Excalibur's medieval, King Arthur theme and the MGM Grand's glamorous Hollywood motif, while New York-New York is the first of several planned casinos that nostalgically re-create famous urban landscapes.

Casino themes are not only increasingly elaborate on the outside, they also include detailed reproductions and simulations in the interior of their buildings, reinforcing a fantasy environment for visitors that may, for some, seem overwhelming. In addition, out on the street the increasingly close proximity of the new resorts has produced a tightly-knit urban texture, providing a phantasmagoric landscape that transcends individual buildings. Since the 1990s observers have commented on an emergent pedestrian street scene on the Strip, a direct result of the robust theming of building exteriors. Visitors no longer stay within their respective hotels for entertainment but stroll along Las Vegas Boulevard to admire the themed architectural creations that characterize the new style of casino construction (see Gottdiener 1997).

Entertaining pedestrian culture is new to Las Vegas and has brought about an altered relationship between people and casino gambling in the town. In the past, casinos tried to maintain a captive audience by providing for their guests' every need within the building – restaurants, entertainment, dry cleaning, hair salons, clothing and shoes – so that they did not leave the resort and would continue gambling. As competition among the casinos helped create an active street culture along the Strip, downtown interests in response have developed the Fremont Street Experience to make their area pedestrian friendly by eradicating the more sordid elements of the old Glitter Gulch, hopefully fostering the re-emergence of tourist street life downtown as well.

As Las Vegas continues to develop a vibrant pedestrian culture in its most important tourist areas, these parts of the city increasingly resemble other older and more traditional urban centers in the East and Midwest that thrive on an active street life. It could already be argued that there are more pedestrian delights offered to tourists in Las Vegas than, for example, in Los Angeles at the present time.

## The Allure of Gambling

All the previously mentioned attractions, however, function mainly as flashy enticements to the main event that makes Las Vegas Las Vegas: casino gambling. As an age-old form of entertainment, gambling also has its own inherent allure which Las Vegas casino operators, and increasingly others around the nation as well, exploit relentlessly. There is perhaps no more potent symbolic example of this defining feature of the Las Vegas image than the way it is depicted in Hollywood films.

In the 1960s James Bond film *Dr NO*, for example, an impeccably attired Sean Connery sits at a baccarat table in an elegant Monte Carlo casino. All around him are men and women of wealth. He catches the eye of an attractive woman in a low-cut dress as he wins hand after hand. When the scene ends, Bond stuffs his winnings into his custom-tailored suit and escorts the woman to his room. Certainly the equation between eroticism, an upper-class lifestyle, and the power of winning at gambling has not been lost on casino-industry publicists. As one observer notes: "Gambling and sex go together ... or to put it more precisely, one follows the other ... because the thrill of gambling is bound up one way or another with the libido" (Spanier 1992: 135).

In a society where the attainment of money, power, and sexual gratification are so closely intertwined, gambling is a high-risk activity that holds a strong attraction for millions of people.

At a more mundane level lies a second allure of gambling: the possibility of sudden economic transformation. Promoted again by innumerable Hollywood films, as well as in advertisements featuring cameo shots of real-life "instant winners," is the prospect of attaining unimaginable wealth with the simple roll of the dice or pull of a slot lever. The reality of casino gambling, however, is far less appealing, as the economics of gambling clearly demonstrate that the house always wins:

> The game of roulette best illustrates the house advantage. There are 38 numbers on the wheel: 1 through 36, plus a zero and double zero. If the ball drops into number 23 and you have a dollar on it, the correct payoff would be $37 (37 to l, which equals the 38 numbers). However, the house only pays $35. It withholds 2 out of 38 units, which translates to a 5.26-percent advantage for the house. ... Of course, luck will play a significant part in the gambling proceedings in the short run, but the longer you play craps, roulette, or any casino game where the house holds the advantage, the more your losses will add up to the percentage. (Castleman 1996: 151)

Slot and video poker machines, however, provide the bulk of gaming revenues in Nevada, in 1997 in Clark County alone topping $6 billion. In the large casinos they range from requiring anywhere from 5 cents to 5 dollars a play. The house advantage ranges from 20 percent on the smallest bets to 5 percent and under on the largest denominations. These machines are extremely popular for several reasons. They do not intimidate inexperienced gamblers, and emit an eerily hypnotic sound, satirized by writer Tom Wolfe as, "Hernia, Hernia, Hernia, Hernia" (1965: 1), that mesmerizes players. Also, the frequency of small payoffs conveys a false image of winning and serves to positively reinforce the almost automatic behavior of continually feeding coins into the slot or punching the "Bet maximum" button from stored credits. Boisterously loud sirens that blare when someone does win a significant payoff conceal the fact that most players will not walk away winners. There is little glamor attached to this activity, but jackpot winners are publicized more actively than presidential candidates, contributing greatly to the attractive image of Las Vegas. The kings of Las Vegas slot games, the networked "Megabucks" machines, require $3 per play, and are progressively structured in payoffs just like a state lottery. Starting out each time with a $5-million pot to attract new players, they offer customers about the same probability of becoming winners as they have of hitting the jackpot of the lottery back home. The incredible publicity given to the lucky winner, however, pumps up the attraction of the game every time. In fall 1998 the "Megabucks" jackpot had surpassed $26 million.

According to Castleman (1996: 152), wheel games range from a house take of 11% to over 20%. Keno is a convenient game that gamblers play while dining in coffee shops or while waiting for more exciting opportunities. Its house percentage is over 20%. Roulette, if played without a knowledgeable system, has a take of over 30%. At the other extreme, craps and blackjack have a lower house percentage and skillful play can reduce the risk. Yet, even in these games, the house advantage always prevails.

Although casino gambling is clearly a losing proposition, legalized gambling has become an explosive nationwide industry in recent years, no doubt in part as an act of desperation in economically depressed areas: "As recently as 1988, *casino* gambling was legal in only two states: Nevada and New Jersey. By 1994, six years later, casinos were either authorized or operating in twenty-three states and were proposed in many others. ... During the six years ... total yearly casino revenues nationally nearly doubled – from $8 billion to about $15 billion" (Goodman 1995: 2). Some form of gambling is now legal in 48 states, and Indian gaming alone has surpassed gross revenues on the Las Vegas Strip (Collins 1993). Despite the megaresort construction of "must see" themed resorts on the Strip, in the late 1990s the most profitable casino in the United States was not located in Las Vegas. The Foxwoods casino, run by the Mashantucket Pequot tribe, took that honor. Located near the coast of southeastern Connecticut, the resort boasts more than 2.5 million square feet, 5,540 slot machines, 11,000 employees, and three hotels, making it the largest casino in the Western Hemisphere.

Civic authorities across the country have pushed to legalize some form of gambling, accompanied by aggressive publicity to promote government-sponsored games of chance. This advertising blitz has greatly enhanced the image of casino gambling and, inadvertently, has aided the image of Las Vegas as a place that offers unparalleled gambling excitement:

> Instead of referring to "gambling" with its negative overtones of seedy characters in smoky rooms, politicians would now talk about "gaming," "casino entertainment," and other such euphemisms. An industry created by gangsters ... financed through laundered drug money and other ill-gotten funds, was now operated by business school

graduates, financed by conglomerates, and listed on the New York Stock exchange."   (Goodman 1995: 5)

Commercials for casino gambling around the country clearly reveal that the valorization of the activity depends heavily upon the promise of instant riches. The presentation of gambling also draws on social status symbols of affluence, implying that "you too, can be wealthy, just take a chance." Television ads for local casinos in upstate New York, for example, are composed of images that feature bright neon lights, extravagant surroundings, opulent dining facilities, well-dressed young couples, i.e., the "beautiful people" and the "good life." A visit to these same places presents a starkly contrasting reality. Non-smiling patrons wearing sneakers, sweatshirts, and fanny packs (bumbags) seem grafted to the quarter slot machines while smoking themselves to death. None of the ads, none of the television commercials, none of the colorful images hint at the slightest possibility that people who gamble can lose money, not to mention the possibility of personal ruin due to an uncontrollable obsession for games of chance. Of course society has a similar problem with advertising for tobacco and alcohol, which tries as well to trade on images of glamor.

Gambling is also presented as a form of light-hearted entertainment. Casino operators consider the house percentage to be the price of admission for a good time. Some tourists even budget their losses accordingly into the price of their vacation, and relatively inexpensive room rates and bargain buffets help them to rationalize their gambling losses.

The gambling industry promotes this image of good-time vacation fun vigorously. Public service announcements suggest that obsessive gambling is an uncommon deviation, and many local and state governments have turned to gambling ventures, such as state lotteries and casinos, to make money. These same public entities ignore the problems associated with legalized gambling, which critics claim cost society millions of dollars each year. Instead, government officials stress legalized gambling as a means for the creation of jobs, for the revival of recreational tourism, or for the increase of revenues. The problems associated with obsessive gambling, such as family breakup and abuse, bankruptcy, criminal acts of fraud and embezzlement, and problem drinking are downplayed: "Estimates of the yearly average combined private and public costs of each problem gambler have ranged between $20,000 and $30,000 in 1993 dollars. ... The U.S. Gambling Study ... arrived at a much more conservative estimate of $13,200 per problem gambler per year in 1993 dollars" (Goodman 1995: 51). Local voters in some areas have actively begun rejecting gaming ventures in their municipalities, however. Twice multi-million-dollar referendums for casino gambling have failed in Florida, and in California officials have thus far denied slot-machine operations to Indian gaming.

The social problems associated with gambling, of course, are not new. What is new is the widespread societal acceptance of gaming, the removal of its immoral stigma. That trend may have begun when churches abandoned the image of gambling as sin and sold out for revenue sources such as Bingo or Las Vegas Nights, paving the way for the national expansion of gambling run by states, Native American tribes, and private operators. Even church Bingo games had their share of compulsive gamblers, with their woes of financial ruin and shattered lives, as before the spread of legalized gaming across America it was estimated that the nation had more than a million compulsive gamblers (Collins 1983b). Once "gaming" was no longer sinful, the floodgates opened, its acceptance spread, and the scale of gambling-related problems grew.

None of the problems associated with gambling, however, are in evidence at Las Vegas casinos, patronized by more than 30 million visitors each year. Caesars Palace surrounds gamblers in the opulence of ancient Rome and the Luxor does the same with ancient Egyptian décor, while the Monte Carlo simulates the carved marble palaces of Europe. Even cut-rate places like Circus Circus, never accused of having glitzy, upscale décor, provides a circus-like atmosphere to project a "fun-filled" setting. In all these cases, the creation of fantasy environments glorifies only the positive allure and, like any ideology, hides the banal and sometimes ruinous reality of casino gambling.

Concluding our discussion of the Las Vegas image in this chapter with a section on the economics of gaming, emphasizes a crucial point overlooked by more sensationalized accounts of Las Vegas by post-modern cultural critics such as Jean Baudrillard (1989). Behind the glittering façade of "archi-tainment" and other Vegas-style "hyper-real" spectacles lies the "real" logic of commodity production. The self-styled "entertainment capital of the world," Las Vegas, embodies, in the most extreme form, the relentless pursuit of profit in the leisure sphere, first described in detail by the critical theorists Max Horkheimer and Theodor Adorno (1972 [1944] ) in their analysis of the American culture industry. In this sense, although he never mentions the city, the little known French theorist Guy Debord provides a more perceptive account of the Las Vegas phenomenon in his slim volume *The Society of the Spectacle* (1967), as he identifies the commodified spectacle as the defining characteristic of culture in advanced industrial societies like the US.

Debord's work also implies another important point here, that Las Vegas is not as atypical as its detractors seem to think. Media critic Neil Postman (1985) makes the same point more explicitly when he describes Las Vegas as "the symbolic capital" of the contemporary US. The thesis, and title, of Postman's book is that we are in danger of "amusing ourselves to death," so, as "a city wholly devoted to entertainment," Las Vegas represents only the most advanced outpost of a general cultural trend in American society. In chapters 5 and 6 we will address this important issue from the opposite angle, by focusing on how Las Vegas is becoming more like other American cities. But there is no doubt that over 30 million people visit Las Vegas every year to participate in a fantasy. That spectacle is the careful product of decades of hype and active media construction. Sex, gambling, and glitter are woven together by Las Vegas' themed environments with some seminal themes from American culture: the Wild West, gangsters, tropical paradise, pirate treasure, Arabian Nights, the splendor of Egypt and Rome as depicted by Hollywood, or the excitement and macho thrills of King Arthur's feudalism (see Gottdiener, 1997, for an extended discussion of these Las Vegas themes). For a three-day visit, losses to "one-armed bandits" seem a small price to pay, for most of the tourists who regularly come here.

# 4 The Advent of Metropolitanization: Rapid Population Growth and a Booming Economy

## Boomtown in the Desert

Las Vegas is the nation's fastest growing metropolitan area, Henderson and North Las Vegas its fastest growing medium-sized cities, and Clark County its fastest growing county. Add to that the region's employment prospects, inexpensive housing, low taxes, relatively safe streets, recreational opportunities, and warm southwestern climate, and Las Vegas clearly has become the latest chapter in the history of Sunbelt migration that began fifty years ago in Los Angeles, prompting some to refer to the Las Vegas area as the New California. Since the 1980s, the "old" California has lost much of its luster due to high crime rates, traffic congestion, tax revolts, drive-by shootings, urban riots, smoggy air, and high-priced homes. Although some of these same problems are beginning to plague the Las Vegas area as well, skyrocketing growth continues to be the norm.

Clark County, which covers nearly 8,000 square miles and includes the cities of Las Vegas, North Las Vegas, Henderson, Boulder City, as well as a number of unincorporated communities, between 1960 and 1990 grew by 483.8%, from 127,016 to 741,459. By 1998, the area's total population exceeded 1.26 million (Judson 1998) – see table 4.1.

Along with its explosive growth, the population of Clark County is also becoming more racially and ethnically diverse. As indicated in table 4.1, between 1960 and 1990 the white population increased by 424.4%, African-Americans by 542.8%, and all other minorities by a staggering 6,167.3% (Bureau of the Census 1960, 1990). Thus, while minority populations have grown more rapidly than the white population, all groups have experienced incredible growth. In 1997 whites constituted 72.2% of the total county population, Hispanics 12.3%, African-Americans 8.7%, Asians and Pacific Islanders 5.8%, and Native Americans 1% (Metropolitan Research Association 1998: 7).

**Table 4.1** Selected socio-demographic characteristics of Clark County, 1960–90: I

| | 1997 | 1990 | 1980 | 1970 | 1960 | Percent change 1980–90 | Percent change 1960–90 |
|---|---|---|---|---|---|---|---|
| Population | 1,133,000 | 741,459 | 463,087 | 273,288 | 127,016 | 60.1 | 483.8 |
| Race | | | | | | | |
| White | 818,026 (72.2%) | 602,658 (81.3%) | 390,959 (84.4%) | 244,538 (89.5%) | 113,925 (90.5%) | 54.1 | 424.4 |
| Black | 98,571 (8.7%) | 70,738 (9.5%) | 46,268 (10.0%) | 24,760 (9.1%) | 11,005 (8.70%) | 52.9 | 542.8 |
| Other | 216,403* (19.1%) | 68,063 (9.2%) | 25,860 (5.6%) | 3,990 (1.4%) | 1,086 (0.8%) | 163.2 | 6167.3 |
| Sex | | | | | | | |
| Male | 523,446 (46.2%) | 376,108 (50.7%) | 233,872 (50.5%) | 138,892 (50.8%) | 65,657 (51.7%) | 60.8 | 472.8 |
| Female | 609,554 (53.8%) | 365,351 (49.3%) | 229,215 (49.5%) | 134,396 (49.2%) | 61,359 (48.3%) | 59.4 | 495.4 |

*Includes Hispanic population of 139,359 (12.3%)

*Sources: County and City Data Book, 1994, 1983, 1972, 1962, respectively: Census of Population, 1990, 1980, 1970, 1960, respectively.* US Department of Commerce, Social and Economic Statistics Administration, Bureau of the Census, Metropolitan Research Association, 1998.

**Table 4.2**  Selected socio-demographic characteristics of Clark County, 1960–90: II

| | 1990 | 1980 | 1970 | 1960 | Percent change 1980–90 | Percent change 1960–90 |
|---|---|---|---|---|---|---|
| **Age** | | | | | | |
| Under 5 years | 57,092 (7.7%) | 33,342 (7.2%) | 25,962 (9.5%) | 15,750 (12.4%) | 71.2 | 262.5 |
| 6 to 17 years | 124,565 (16.8%) | 94,933 (20.5%) | 72,148 (26.4%) | 29,341 (23.1%) | 31.2 | 324.5 |
| 18 to 64 years | 481,948 (65.0%) | 299,617 (64.7%) | 161,240 (59.0%) | 76,210 (60.0%) | 60.9 | 532.4 |
| 65 years and over | 77,853 (10.5%) | 35,195 (7.6%) | 13,938 (5.1%) | 5,716 (4.5%) | 121.2 | 1262.0 |
| Median age | 33.0 | 29.6 | 26.9 | 28.6 | 11.5 | 15.4 |
| **Educational attainment** | | | | | | |
| Persons 25 years and over | 427,080 | 272,445 | 144,993 | 70,068 | 56.8 | 509.5 |
| Less than high school | 96,948 (22.7%) | 70,836 (26.0%) | 50,458 (34.8%) | 33,195 (47.4%) | 36.9 | 192.1 |
| High school | 271,195 (63.5%) | 167,279 (61.4%) | 80,036 (55.2%) | 31,687 (45.2%) | 62.1 | 755.8 |
| More than high school | 58,937 (13.8%) | 34,330 (12.6%) | 14,499 (10.0%) | 5,186 (7.4%) | 71.7 | 1036.5 |

*Sources:*  *County and City Data Book*, 1994, 1983, 1972, 1962, respectively; *Census of Population*, 1990, 1980, 1970, 1960, respectively.
US Department of Commerce, Social and Economic Statistics Administration, Bureau of the Census.

In terms of gender, males slightly outnumbered females as a percentage of the total Clark County population up until 1990 (Bureau of the Census 1960, 1990) – see table 4.1 – although the difference has since been reversed, with females in 1997 slightly in the majority in the county, 53.8% to 46.2% (Metropolitan Research Association 1998: 7).

According to table 4.2, the age distribution of the county's population shows the majority to be 18 to 64, though since 1960 the proportion of elderly, i.e., of people over 65, has quadrupled to 17.8% in 1997. In 1960, Clark County children aged five and under constituted 12.4% of the population, 60% were aged 18 to 64, with 4.5% in the over-65 age category. Thirty years later, young children comprised 7.7% of the population, those 18 to 64, 65%, and those over 65, 10.5%. Over the same time span, the number of children five and under increased by 262.5%, those in the 18–64 group by 532.4%, and the over-65 group by 1,262% (Bureau of the Census 1960, 1990), making the over-65 population by far the most rapidly increasing age group in Clark County. In the ten years between 1980 and 1990 alone, the number of seniors expanded 121.2%, while that of children under five also grew by a significant 71.2%. These figures are further reflected in the rise of median age among Clark County residents, from 28.6 years in 1960 to 33 years in 1990 (Bureau of the Census 1960, 1990), to 45.8 in 1997 (Metropolitan Research Association 1998: 7).

Clark County continues to grow at an amazing rate. In 1997 more than 7,000 new residents arrived each month (Metropolitan Research Association 1998: 3). Reasons for moving to the region however, have changed over the last few years, reflecting, in part, the growing ability of the non-gambling segment of the local economy to attract workers and retirees. In 1990, 15% of newcomers said they came because of job transfers (Metropolitan Research Association 1997), compared with 21.3% in 1997 (Metropolitan Research Association 1998: 10); and 10.5% in 1990 said they moved to be near relatives, while in 1997 double that number, 21.9%, gave this as their primary reason for moving (see table 4.3). Other significant reasons cited for moving to Clark County in 1997 included 17.4% to find a better job, 13% for a better lifestyle, and 10.2% to retire (Metropolitan Research Association 1998: 10). Given the fact that 25.5% of the newcomers were aged 55 or over, a significant number may be moving to work for a few years while establishing a retirement residence.

California continues to be the most common area of origination for newcomers to the Las Vegas Valley, at 39.1% in 1997, with southwestern and northeastern states a distant second and third, at 17.5% and

**Table 4.3**   Reasons for moving to Las Vegas

|                     | 1990 | 1997  |
|---------------------|------|-------|
| Like the area       | 23%  | 7.9%  |
| Job transfer        | 15%  | 21.3% |
| Better lifestyle    | 14%  | 13.0% |
| Near relatives      | 11%  | 21.9% |
| Retirement          | 9%   | 10.2% |
| Seeking employment  | 9%   | 10.5% |
| Other               | 19%  | 11.8% |

*Sources*: *Las Vegas Perspectives*, 1996 and 1998, Metropolitan Research Association, Las Vegas.

17.4% respectively (Metropolitan Research Association 1998: 10). Among these, the largest numbers come from Arizona and New York (see table 4.4).

About half of the Clark County population between 1980 and 1997 had household incomes between $25,000 and $49,999 (see table 4.5), with median income increasing steadily, reaching $40,514 in 1997

**Table 4.4**   Department of Motor Vehicles driver's licenses surrendered

|                 | 1986   | 1990   | 1995   |
|-----------------|--------|--------|--------|
| Arizona         | 1,855  | 4,971  | 3,900  |
| California      | 7,949  | 17,344 | 26,321 |
| Florida         | 1,088  | 1,656  | 2,830  |
| Illinois        | 1,203  | 1,877  | 2,675  |
| New York        | 1,015  | 1,711  | 2,950  |
| Texas           | 1,690  | 3,133  | 2,950  |
| Colorado        | 1,093  | 2,339  | 1,880  |
| Michigan        | 747    | 2,225  | 1,667  |
| Delaware        | 25     | 37     | 58     |
| Washington, DC  | 17     | 23     | 29     |
| Maine           | 49     | 89     | 90     |
| North Dakota    | 93     | 176    | 116    |
| Rhode Island    | 38     | 114    | 128    |
| Vermont         | 16     | 41     | 64     |
| West Virginia   | 51     | 94     | 78     |
| Total           | 28,652 | 53,702 | 67,144 |

*Source*: *Las Vegas Perspectives*, 1997, Metropolitan Research Association, Las Vegas.

**Table 4.5** Selected socio-demographic characteristics of Clark County, 1960–90: III

| | 1990 | 1980 | 1970 | 1960 | Percent change 1980–90 | Percent change 1960–90 |
|---|---|---|---|---|---|---|
| Households | 287,025 | 173,891 | 87,728 | 40,400 | 65.1 | 610.5 |
| Income | | | | | | |
| Median family income ($) | 35,172 | 21,029 | 10,870 | 7,010 | 67.3 | 401.8 |
| Families with income below poverty rate (%) | 7.5 | 6.7 | 7.0 | 11.3 | | |
| Civilian labor force, total | 397,216 | 240,320 | 123,669 | 53,645 | 65.3 | 640.5 |
| Unemployment rate (%) | 6.7 | 6.4 | 5.2 | 6.7 | | |
| Female | 178,114 (44.8%) | 104,058 (43.3%) | 41,284 (33.4%) | 18,025 (33.6%) | 71.2 | 888.1 |

*Sources: County and City Data Book,* 1994, 1983, 1972, 1960, respectively; *Census of Population,* 1990, 1980, 1970, 1960, respectively.
US Department of Commerce, Social and Economic Statistics Administration, Bureau of the Census.

(Bureau of the Census 1980, 1990; and Metropolitan Research Association 1998: 7). At the poverty level, the percentage of households with incomes under $15,000 remains at about 11%, which is an increase of 4% from 1990 (table 4.5). Significantly, the fastest growing category was the above-$75,000 household-income group, rising from 5% in 1990 to 17.3% in 1997 (Bureau of the Census 1990; Metropolitan Research Association 1998: 7), which indicates graphically the growing gap between the wealthy and the poor in the region. Overall the data suggest that, as the region has matured and developed, income polarization has increased. Also, in 1990, 51% of local retirees reported median household incomes of $20,000 to $49,999, with 7% having incomes over $50,000, and 15% under $10,000 (Bureau of the Census 1990). By 1997, however, senior income figures showed increased polarization with 47.1% of local retirees reporting median household incomes of $20,000 to $49,999, with 22.7% having incomes over $50,000, and 18.5% under $10,000 (Metropolitan Research Association 1998: 9). In the future it is expected that the percentage of less affluent seniors will increase, as the elderly population grows older (see below).

Growth of the permanent residential population is further reflected in the tremendous expansion of the Clark County School District. In 1990 it was the fifteenth largest district in the nation with 147 schools, but by 1998, it was the ninth largest school district. With more than 203,777 students, the district faces the challenge of building a school per month, a classroom per day, just to keep pace with growth (see chapter 6).

A marked upward trend in educational achievement levels also can be seen among southern Nevada residents over the last 30 years. Between 1960 and 1990 the percentage of all Clark County residents over 25 with some college education increased by 1,036.5% (Bureau of the Census 1960, 1990), see table 4.2. More recently, between 1980 and 1990 the percentage of those with some college education increased by 71.7%, although the percentage of those without a high school degree also increased by 36.9% (Bureau of the Census 1980, 1990), contributing to the social polarization of the region. It is not necessary, for example, to have a high school diploma for many casino jobs (see below).

Over the last thirty years rapid growth has brought a comparable increase in the number of households. According to table 4.5, in 1960 the county had 40,400 such households, but by 1990, that figure had grown to 287,025 (Bureau of the Census 1960, 1990) and in 1997, to 439,656 (Metropolitan Research Association 1998). Here, as elsewhere, the regions outside the city of Las Vegas experienced more rapid growth until 1990, when city growth increased significantly as large segments of annexed city land were developed.*

## Las Vegas Sub-Populations

### Hispanics

Hispanics have a long history in Nevada as the Spanish and, later, Mexicans were the first non-native explorers of the area. More sustained Hispanic migration into southern Nevada, however, began in the early twentieth century with the construction of a railroad line between Salt Lake City and Los Angeles that passed through Las Vegas. Mexican laborers, along with the Chinese, made up the bulk of the railroad's workforce (Bowers 1996: 34–5).

The second major wave of Hispanic migration to Las Vegas began after World War II, when large numbers of Hispanic men arrived as construction workers and soldiers. Like the African-Americans, these new residents were segregated as a result of discriminatory housing practices. Since the 1960s the Hispanic population of Las Vegas has become more diversified: first with an influx of Cubans, many of them former employees of Havana casinos following the revolution there, then with the migrations of Puerto Ricans from the East, and in the 1980s with the arrival of refugees from war-torn Central America. In the 1990s the majority of Hispanics moving to Las Vegas have come

---

*Comparable figures for the city of Las Vegas alone are: 400% growth in population from 1960 to 1990 and a 1997 population of 417,462 residents.

Overall figures for the city largely parallel those for the county. Racially and ethnically, the city of Las Vegas has a slightly higher percentage of African-Americans than the county as a whole.

Regarding gender in the city, males outnumber females and the percentage of females has dropped from 49.9% in 1960 to 49.3% in 1990.

Comparable age figures for the city in 1990 are children, 8.3%; 64.7% in the 18–64 group; and those aged 65 and over, 10.3% (a doubling of the percentage of seniors). The median age rose less drastically in the city, however, from 31.6 years in 1960 to 32.5 in 1990, although this has since changed with the development of Sun City within the city limits.

Regarding educational achievement, between 1960 and 1990 the percentage of Las Vegas city residents with some college education increased by 530.4%, while between 1980 and 1990 those without a high school degree increased 27.6% and those with some college education increased by 74.9%.

Finally, the Las Vegas city figures for family households with two or more residents grew from 21,513 in 1960 to 99,735 households in 1990, (Bureau of the Census 1960, 1990), and by 1996, the figure reached 154,130.

not from foreign lands but from southern California, Texas, Florida, and New York.

Hispanics now constitute the largest and fastest growing ethnic sub-population in Las Vegas. In 1990 Hispanics represented 11.2% of the Clark County population, growing to more than 13% in 1997, an increase of 116% (82,904 to 179,061) (Kanigher 1998). According to Fernando Romero, Mirage Resorts' government-affairs manager: "Hispanics have been attracted to jobs in construction and in hotels that others may not want ... the cost of living is low compared to other states, and there is a relatively short commute to jobs" (Kanigher 1998). Continued growth of the Hispanic population in the Las Vegas area seems likely, even without immigration, given the young average age of Hispanic residents (more than 20 percent of Clark County's elementary school children are Hispanic) (Rodriguez 1997).

Despite their growing numbers, Hispanics have not yet emerged as a cohesive political force in southern Nevada, with far less representation in high-profile political positions than African-Americans. Only 3 of Nevada's 71 elected education officials (university regents, state board of education and local school board members) and 10 of Nevada's 424 municipal and county officials are Hispanic (Rodriguez 1997). Many local observers predict that this situation may soon change, however, as Hispanic purchasing power increases and with 3,000 new Hispanic voters registered in 1998. Hispanic influence is also reflected in the growing number of Spanish-language media outlets that provide an enhanced Hispanic voice and forum in local affairs. The first local Spanish-language weekly newspaper, *El Mundo,* was published in 1979, and from 1982 to 1985 was printed by the *Las Vegas Sun* and distributed with its Saturday edition. By 1997 the expanding Hispanic community boasted two Spanish-language radio and two television stations, along with an additional newspaper.

Non-Hispanic advertisers also are turning to Hispanic media because of the realization that Hispanics overall have the highest disposable income of any minority. The first advertisements targeted towards Hispanic-speaking consumers in the mainstream Las Vegas media appeared in the mid-1980s when a personal injury attorney, Edward Bernstein, aired television commercials in Spanish. Although he received a great deal of criticism, including hate mail, at the time, the campaign ultimately was successful (Bell 1996b) and has since been copied by other businesses, including local casinos, which have launched aggressive advertising campaigns in the local Hispanic media.

The owner-manager of Hispanic radio station KLSQ claims that there are more Hispanics in Las Vegas than official statistics suggest

**Figure 4.1**   Cinco de Mayo (Mexican Independence Day Celebration)

because older Spanish-speaking residents and undocumented workers don't respond to census inquiries. He estimates that Hispanics comprise 14 to 18 per cent of the Clark County population and will have 250,000 residents by the year 2000 (Bell 1996a). His estimates have been backed up by an analysis of US Census Bureau data in 1996 by the *Reno Gazette Journal,* which suggests that more than a quarter of Nevada residents by 2025 will be Hispanic *(Reno Gazette Journal* 1996). Today, most of these new Hispanic residents in Nevada will either be born in Nevada or arrive from other American states rather than from outside the country.

## African-Americans

A smaller and less rapidly increasing Las Vegas area sub-population is the African-American community. African-Americans first moved to Las Vegas in significant numbers in the 1940s, attracted by jobs at the Henderson industrial plants during World War II. As the fledgling desert community was strictly segregated at the time (see chapter 1), many black people settled in an area just north and west of downtown Las Vegas referred to as the "Westside." Though they lived in makeshift tents and shacks, these hardly stood out in the Las Vegas community, which in general was comprised of modest desert dwellings, unpaved main streets, and primitive dirt-floor casinos. Many southern black women moved to Las Vegas to find jobs as maids and food-service workers in the hotel-casinos so that in the 1940s "all Las Vegas hotel maids were black" (Potters 1996). In 1940 Las Vegas had only 147 black residents, but by 1955 the number had grown to more than 13,000 (Potters 1996). Eighty percent of the people comprising this African-American population increase came from just two small southern towns, Fordyce, Arkansas, and Tallulah, Louisiana, and to this day there is a constant flow back and forth between these towns and Las Vegas.

Formal segregation of black people in Las Vegas continued into the 1950s, as black performers such as Sammy Davis, Jr were banned from staying in the hotels where they entertained as headliners. De facto racial segregation in the area continued into the 1970s as black people still were systematically banned from dance clubs and other social venues.

The 1990 Census figures showed that African-Americans comprised 9.3% of the total Clark County population, while in 1997 they constituted 8.7% of the growing local populace (see table 4.1; Bureau of the Census 1990; Metropolitan Research Association 1998: 7). Their numbers are increasing in absolute terms, however, as 1997 Census Bureau estimates reflect a 58.8% increase from 1990 to 1997 (Kanigher 1998). Despite a decline in overall percentage of the population, more than any other ethnic group, African-Americans have made significant inroads in the local political structure. The Clark County fire chief, the North Las Vegas police chief and former city manager, some long-time state legislators, and the Chair of the powerful Clark County Commission are all African-Americans. Black judges also sit on the bench in District Court and, in 1998, a woman became the area's first African-American federal judge.

African-Americans' main informal source of political influence comes through the Westside churches, whose pastors are assiduously courted by local politicians. However, according to the Urban Chamber of Commerce, there is no centralized African-American community because less than 12 percent of the Las Vegas black population now lives on the Westside, with the rest dispersed throughout neighborhoods across the valley. An African-American weekly newspaper, the *Las Vegas Sentinel Voice,* was created in the late 1950s. With a circulation of 5,000 to 7,000, it remains the only publication serving that community in Nevada.

While predominantly minority districts such as the Westside have been represented as separate political entities on the city council and county commission, this is in the process of changing as the community grows. Federal guidelines mandate that city-ward and county-commission-district populations must be within ten percentage points of each other, so rapid growth in suburban areas is diluting the inner-city districts via redistricting. The city of Las Vegas redistricted its formerly black and Hispanic inner-city council wards, combining the two minority groups as part of Ward 3. Other extremely poor, inner-city neighborhoods such as Meadows Village were redistricted to join with some older wealthy neighborhoods, as well as with residents of the city's western suburbs, as part of Ward 1. Some city leaders have argued that the action preserved a minority-coalition district; however, minority representatives see the redistricting as having created a ghetto district (Sebelius 1996). A counter-proposal to preserve separate representation for the predominantly black city ward, and for a predominantly Hispanic ward as well, by increasing the city council from five to seven members, was defeated in 1997 but will be reconsidered in 1999. The city ward structure is up for further redistricting in the near future, however, as the suburban population continues to grow while the more established east and west central areas have all but stopped growing.

The Clark County commission is facing similar redistricting issues but is waiting for Census 2000 data. The commission district that covers the Westside is represented by Yvonne Atkinson-Gates, the African-American, female Chair of the commission, who represents only 39,000 residents, while two of her fellow commissioners represent more than 111,000 constituents each, a gap that literally grows larger each day.

In 1992, the Westside was rocked by violence and rioting related to the trial verdict concerning the Los Angeles police officers accused of beating Rodney King. Following more than 24 hours of heavy media coverage of rioting in Los Angeles, hundreds of Las Vegas blacks living in the Westside burned and looted a local NAACP (National Association for the Advancement of Colored People) office, a post office, a welfare office, a medical center, and neighborhood businesses. A police sub-station and several apartments also went up in flames, while rioters shot at rescue vehicles, fire and police personnel, and news crews.

Many long-time Westside residents were furious at the damage inflicted on their neighborhood by the rioters. Although sympathizing with the outrage at the trial verdict, they criticized those who caused $6-million damage and destroyed many businesses crucial to the local community. Overall, 37 people were injured, 111 were arrested, and many others were left homeless or lost their livelihoods as a result of the riots. Criticisms also were raised against the Las Vegas Metropolitan Police Department for setting up barricades on the few roads leading out of the Westside in order to prevent rioters from reaching the downtown Las Vegas area.

Within the next few years, however, a concerted community effort replaced many of the lost businesses. A major supermarket, the West Las Vegas Library, the Andre Agassi Boys and Girls Club, and a Veterans' Hospital, all constructed after the riots, resulted from an out-pouring of private, city, county, and federal funding to help renovate the area.

## Asians

Chinese immigrants began arriving in Nevada in the mid-nineteenth century, first as part of the Gold Rush and later as workers on the Central Pacific Railroad. Although in both cases they were concentrated primarily in the northern part of the state, the vicious discrimination that the Chinese experienced was a statewide phenomenon in the form of both racist legislation and violent physical assaults (Bowers 1996). Despite these enormous obstacles, however, the Chinese in Nevada, including Las Vegas, have persevered and even prospered, and have more recently been joined by a growing influx of other Asians, especially from the Philippines, Japan, and Korea.

The 1990 census figures show that Asian and Pacific Islander residents comprised 3.3% of the Clark County population, while in 1996 their numbers nearly doubled to 5.8% of the growing county populace (Metropolitan Research Association 1998: 7). This reflects a 96.8% increase, the second largest among ethnic minorities, according to 1997 Census Bureau estimates (Kanigher 1998).

Perhaps one of the most visible signs of the expanding Asian subpopulation in Las Vegas is the 90,000-square-foot Chinatown Plaza, located on Spring Mountain Road a few miles west of the Strip. This colorful commercial center boasts a variety of restaurants, a full-size supermarket, bookstores, wedding chapels, and other retail outlets. The mall serves both the local Asian and non-Asian community, as well as tourists. Opened in 1995, the plaza defies traditional wisdom, as it is not located in a Chinese-American neighborhood and probably would not survive if it relied solely on the local Asian-American population.

Another example of the growing significance of Asian cultures in Las Vegas is the city's formation of its first cooperative sister-city agreement in 1987, with a Korean city, An San. Although the city of Las Vegas has been criticized for spending more than half a million dollars on the program, the city council voted to extend expenses in 1998 for a $30,000-per-year consultant, a $25,000 annual grant, and $40,000 for three city employees to administer the program. Thus far, however, the partnership has not lived up to the expectations of its sponsors. One Korean business, Continental Wire American, did purchase eight acres of land at the Las Vegas Technology Park in 1993 for $1 per square foot, approximately one-fourth the going rate. No construction ever took place, however, and the city is suing to regain the undeveloped land, now worth approximately $6 per square foot.

## Seniors

More than any ethnic group, senior citizens constitute the largest and most rapidly increasing Las Vegas sub-population. The increase in numbers of early retirees and those nearing retirement (aged 55+) is even more startling. Of the 85,648 newcomers who moved to the Las Vegas Valley in 1997 alone, one of every four (25.6 percent) was 55 or older, and most were retired or in pre-retirement (Metropolitan Research Association 1998: 3, 9,10). These numbers are not expected to let up soon, since it is estimated that as many as 20 percent of the 76 million baby boomers will move when they retire, and a percentage of that population are likely to come to Las Vegas.

According to the Nevada State Demographer, an estimated 21.1 percent of the Clark County population now falls into the 55+ (senior/retired) category, with nearly half of that group aged 55 to 64 (Judson 1998). Although it is estimated that up to two out of five individuals who move to Clark County eventually move on, few of these out-migrants are seniors (Calder 1997: 12). Thus, as many as one-third of Clark County's permanent in-migrants may be seniors. As the indigenous population ages in place, joined by a strong in-migration of retired baby boomers, the "graying of America" could have a much greater impact in Las Vegas than in most other communities.

National statistics also show that seniors who move to retire tend to have incomes that average $30,000 per year and Las Vegas is typical of this trend: in 1997, southern Nevada retirees had a median income of $29,628 (Metropolitan Research Association 1998: 9). Retirees who relocate from other areas are often much wealthier, with an average estate value of more than $300,000, making them attractive residents

as their incomes are virtually recession-proof. Recognizing their economic potential, states now compete vigorously to attract retirees as
people 55 and older constitute a $900-billion market, controlling half
of all discretionary income and 75 percent of the nation's financial
assets (Associated Press 1997a). Arizona, for decades a magnet for
seniors, began an organized campaign to entice well-to-do retirees
and aging baby boomers by creating a separate Arizona Office of
Senior Living within its state Commerce Department. In 1996, people
over age 55 spent $13.6 billion in Arizona alone, according to the
Arizona State University Center for Business Research. Other studies
have shown that each new retiree who relocates to Arizona generates
almost two jobs as a result.

Thus far, southern Nevada political entities have made no such
formal effort to attract retirees, though the area is one of the nation's
fastest growing retirement destinations, relying instead on the state's
favorable tax structure, climate, and entertainment variety as pull
factors. Some of the 30 million tourists who visit Las Vegas each year
decide to retire in southern Nevada and the area is consistently listed
in national Top Ten retirement lists. Also, the Del Webb Corporation,
developers of Sun City, prominently advertises its two Las Vegas
retirement communities in numerous national publications (see
the end of this chapter for the economic impact of seniors in Las
Vegas).

One major characteristic of the migratory senior population is that
they are less likely to have traditional family support structures.
Retirement relocation usually means moving away from the community where they lived, worked, and raised their families, although
some are moving to Nevada to join other family members. People
who retire in the community where they have lived and worked for
years usually have a strong support network in place, and moving to
a new community to retire means having to replace that structure. It
is not yet known what long-term impact this factor will have in Las
Vegas. However, one study of Clark County seniors found the personal factor of loneliness to be related more to income level, with no
correlation found to length of residence in Clark County (Nevada
Division of Aging Services 1994).

However, not all seniors are wealthy. There is a sharp economic contrast between the seniors who move to Clark County to retire and the
aging indigenous population, which includes a large number of
workers from the service sector. A large percentage of these long-time
residents were minimum-hourly-wage workers who relied on tip
income and do not have substantial pensions or retirement-program
options. Lower salaries, frequent job changes, and lack of retirement

planning could make their retirement years a struggle from the beginning. Many indigenous seniors also live in older neighborhoods and experience problems associated with lack of services (see chapter 5), and crime (see chapter 7).

While they are healthy and financially secure, in-migrating retirees are a fiscal asset to Clark County; in fifteen years many will be neither as healthy nor as financially comfortable. These seniors, along with the aging local population, could ultimately place a tremendous burden on medical care and emergency services in Clark County (Collins 1999). Nevada must take a hard look at this issue, as should Arizona and the other Sunbelt states, but it has not done so thus far.

Seniors are becoming a potent political force in Las Vegas (see chapter 8). According to the Clark County Election Department, in 1998 nearly one-third of the county's registered voters were aged 55 and over. Equally significant, seniors turn out to vote in elections in much larger proportions than other age groups.

Given their inordinately high numbers and rapid growth, seniors who move to retire in Las Vegas are having a significant impact on the local economy. During the first few years after arriving, many pay cash for their homes and spend money not earned in the community on furnishings, water treatment systems, solar screens, landscaping, and other home improvements. As consumers they are highly sought after by Las Vegas businesses, who encourage them by offering senior discounts. Age-restricted communities such as Sun City Summerlin have attracted the attention of shopping centers in the northwest part of the valley, who provide a complimentary shuttle service to transport elderly customers to their businesses, as do many local casinos (see chapter 7).

Businesses catering specifically to affluent seniors are also sprouting up around Las Vegas. Elder law practices and medical service providers that cater to the elderly are expanding rapidly. Another rapidly growing phenomenon is the increasing number of assisted-living residences, marketed as home-like facilities that provide aid to people who are ambulatory but have lost the ability to perform, without assistance, two or more Activities of Daily Living (ADLs). Many seniors are coming to southern Nevada to move into these new residences. By mid-1997, Nevada had more than 300 assisted-living residences, each housing from 5 to 130 seniors (Nadler 1997). Costing $1,500 to $2,000 per month, they are designed as alternatives to nursing homes, which can cost $35,000 to $40,000 per year for 24-hour care. Aging in place is the goal of these residences, which provide restaurant-style meals three times a day, plus snacks, weekly housekeeping, laundry service, all utilities except telephone, recreational activities, 24-hour supervision, and personal care in private and semi-private suites.

Recently, a large number of apartment complexes and other living communities catering to seniors also have been constructed throughout the southern Nevada region. Most are designed for the elderly with relatively large amounts of discretionary income and feature a variety of amenities, from concierge assistance to recreational activities and special transportation services. Townhomes in the $125,000 range are specifically targeted at seniors, referred to by one Las Vegas builder, Trophy Homes' CEO Mitchell Rouda, as "retirees on a budget, who come here to gamble and want the city lifestyle" (Calkins 1996).

The real-estate market in Las Vegas is thus adapting in response to changing needs of homebuyers such as senior retirees and aging baby boomers. Because the majority of retirees moving to Las Vegas purchase their homes, they have created the demand for retirement communities like Sun City Summerlin and Sun City MacDonald Ranch. Seniors for the most part want single-story homes, and if aging baby boomers purchase a two-story home, many of them are looking for a master bedroom at ground level. This large group of homebuyers is thus changing home design patterns in southern Nevada's new residential construction. In a booming real-estate market where nearly two thousand homes are built and sold each month, land prices are escalating. Buyers must pay a premium for a spacious single-story home yet many seniors and aging baby boomers are willing to do so. In order to cater to this consumer group all homes built in Sun City Summerlin and MacDonald Ranch are single-story.

In addition to the substantial financial resources in-migrating seniors bring with them, many retirees also have valuable work skills, knowledge, and other talents developed over a lifetime. Thus, while seniors may be seen as a potential drain on social resources, they may also be seen as a community asset, with their active participation in and contributions to the local labor force making them an unexpected and cost-effective addition, in the short term at least, to the community in both paid and volunteer positions. Nationally, in 1994, 18 percent of retirees' income came from post-retirement employment (Doup 1997). The National Bureau of Labor Statistics found that the number of workers age 65 and older rose 31 percent to 3.8 million, between 1985 and 1995 (Associated Press 1997c). Many large national companies, such as the Gap and McDonalds, are looking for reliable older workers who bring a work ethic and loyalty harder to find in younger, part-time employees. Senior employees have the additional advantage for businesses of not requiring child-care, health, or retirement benefits. Las Vegas is beginning to feel the impact of this labor pool as local employment service agencies claim that older workers are much in demand in Las Vegas (Caruso 1998a). Such participation also provides a boost to some retirees in terms of leading a longer, happier, and healthier life, as even relatively affluent seniors who retire and buy homes in the more upscale communities are working in a variety of part-time positions, from light maintenance to security jobs, largely to have "something to do," or to "keep me out of the casinos."

The overall impact of the senior workforce on the Las Vegas economy is a controversial point to some, however. Specifically, are these seniors taking part-time, low-pay, no-benefit jobs that other, younger workers could fill full-time for more money, or are they a low-cost resource? There are, to date, no studies of the southern Nevada region that address this important question, but it will no doubt become an important local public-policy issue in the near future.

## Rapid Economic Growth

The rapid economic growth that has taken place in Las Vegas since 1960 is reflected in labor force statistics. Total full-time employment within the county grew from 47,048 to 370,583 from 1960 to 1990 (see table 4.7) and since 1987 the Las Vegas metropolitan area has consistently led the nation in job creation. Most of these positions, however, are relatively low paying service-sector, resort-industry jobs (see table 4.6). Employment expansion of this kind is precisely what has caught the attention of declining urban areas in the rest of the country, although many large cities are debating whether bringing in legalized gambling is a panacea for the ills of deindustrialization. Nonetheless, employment expansion in Las Vegas has continued unabated, with the metropolitan area's job growth increasing at a rate between 6% and 7% annually, gaining 209,400 new jobs between 1992 and 1997 alone (Caruso 1998a). Also, while the national unemployment rate hit a 24-year low of 4.6% in 1997, unemployment in Clark County was even lower, an amazing 3.9% in December, making it difficult for local employers to find workers. Salaries in Las Vegas are also rising because of the labor shortage, with "double digit wage inflation in numerous categories" (Caruso 1998a).

As in the rest of the country, another significant change since 1960 has been the increasing number of women who have entered the full-time workforce. In 1960, 33.6% of the total number of workers in Clark

0**Table 4.6**    Job growth in Clark County's ten largest occupations

| | Clark County employment | | Percentage job growth | |
| --- | --- | --- | --- | --- |
| | *1996* | *1987* | *1985* | *1985 to 1996* |
| Retail salespersons | 20090 | 10050 | 8820 | 127.8% |
| Waiters and waitresses | 19200 | 1049 | 9310 | 106.2% |
| Cashiers | 16090 | 8630 | 7710 | 108.7% |
| Janitors and cleaners | 13190 | 7770 | 7000 | 88.4% |
| General office clerks | 13050 | 4910 | 3880 | 236.3% |
| Maids and housekeeping cleaners | 12560 | 7450 | 6160 | 103.9% |
| Blackjack dealers | 12370 | 7990 | 6160 | 100.8% |
| General managers and top executives | 10860 | 6960 | 5300 | 104.9% |
| Guards | 10720 | 5550 | 4560 | 135.1% |
| Carpenters | 10240 | 2960 | 2320 | 341.4% |

*Source*:  Research and Analysis Bureau, State of Nevada Department of Employment, Training, and Rehabilitation, Carson City, Nevada, 1998.

County were women, but by 1990 the figure was 44.8%, almost half the total, (see table 4.5).

A more precise picture of economic changes in the region may be obtained by examining the figures for employment by sector. In Clark County, increases were seen in the following categories from 1960 to 1990: wholesale and retail trade increased from 17.7% to 19.2%; finance, insurance, and real estate rose from 3.7% to 6.4%; and the service sector grew from 43.5% to 48.4%. Declines from 1960 to 1990 were reflected in other categories: agricultural employees decreased from 1.7% to 1.1% of the labor force; mining declined from 0.6% to 0.3%; construction workers fell from 9.8% to 9.3% before the Strip construction boom of the 1990s; manufacturing dropped from 7% to 4.7%; transportation and public utilities fell from 7.4% to 6.5%, and public administration fell from 6.8% to 4.1% (Bureau of the Census 1960, 1990). Here again, employment in Clark County, like that of the rest of the nation, is becoming increasingly concentrated in services, commerce, and financial/real-estate enterprises (see table 4.8).

Unlike the rest of the nation, however, the regional economy of Las Vegas has always been highly concentrated in the service and com-mercial-trade industries, which together account for more than 70% of

**Table 4.7**   Employment by industry: Clark County, 1960–90

| | 1990 | 1980 | 1970 | 1960 | Percentage change 1980–90 | Percentage change 1960–90 |
|---|---|---|---|---|---|---|
| Industry total | 370,583 | 224,869 | 107,750 | 47,048* | 64.8 | 672.9 |
| Agriculture | 4,137 | 1,539 | 904 | 799 | 168.8 | 417.8 |
| | (1.1) | (0.07) | (0.08) | (1.7) | | |
| Mining | 1,205 | 585 | 449 | 296 | 106.0 | 307.1 |
| | (0.3) | (0.3) | (0.4) | (0.6) | | |
| Construction | 34,305 | 17,484 | 9,153 | 4,707 | 96.2 | 628.8 |
| | (9.3) | (7.8) | (8.5) | (9.8) | | |
| Manufacturing | 17,368 | 9,738 | 4,955 | 3,344 | 78.4 | 419.4 |
| | (4.7) | (4.3) | (4.6) | (7.0) | | |
| Transportation and public utilities | 23,964 | 15,994 | 8,118 | 3,528 | 49.8 | 579.3 |
| | (6.5) | (7.1) | (7.5) | (7.4) | | |

*While industry categories in 1960 Census of Population include "industry not reported," table 4.7 excludes it. Numbers in parentheses are percentages, which may not add to total due to rounding.

Sources: *County and City Data Book, 1994, 1983, 1972, 1962*, respectively; *Census of Population, 1990, 1980, 1970, 1960*, respectively; US Department of Commerce, Social and Economic Statistics Administration, Bureau of the Census.

**Table 4.8** Employment by industry: Clark County, 1960–90

| | 1990 | 1980 | 1970 | 1960 | Percentage change 1980–90 | Percentage change 1960–90 |
|---|---|---|---|---|---|---|
| Wholesale and retail trade | 71,004 (19.2%) | 42,094 (18.7%) | 19,884 (18.5%) | 8,478 (17.7%) | 68.7 | 737.5 |
| Finance, insurance and real estate | 23,845 (6.4%) | 13,812 (6.1%) | 4,401 (4.1%) | 1,762 (3.7%) | 72.6 | 1253.3 |
| Services | 179,537 (48.4%) | 111,171 (49.4%) | 52,920 (49.1%) | 20,867 (43.5%) | 61.5 | 760.4 |
| Public administration | 15,218 (4.1%) | 12,452 (5.5%) | 6,966 (6.5%) | 3,267 (6.8%) | 22.2 | 365.8 |

*Sources: County and City Data Book, 1994, 1983, 1972, 1962, respectively; Census of Population, 1990, 1980, 1970, 1960, respectively; US Department of Commerce, Social and Economic Statistics Administration, Bureau of the Census.*

total employment. Figures that focus more specifically on employment by occupation reveal that, while most categories, such as management and professional/technical workers, exhibited roughly the same importance in the economy of 1990 as they did in 1960, the percentage of employment in sales doubled at the county level, from 6.4% in 1960 to 13.2%.*

## Labor Issues

Nevada is a "right to work" state yet Las Vegas has an active union population. Its large service-sector population has a powerful union presence in the form of Culinary Local 226, with more than 40,000 members the state's largest labor organization. The Culinary Union had tight control of the town until 1977 when its long-time leader, Al Bramlet, was murdered following a series of controversial events attributed by some to Bramlet's influence, including the firebombing of local restaurants that would not unionize.

Even before Bramlet's demise, however, Las Vegas was the scene of several hard-fought labor struggles, including a fifteen-day Culinary Union strike in 1976 that cost an estimated $130 million. A subsequent 1984 strike cost an estimated $3 million a day when striking culinary workers, bartenders, musicians, and stagehands who were union members closed resort showrooms and curtailed restaurant service. The strike was called at a strategic time, as 25,000 delegates to the

---

*Comparable figures for the city of Las Vegas alone are: an increase in median family income from $7,662 in 1960 to $35,300 in 1990, slightly higher than in the county. A lower level of poverty, 10.6%, was seen in 1960, but by 1990 the rate was higher than in the county at 8.2%.

Las Vegas had 86,114 people employed full time in 1960, a figure that was larger than the rest of the county, and in 1990 140,298 were employed. These statistics indicate that the county experienced a more rapid increase in the creation of jobs than did the city in those three decades, partially reflecting growth of Las Vegas Strip resorts.

The city of Las Vegas experienced a similar change in work distribution by gender, going from 34.1% of the labor force constituted by women in 1960 to roughly the same percentage as the county, or 44.7%, in 1990.

Sector employment figures for the city are slightly different. Between 1960 and 1990 the percentage employed in construction rose from 7.9% to 10.2%; wholesale and retail trade increased slightly from 18.2% to 18.7%; and finance, insurance and real estate increased from 4.3% to 6.5%. During the same period, and unlike the county, services decreased from 52.4% in 1960 to 48.3% in 1990. Other declines matched county trends, with manufacturing dropping from 4.8% to 4.3% of the total employment, transportation declining from 7% to 6.3%, and public administration down from 5% to 4.1% (Bureau of the Census 1960, 1990).

National Association of Broadcasters' convention, most of them television station general managers and news directors from around the country, had to make their own beds while staying at premier Strip resorts. The impact was felt for years locally as well, as workers who had gone without paychecks struggled to catch up on house payments and other bills. The Musicians' Union also lost a major contract battle in the 1980s, when live music was no longer required for local shows as part of the new bottom-line corporate mentality at the resorts.

The longest labor dispute in Las Vegas' history is also the longest in the nation's history. It began on September 21, 1991, when 550 Frontier Hotel employees, members of Culinary Workers' Local 226, Bartenders' 165, Teamsters' 995, Operating Engineers' 501, and Carpenters' 1780, walked off their jobs. The strike was called when the Frontier refused to sign the same labor contract that had been ratified by most of the city's other hotel-casinos, saying it could not provide the same benefits as those paid by the larger Strip resorts. The 30-year-old Frontier, which had been part of the old Howard Hughes empire, had been bought by the Elardi family in 1988 from the Summa Corporation. Many of the older family-owned gaming operations, such as the Horseshoe in downtown Las Vegas, had similar complaints about not having the large profit margins of the new mega-resorts.

In April 1993, violence from the long-running strike erupted on the Strip when a California tourist was severely beaten by Frontier picketers, in front of his wife. Video of the brutal incident was broadcast on national newscasts, tarnishing Las Vegas' image for a while. Seven strikers received criminal citations and the couple was awarded an $800,000 settlement by the Clark County District Court. Union members counter-charged that the hotel was spying on strikers and had hired a high-tech dirty tricks squad that fired a large water gun at the strikers, placed manure where they were eating, and jammed their hand-held radio frequencies. Frontier Hotel representatives, in turn, responded that the union was making money on the strike, collecting more than $7 million per year ($15 per month from 40,000 union workers), but paying out much less in strike benefits.

After six and half years, the nation's longest labor strike finally came to an end in 1998 when the Frontier was purchased by Kansas businessman Phil Ruffin, owner of a dozen Marriott hotels, for $167 million cash. Workers returned to the resort in exchange for wages that averaged $2 an hour higher than before the strike.

Another major challenge to the Culinary Union came in 1993 when the 5,000-room MGM opened as a non-union shop, paying employees higher wages and benefits than they would have received through union membership. What locals refer to as "the great sidewalk battle" ensued – an unscheduled feature of the opening festivities for the world's largest hotel. Anticipating conflict with the union, the MGM asked the Clark County commission to designate the sidewalks along Las Vegas Boulevard and Tropicana Avenue in front of the MGM as private property. The county agreed, limiting access of the unions to picket the property when it opened and causing hundreds of union protesters to be arrested for trespassing. A similar sidewalk-privatization request was granted to the Mirage in an effort to eliminate the proliferation of smut peddlers who were harassing tourists and restricting sidewalk access there. In an interesting turnaround, new MGM management in 1996 wanted to cut operating costs, so they allowed the union to solicit workers and negotiated a contract in 1997 that meant lower wages because of unionization. Many MGM workers complained publicly at the loss of benefits that came with the new union deal.

Another controversial labor practice, subleasing restaurants within their properties, began in some Las Vegas resorts in the 1990s. The MGM and other Strip properties leased the bulk of their restaurants to non-union operators in order to move away from the expenses of food service, as part of the overall corporatization of Las Vegas casinos. Non-union subcontractors could run profitable operations with the hotel acting merely as landlord and therefore not violating union contracts. This practice became a major source of contention with the opening of New York-New York, where all food-service establishments run by ARK Restaurants Corporation were non-union. Approximately 800 food-service workers at New York-New York, many making $4 per hour less than prevailing union wages, received no retirement benefits and only limited health coverage. By contrast, at the Mirage, California Pizza Kitchen workers are employees of the hotel and therefore are covered by the Culinary Union contract.

The next major battle with the union over the opening of a non-union megaresort will come at the Venetian, owned by developer and union critic Sheldon Adelson, who claims that he will let his employees decide if they want union membership, adding, "I'm not going to be intimidated by the union" (Macy 1997).

Despite their recent troubles with the new megaresorts as well as at older establishments, the major unions are mobilizing for a concerted effort to defend, and even increase, their presence in Las Vegas. In 1997, John Wilhelm, secretary-treasurer for the Hotel Employees and Restaurant Employees International Union (HEREIU), parent of the Culinary Union, pledged to spend millions of dollars in Las Vegas to strengthen the union's presence. Las Vegas was targeted because of the growth in its construction industry and the existing strength of the Culinary Union. At a union rally one month after Wilhelm's announcement, AFL-CIO president John Sweeney called Las Vegas "the fastest growing union city in America," adding that "just as surely as New York set the [labor union] standards for the past 100 years, Las Vegas will be setting them for the next 100 years" (Associated Press 1997b). Union officials point to the tourism industry in Los Angeles as an example of a low-wage, no-benefit industry and claim that a similar situation would be disastrous for the Las Vegas economy.

Even as they compete for bottom-line dollars, however, the relationship between the gaming industry and Culinary Union remains a symbiotic one. Gamers serve on the union's health and welfare fund and labor lobbyists help the gamers on federal tax policy. For example, in 1997, HEREIU lobbied Congress to free up federal transportation dollars necessary to widen Interstate 15 in the area between Barstow and Victorville. The highway, the main land-transportation route between Los Angeles and Las Vegas, is such a vital tourism pipeline that what is normally a four- to five-hour trip between the two cities usually takes more than eight at the beginning and end of three-day weekends. The union's support of the Las Vegas tourism lifeline came as forty Las Vegas resort contracts with the Culinary Union were expiring and contract negotiations were underway. From past experience corporations now know that unions can help them *control* wages rather than pushing for excessive labor costs.

## The Casino/Tourist Economy

### Tourism

As a prime tourist destination, Las Vegas received visitors totaling 30,464,635 in 1997, up 10.7% from the previous year, with a total economic impact of nearly $25 billion (Metropolitan Research Association 1998). Of that figure, 52% came by ground transportation (auto, bus recreation vehicle), while 47% came by air.

In 1997, 3,749 conventions brought 3,519,424 delegates to Las Vegas, helping produce a 90.3% average hotel occupancy rate. A 1997 visitor profile revealed that, of all respondents, 70% were married, 65% were employed, and an additional 26% were retired. Also, 84% were white, 68% were 40 years old or over, and 44% came from the western states (28% from California). Finally, more than half, 57%, had household incomes of $40,000 or more (Las Vegas Convention and Visitors Authority 1997).

While it is common knowledge that more than $6 billion in casino revenues come from gambling, the overwhelming majority of respondents to the visitor survey, 72%, said they came to Las Vegas principally for a vacation. Only 4% stated that gambling was the principal aim of their trip, down from 10% in 1994 Las Vegas Convention and Visitors Authority (1997: 2). Many visitors come to Las Vegas more than once a year, 30% came to the area 2 or 3 times and 6% visited 4 or more times (Las Vegas Convention and Visitors Authority 1997: 16). Although most visitors are from other western states, 19% of the respondents came from foreign countries, 9% from eastern states, 13% from the south, and 15% from the Midwest (Metropolitan Research Association 1998: 73).

Visitor volume and hotel capacity have always been highly correlated in Las Vegas, as the different properties offer competitive package deals to attract tourists. Since the advent of the megaresorts in 1989, tens of thousands of rooms have been added and the number of visitors has doubled. Although hotel occupancy has traditionally exceeded 90%, the additional 12,000 rooms opened in 1997 were met with no increase in visitor volume and gaming revenues, while hotel occupancy rates were 90.3% and motel rates averaged 68.8%.

## Gambling

Despite impressive growth in other areas, the heart of the Las Vegas regional economy remains casino gambling. Gross gambling revenue for Clark County has doubled in ten years from $3.1 billion in 1988 to $6.2 billion in 1997. Combined with gaming, tourists spent a whopping $25 billion in 1997. This includes hotel rooms, food, and other services, a more than 300% increase from 1991. The average "gaming budget" for each tourist is approximately $515 per visit (Las Vegas Convention and Visitors Authority 1998: 5).

How exactly do casinos profit from gambling? As more corporations that must report to stockholders take over casinos, more exact figures on the take from gambling operations are becoming available. According to a director of Smith Barney, Harris Upham, and Company: "As a rule of thumb, the typical table game, whether blackjack or craps or roulette, is basically set so that the house will win 2 to 4% per play" (Morris 1992: 1).

Slot machine and video-poker paybacks range from 80% to 97%. In places such as bars or laundromats, which also contain the ubiquitous gambling machines, customers can lose as much as 20% to the house. However, word spreads fast and gamblers tend to avoid patronizing places with low-payoff, or "tight" machines. Even on the better-paying machines, an announced payback of 97% on slot machines means that, because it is less than 100%, the house maintains the edge.

Baccarat is considered a "high roller" game because it has the largest payoff for winners, yet the lowest chance of winning, among table games. A typical house take on baccarat is between 15% and 17%, but many players lose (or win) more (Morris 1992). Noticeable fluctuations in the Strip's win percentages are often explained by large house losses to major baccarat players. The state's twenty casinos that offer baccarat generated $534 million in revenue in the twelve months from December 1996 to November 1997. During that same period, Nevada casinos as a whole generated $8.3 billion in total revenue, with $6.2 billion of that coming from Clark County.

Occupational estimates from the state suggest that when a major megaresort opens, it creates upwards of 4,000 new positions. Most of these, however, are relatively low-wage service jobs in the hotels and casinos. There are some exceptions, however, even among minimum-wage casino employees, such as those operating blackjack and craps at the major resorts. These workers are often able to dramatically increase their income through tips or "tokes" they receive from players.

Many entry-level workers in the casino-based service sector possess minimal educational skills, especially in mathematics and writing. The lack of writing skills, in particular, "has created an interesting niche market in Las Vegas – that of writing résumés for entry-level workers. Some thirty companies offer this service for hefty fees (R. Smith 1994). Casino operators are more interested in hiring workers who "understand the team-player nature of the environment" (Morris 1992: 1).

Following a national trend, another market niche has been created in the Las Vegas economy by the resorts' practice of drug-testing employees. Casinos consider drug use by employees a very serious problem, especially since large amounts of money are handled as part of their jobs, so most test job applicants and many spot-test their workers. For example, when the new MGM Grand opened, every one of its more than 10,000 employees was tested (Havas 1995). Consequently, several companies that specialize in this type of testing have opened facilities in the Las Vegas area.

A final unusual aspect of Las Vegas employment stems from its casino-based mystique as a 24-hour town where "the action never stops." By employing workers around the clock in three shifts, the casinos are able to conform to union requirements for an eight-hour "workday" for their workers, which more importantly enables them to earn round-the-clock revenue. At the same time, other businesses, such as dry cleaners, fast-food restaurants, and grocery stores, also benefit from the 24-hour lifestyle, remaining open all night as well (Martin 1992).

## Shopping

Another recent trend that is helping to diversify the casino/hotel economy into a tourism/resort economy is the construction of shopping malls inside the larger resorts. A 1998 study conducted by the Las Vegas Convention and Visitors Authority found that shopping and fine dining have replaced gambling as the city's primary attractions. As more tourists spend more money on non-gaming activities, shopping is becoming a major part of the Las Vegas experience. Caesars Palace was the first resort to exploit the mall concept in a major way and it later expanded and enhanced its shopping area to remain competitive with its new neighbor, the Mirage. A 1992 upgrade, the first of several multi-million-dollar expansions at Caesars in the 1990s, included a Roman-themed upscale shopping mall, the Forum Shops, which rapidly became the nation's most profitable shopping center, posting earnings of $1,200 per square foot, compared with the national average of $300 per square foot. Designed as much for entertainment as for shopping, the Forum enables shoppers to wander beneath a constantly changing sky dome that shifts from dawn to dusk as they stroll past bubbling fountains to dine at Spago or Planet Hollywood and shop at Gucci, Escada, or the Disney and Warner Brothers Store. At the same time, they can watch a laser light show featuring a wine-swilling Bacchus and other animatronic Roman statues. Elaborately themed façades depict the classical Roman period and the shops are open year-round, including Thanksgiving and Christmas Day, when they report phenomenal sales. According to a hotel spokesman: "The idea is to offer attractions, not just a shopping center, but entertainment dimensions not available anywhere else in the Las Vegas area. The average visitor stays in Las Vegas for three days, but you don't just gamble for three days straight" (Jones 1992).

In 1997, the Forum Shops opened a $90-million addition, expanding its total size to 1.8 million square feet, making it nearly twice the size of most regional malls (see figure 4.2). The Atlantis entertainment

**Figure 4.2**   The Forum Shops, Caesars Palace

attraction features interaction between humans and animatronic characters in a show replete with water and fire. A three-story F. A. O. Schwartz children's toy store is the largest in the chain and features a two-story-high Trojan horse playhouse and the Monopoly Café. Still to come is a planned Caesars Maximus, a $220-million retail and entertainment complex, to be located at the front of the resort property. Retailers are attracted by the unique combination of a strong and growing local economy plus a robust tourism market.

In short, the retail-sales industry on the Las Vegas Strip is booming. In 1997, 3.7 million square feet of new retail space, much of it geared toward high-end, upscale shoppers, was coming on line or was on the drawing boards at resort properties in the heart of Las Vegas' gaming industry. Bellagio opened in 1998 with upscale shops that included Tiffany, Chanel, and Hermes, and the Venetian opens in 1999 with 1 million square feet of shopping space. While visitor volume in Clark County rose a modest 2.2% in 1996 (the eighth largest increase in the nation) and gaming revenues only 1.1%, tourist spending on shopping, rooms, and entertainment increased 8.9%. Resort owners thus have been quick to respond to this latest trend in Las Vegas tourism.

## Economic Diversification of the Region

### Public-Sector Diversity

In a sense the regional Las Vegas economy, despite its heavy reliance on casino gambling, has always been diversified, given the substantial revenues it receives from the federal government. Massive Washington spending began in earnest during the 1930s with the construction of the Hoover Dam, as discussed in chapter 1. This "federal trigger" (Moehring 1989) provided a basis for economic expansion and attracted many permanent residents to the area. The lion's share of federal money, however, has come from the billions of dollars transferred to the Las Vegas region each year by the Departments of Defense and Energy.

The Defense Department maintains Nellis Air Force Base, located eight miles north of Las Vegas. The base was built during World War II and has been a major economic presence in Clark County ever since. Defense spending cutbacks have affected Nellis Air Force Base less than most other military installations, given its unique status as a training facility with a massive range comprising 3 million acres of ground space and 5 million acres of airspace. However, military consolidation has been felt as more tenant units occupy the base. Economically, Nellis had an annual payroll of more than $300 million in Fiscal Year 1996, a substantial windfall to the regional economy despite the fact that the 9,000 military and civilian workers that year represented a decrease from a high of 14,000 in 1985. Also, another 16,000 military retirees in the area receive an additional $252 million annually (USAF 1997).

The Nevada Test Site, the major source of Department of Energy (DOE) funds, constitutes a different story, as the cessation of nuclear testing has had a huge impact on its operations. Located 65 miles northwest of Las Vegas, the test site is an enormous expanse of high desert and mesas. In 1963, above-ground nuclear testing was banned in favor of underground testing, and by 1988, the test site reached its peak level of employment with 11,000 workers, many of them in high-paying jobs requiring highly educated personnel. The test facility had half a million square feet of office space on 1,400 square miles of land and its main employer was Reynolds Electrical Engineering Company (REECO). In 1992, a moratorium on nuclear testing was imposed, and by 1997, the multi-billion-dollar budget had been reduced to $390 million and 900 of the 2,000 buildings were closed, with only 5,300 DOE and contract employees remaining. The test site budget in 1998 totaled $684 million, with about half of that going to research the suitability of Yucca Mountain as a nuclear storage site.

Nevada Test Site Development Corporation is exploring future uses for the site, which is approximately the size of Rhode Island. Its high-technology capabilities and the site's relative isolation suggest possible uses such as solar-energy development, a hazardous-spill center, and a counter-terrorism training camp, in addition to the nuclear-waste dump, tentatively slated for location at Yucca Mountain on the western edge of the test site.

The combined budgets of the test site and Nellis Air Force Base, along with the additional income of military retirees, put more than a billion dollars annually into the southern Nevada economy, which is enhanced further by multiplier effects. Regardless of the ultimate success of diversification attempts in the private sector, the economic miracle of casino gambling in Las Vegas continues to be bolstered significantly by a massive injection of federal funds each year.

## Private-Sector Diversity

When recession hit the southern California economy in the late 1980s, as aerospace industry cutbacks, base closings, burdensome business regulations, and higher operating costs took their toll, many southern California firms began considering relocation to Las Vegas. Over the 1990s economic interests in the Las Vegas metropolitan region, including the Chamber of Commerce and Nevada Development Authority, have aggressively pursued these and other businesses from around the country. Economic diversification is designed to decrease the reliance on casino gambling, although that sector continues to dominate local employment; in 1990 it was estimated that the gambling industry's share of local employment, both direct and indirect, was about 55 percent (Gabriel 1991).

Between 1985 and 1990, new non-gaming-oriented firms moving into the area increased by 31 percent and from 1989 to 1991 alone 120 new industrial firms opened in the region. Significantly: "the majority of relocating firms came from California or were weighing a move to California at the same time as Nevada" (Gabriel 1991). The region continued to attract new businesses throughout the 1990s, as Clark County passed the 1 million population mark and new businesses moved in to capitalize on the rapidly growing market. In 1997 alone, more than 37 companies, employing 3,048 workers and with payrolls totaling $65 million, moved to Las Vegas, adding $150 million to the economy in major industries other than ... gaming (Metropolitan Research Association 1998: 37). Again, the largest number came from California, with the second largest group coming from New York.

Many of these new companies were manufacturers and retailers attracted by low business costs and the region's proximity to major western markets. Business operation costs for industries in Las Vegas are among the lowest of any southwestern city and Nevada is one of the few states with no income or franchise tax.

With easy links to adjacent states in the southwest, McCarran International Airport also provides a major boost to non-casino-based economic expansion in several ways (see chapter 2). The establishment of Foreign Trade Zone 89 in 1986 has helped the area become an international business destination and more than 100 companies utilize 300,000 square foot of storage space at the facility (Metropolitan Research Association 1998: 36). The airport's Air Cargo Center has experienced double-digit growth in cargo handled each year since 1993. The 170,000-square-foot facility is located less than a mile from major interstate highways, railroad access, and the airport's main terminal (Metropolitan Research Association 1998: 41). The area is also served by a first-class rail service, providing access not only to the rest of the nation but also to several local industrial sites.

Much of the influx of non-gambling businesses is a direct result of Las Vegas' excellent highway and rail-transport links to the rest of the West. The facilities of discount clothing chain T. J. Maxx, for example, sit alongside the northern edge of Interstate 15, where plentiful warehousing facilities are situated. Lately, what has been true of warehousing is also becoming true of manufacturing. According to an official of the Nevada Development Authority: "If you do business in Southern California, Las Vegas is a logical place to relocate. We're now seeing more interest in manufacturing firms rather than warehousing firms, and that's what brings more jobs, too" (Martin 1992).

Another important factor for diversified business development is the availability of plentiful and affordable office space. More than 1.5 million square feet of new office space was completed in 1997, bringing the total Las Vegas inventory to more than 15.3 million square feet (Caruso 1998b).

One prominent recent trend involves the relocation of business "back-office" operations, such as warehousing and credit centers, to Las Vegas, while corporate headquarters and other "front-office" activities remain closer to large markets. West Coast warehousing centers have been established by Levi Strauss, T. J. Maxx, and Hanes Hosiery and light manufacturing business is represented by companies such as Ocean Spray and Kidd Marshmallow.

Las Vegas also has attracted significant banking, credit, and catalog-sales businesses. Citibank chose Las Vegas over southern California as its national credit-operations center, for example, employing more than 1,600 people, and Montgomery Ward opened a national head-quarters for its credit operations in the area. In 1998, Citibank planned to add 300 to 500 employees, and also began consolidating its national credit-card centers, moving jobs from Georgia, Florida, Denver, and Salt Lake City to Las Vegas (Edwards 1998b). Other new related businesses in the region include Marin Credit Card Services with 600 employees, Williams Sonoma mail-order sales center with 500, Household Finance Credit Card Center with 1,300 employees, and Softbank Services Group's computer support-services calling center with 450 employees. Some high-tech businesses have also been attracted to the area. Most prominent among these is Lockheed Engineering, which recently built a $10-million testing lab in Las Vegas.

Overall, these companies seem satisfied with the southern Nevada economy. A 1998 survey found that two-thirds of local businesses "believe they're better off than they were two years ago and 60 percent said the business climate has improved over the past five years" (H. Smith 1998c). The largest problem identified by the survey was that of finding quality workers, given the state's unemployment rate of only 4.7 percent. Some business owners also pointed to inadequacies in the local school system. Nearly two-thirds of them ranked Clark County schools only as "fair" or "poor" in preparing their graduates for the business world and nearly half said the schools did not adequately support workforce needs. Local higher education fared slightly better, with nearly half the businesses saying they did an "excellent" or "good" job of preparing graduates for business (H. Smith 1998c). Although there are no plans to aggressively diversify the metro economy, clearly such a pattern will continue in the future.

# 5 The Normalization Process I: The Construction of Community Life by the Private Sector

The story of Las Vegas' development is often framed solely in terms of the history of casino gambling. Yet more than a million people live in the area, although establishing such a vast residential market in the desert was not an easy task. While the history of gaming has its famous personalities, like Bugsy Siegel, Moe Dalitz, Kirk Kerkorian, and Steve Wynn, the story of how Las Vegas became a multi-billion-dollar housing market includes other special personalities, such as Hank Greenspun and Howard Hughes. As the region consists mainly of what the Bureau of Land Management calls arid, "disposable" desert, however, a handful of individual entrepreneurs alone, no matter how gifted, could not have produced Las Vegas' community growth. Creating a mass market for housing and ultimately a shaped sense of neighborhood life was, rather, a combination of economic opportunity, shrewd business sense, good timing, and a heavy dose of luck.

In this chapter and the next we seek to describe how Las Vegas emerged as a region with a distinct sense of community in terms of a process we call *normalization*. By normalization we mean the process by which a new residential area develops the practices and institutions of civic life that are essential characteristics of communities in more developed parts of the country and which contribute to the social stability of the urban region. We thus seek to analyze the fundamental transformation of the Las Vegas region from one with a political culture oriented almost solely towards the business needs of tourism and gambling to an ongoing, permanent residential milieu of conventional families, lifestyles, and neighborhoods with a local political agenda that reflects the needs of daily living.

To be sure, the sheer volume of the influx of permanent residents and of new home construction since the 1980s implies that the Las Vegas region is much more than just a tourist destination for legalized gambling. Yet these figures alone do not necessarily imply the development of a viable, civic milieu, as constructing single-family housing on a mass basis in itself might only lead to population aggregation and anomie. Community life requires social institutions and spatial arrangements that promote interaction, daily contact, and visible, accessible forums for discussing everyday concerns. Mass development of residential housing in Las Vegas could have occurred as a faceless sprawl of unending suburban housing, with minimal links to public forums and a limited attachment to, or sense of, place. However, Las Vegas attracted not only visionaries fixated on casino gambling, but others who saw the possibility of creating master-planned communities. As a result, an infrastructure of community institutions and a growing sense of civic life have taken root in the harsh desert environment. More importantly, the sheer numbers of permanent residents, through their collective needs, have redefined the local political agenda (see chapter 8). It is precisely these overlapping resident-based changes that we call "normalization."

## Master-Planned Communities

Las Vegas has a long history of planned communities almost as old as the town itself. Master planning began in the early 1930s with the establishment of Boulder City, which was federally planned and constructed to house workers building the dam. Federal funding included well-maintained open park space in the center of town, and water and power infrastructure systems. Residences were constructed to reflect the hierarchy among dam employees, with those in control of the operation living in the largest houses perched at the highest locations, middle management further down the hill, and workers living in smaller dwellings in less desirable locations. Boulder City also had a strictly controlled social environment, with laws banning gambling (still in effect) and liquor sales (repealed in 1969). Visitors who wanted to stay for more than a day had to obtain a permission slip signed by the city manager (repealed in 1948).

Private developers also created early forms of planned communities. Until recently, the largest was Spring Valley, a major residential project conceived primarily for single-family development. Spring Valley does not qualify as a master-planned community because developers did not envision a housing market mix, nor did they provide funding for infrastructure such as schools or parks. That was the old Las Vegas way, still the norm elsewhere, where the private sector develops the land, sells the homes, and forces the public sector to fund the infrastructure. Spring Valley developers also did not specifically plan for commercial development, although property

**Figure 5.1**  The Las Vegas construction boom

located near major intersections was designated as a commercial zone and businesses moved in as needed. The original landowner was Pardee Construction, a branch of the Weyerhauser Corporation, and the original project was approximately one square mile (640 acres) in size. First developed in the mid-1970s, Spring Valley sold well and has subsequently mushroomed into 30 square miles.

A key figure who played a major role in realizing the idea of master-planned community development in the Las Vegas Valley was Hank Greenspun. As a neophyte Wall Street attorney, Greenspun visited Las Vegas with a client in the 1940s. After checking into the Last Frontier Hotel, Greenspun made a spur of the moment decision to leave the blizzards of New York and move to the desert, where he became the publicist at Bugsy Siegel's Flamingo Hotel. In June 1950, Greenspun took over a weekly newspaper started by typographers who had quit the town's leading newspaper, the *Review-Journal*, in a labor dispute.

Greenspun's only prior journalistic experience had come from editing an Army-post newspaper in Louisiana. The *Las Vegas Sun* was losing $10,000 a week when he bought it but he quickly turned it into a successful daily newspaper that provided competition for the *Review-Journal*. The politically minded Greenspun loved owning the newspaper and often used it to attack the Nevada power structure. One of his primary targets was powerful Senator Pat McCarran, who, Greenspun claimed, had an iron grip on the town in collaboration with the *Review-Journal*: "There was a very powerful Senator, aided and abetted by this newspaper, the *Review-Journal*, we broke their control. I'm proud of that. That was one of my proudest achievements, that we opened up the town to competition, otherwise you wouldn't have half the hotels out there today" (Collins 1983a).

Greenspun's attacks on political leaders were not confined to Nevada, however, as his front-page *Sun* editorials were among the first to criticize Wisconsin Senator Joe McCarthy, who Greenspun called a "sadistic bum," which brought him and his paper national attention as well as a federal indictment. He himself liked to call his newspaper "the people's university, the poor man's university" (Collins 1983a). The *Sun* made money and came close to overtaking the *Review-Journal* in circulation until it was struck by a suspicious fire. The paper survived, however, despite overwhelming odds and did not miss an issue as a result of the fire.

Greenspun invested his entrepreneurial profits in local desert land, a move that seemed foolhardy at the time. From 1956 to 1971 he acquired 3,500 acres outside the Las Vegas city limits adjacent to nearby Henderson, a town which had been built around industrial plants during the war. In 1971 Greenspun acquired an additional 4,500 acres in Henderson on the condition that the original acreage would be annexed to the town and that national developers would be brought in to construct housing.

Initially, the only significant development in the isolated area was the Paradise Valley Golf Club, which was a joint venture with Wilbur Clark, who had built the Desert Inn. Golf courses alone rarely make money unless they are connected to a country club or residential housing development, so Greenspun sold the golf course to Howard Hughes in the late 1960s and pledged to build homes alongside it. The Paradise Valley location drew a few wealthy individuals who built custom homes, but not nearly enough of them to support the golf club. The health-obsessed Hughes abandoned the project when he discovered the golf course was watered with sewage effluent and his company sued Greenspun for fraud, initiating a long-term feud between the two personalities.

In 1971, Greenspun was approached by Great Southwest Corporation, a Penn Central Company, to develop his land. The company went bankrupt before the final agreement, however, and Greenspun was next approached by the D. K. Ludwig Corporation, a company active in master-planned community development in California. A joint venture to develop a planned community for the area was entered, but the Ludwig Corporation soon bailed out also, fearing that the proximity to Las Vegas and its reputation would limit interest in the location as a place for permanent residential living.

Several Ludwig Corporation executives subsequently left the company to continue the project with Greenspun, forming the American Nevada Corporation. The fledgling company initially developed a few residential home sites but soon faced bankruptcy, forcing Greenspun to trade land for advertising space in the *Sun*. Severely undercapitalized, American Nevada failed to attract major investment funds and there was virtually no demand for mass-produced suburban housing so far outside Las Vegas, though Greenspun was still under pressure from the city of Henderson to fulfill his end of the development deal.

To avoid bankruptcy, Greenspun took complete control of American Nevada, assuming the debt on the land, and handed it over to his son-in-law, Mark Fine. A young New Yorker with five years' experience in real estate, Fine was a college-educated banker who had worked for the land-development section of Chemical Bank and then with the investment bank Loeb Rhoades Inc. Greenspun told Fine: "You're the president [of American Nevada]. Don't do anything!"

## Green Valley

Fine inherited little except the general idea for a planned community, considerable debt, some sewer lines and the land deal with Henderson, which was now in jeopardy. The immediate goals were to address the current debt, cover existing operating expenses and maintain the property. In 1975, Fine turned to land sales in order to raise capital, dividing up one thousand acres into ten-acre subdivisions. The land was bargain-priced at $25,000 per ten-acre site. The terms were 10 percent down and monthly payments for twenty years, giving American Nevada a recurring cash flow. Today, those same parcels are worth between $500,000 and $750,000.

The Green Valley project, named by Greenspun, was offered to developers as a master-planed community, a concept Fine was familiar with from his days as a real-estate investment banker. Pardee Homes was successfully developing Spring Valley at the time in what was then the western edge of Las Vegas and bought several of the Green Valley parcels in order to construct residential housing there. Three other builders also signed on, Collins Brothers, US Home, and Metropolitan Development Corporation. All four developers built a variety of suburban homes that fitted the master plan. Pardee constructed 3- and 4-bedroom models that sold from $77,000 to $83,000 in 1981, the more costly US Home models ranged from $109,000 to $123,000, Collins Brothers built family homes from $71,000 at "Royal Oaks," and semi-custom, luxury homes from $199,800 at "Valley Oaks," while the Metropolitan Development Corporation built luxury townhouses ranging in price from $86,950 to $119,950.

In 1977–8 developers sold their first homes and Pardee purchased additional land after finishing their first parcel. Fine got Clark County to rename Lamb Boulevard, at the entry to the community, Green Valley Parkway, and by 1980 more than 200 residential homes dotted the area. Also that year, a convenience-store entrepreneur expressed interest in the area, building the first of several mini-marts, which Fine approved contingent upon their being named Green Valley Grocery. Today the chain is one of the most successful in Clark County, boasting more than 50 convenience stores in 1997.

Following its initial success, American Nevada's planning became more sophisticated and a wider variety of housing models was developed to attract a broader spectrum of buyers. Diversification in the housing stock was furnished primarily by the townhouse and luxury-home components of the development, including custom homes, in contrast to the bulk of the early housing, which was dedicated to more affordable, single-family homes. American Nevada under Mark Fine's direction built Green Valley Highlands in 1981 as a joint venture with Metropolitan Development Corporation, built the upscale, semi-custom Fox Ridge Estates by itself, and developed Green Valley Park on land adjacent to the golf course. Land sales continued with the sub-division of a more than 50-acre tract of land into half-acre home sites, called Quail Ridge Estates, at the southernmost section of Green Valley directly south of the golf course. There, Fine envisioned a "gate guarded" and "fully walled" luxury home community development. The half-acre sites were priced at $65,000 and tennis club facilities were provided, along with security guards at the gate.

In the early 1980s, construction in Green Valley slowed somewhat due to the national economic recession, as interest rates topped 15%, and because of concerns by potential investors for the future of Las Vegas since Atlantic City had legalized gambling in 1978. As the recessionary effects wore on, Fine maintained Green Valley growth momentum by reinvesting American Nevada Corporation's land-sale profits in housing construction projects of his own.

Another factor limiting commercial and service development was restricted transportation access to the community and its relatively isolated location more than ten miles and 30 minutes from downtown. At that time one could drive from one end of the developed part of Las Vegas proper to the other in little more than ten minutes. The problem was overcome, however, as highways were constructed linking Green Valley to the rest of the Las Vegas area, with US Highway 93–95 extended east from downtown in the mid-1980s and, in 1996, the opening of the Interstate 215 connector, linking the community to the Strip.

In the mid-1980s the Las Vegas population began to grow even more rapidly, with 2,000 new residents arriving each month. Significantly, the corporate takeover of casino gambling, the opening of the megaresorts, and increased diversification of the economy brought middle-class professionals to the area. American Nevada sought to attract these new families to Green Valley, as many of them were already familiar with the master-planning concept from their home towns. Marketed in its second phase as the consummate suburban address and promoting a superior "quality of life," Green Valley became a hot location for professionals with its miles of walking trails, imported tall trees, a recreation center and 13 acres of park space. The second major phase of development, named Silver Springs, was a primary home community offering a variety of market segments around an open-space amenity that included recreational facilities, an elementary school, and jogging trails. The Legacy Village golf course community soon followed, with many of the same market segments seen in Silver Springs plus residences built alongside the golf course.

An important element in the transition from the first to the second phase of development in Green Valley was the construction of new schools for the community. Since many administrators and teachers from the Clark County school district bought homes in Green Valley, as did a large number of UNLV professors and administrators, some contend that so many influential educators living in the area created a bias within the school district to enhance public education there. Whatever the reason, Green Valley public schools quickly established a reputation for excellence, which in turn helped attract even more middle-class residents. Also, being located in Henderson, Green Valley schools were not subject to the mandate of busing elementary students to sixth-grade centers to meet integration requirements.

When the first school opened in Green Valley it almost immediately went on double sessions because of overcrowding. In order to get a much-needed second school into the area, American Nevada made a deal with the school district, in which the company paid to build the school a year ahead of schedule and was later repaid. Other builders demonstrated their support by donating computers to the schools.

Another significant aspect of the second phase was the development of a state-of-the-art private recreational facility, the Green Valley Athletic Club, which assumed the status of a country club of sorts; 3,000 families joined almost at once as little else met residents' recreational needs in Green Valley at the time. The 120,000-square-foot facility soon became a focal point for the entire development. Although somewhat expensive (in 1996 initiation fees were $300 for a family with $90 monthly dues), the club offered six indoor and seven outdoor tennis courts, two squash and six racquetball courts, 25-meter indoor and 25-meter outdoor swimming pools, an indoor running track, two gyms for basketball and volleyball, an elaborate weight and aerobic training section, a restaurant, and a lounge.

A successful master-planned community often includes special features that help define its distinctiveness and Green Valley is no exception. While attending a real-estate conference in San Antonio, Fine noticed a display of free-standing sculptures of tennis players at the Four Seasons Hotel. Observing the positive reaction of passersby, he contacted the sculptor, discovering that he could lease the bronze sculptures on a rotating basis for $15,000, and decided to feature them as cultural landmarks for Green Valley. The outdoor sculptures were popular with residents and attracted media attention, further contributing to the image of Green Valley as a desirable place to live.

Fine also was approached by the library-district director, who offered to build a library in the growing community (see chapter 6). American Nevada donated the land in order to ensure its placement at the entrance to Green Valley with the bronze sculptures prominently displayed out front and an art gallery, a children's center, and a community room inside. In 1986, a company of Shakespeare-in-the-Park actors came from Los Angeles for a summer program. The series was so successful that it became an annual event at Fox Ridge Park, further enhancing Green Valley's image as an active site for community-oriented cultural events.

In the mid-1980s a shopping center opened in Green Valley along Sunset Road. The Green Valley Shopping Center attracted a national chain, Smith's Foods, which built a 43,000-square-foot, 24-hour supermarket. The master-plan concept was further expanded with the development of a Green Valley Professional Center, a Green Valley

Health Center, a commercial and office park, a warehousing section, and a hotel/commercial/office complex. Thus, within a decade after its first residents moved into their homes, the master-planned community had acquired the diversity of housing, and commercial and health services necessary to establish it as a major residential site in the region. In the mid-1990s Green Valley also got its own regional shopping mall, the Galleria on Sunset Road.

Fine pursued the concept of master planning for Green Valley because he believed it was the best way to market single-family homes in southern Nevada. In a personal interview, he defined three aspects of master-planned communities that create marketing appeal. First, people need to feel that they belong to something: "they need to belong to a community, not a randomly developed, amorphous location within a larger metropolitan area. Having a specifically named community helps newcomers with a personal sense of identity." Secondly, a community with a master plan helps attract developers. Individual builders become part of a larger whole and enjoy the benefits of combined advertising. Finally, master planning allows the developers to expand according to the size of the market, growing as "phased development," so that there is little threat of market saturation. Master planning, in short, means balanced, orderly growth over an extended period of time.

Finally, with a robust market for suburban homes produced by the influx of middle-income families, Green Valley development began to mature and the full dimensions of the master-planned community were realized. By 1990 there were more than 30,000 Green Valley residents. The remaining land was divided by American Nevada into five sections, each containing separate plots that were sold to builders, each with its own village center, parks, schools, golf courses, and other recreational facilities. In all, a projected 35 developments were proposed to cover the original 8,500-acre, site with an expected population of 60,000. Each development would appeal to a particular budget, with homes ranging from the extremely affordable low-end price of around $80,000 to high-end, luxury, custom-built homes on exclusive estate complexes, costing more than $200,000 at 1986 prices.

By creating a well-defined community ambiance in its own right, Green Valley became known as a desirable master-planned suburban place to live, with little to link it to the "sin city" of Las Vegas. Green Valley also distinguished itself from the blue-collar industrial town of Henderson, although it sits within Henderson's city limits and all its municipal services are supplied by the town. This situation created conflicts between long-time, blue-collar Henderson residents and the newer white-collar Green Valley populace, with new residents gaining the upper hand when a young Green Valley lawyer was elected mayor in 1992. When he stepped down four years later, his successor was another lawyer, the son of a powerful Nevada legislator with strong ties to industrial Henderson.

By the 1990s Green Valley also had achieved national recognition as a master-planned community of the same caliber as Reston, Virginia, or Irvine, California. According to an account published in *Harper's Magazine*: "The colors of its homes are muted in the Southwest manner: beiges, tans, dun browns, burnt reds. ... Its graceful, palm-lined boulevards and parkways are conspicuously devoid of gas stations, convenience stores, and fast-food restaurants, presenting instead a seamless façade of interminable, well-manicured developments punctuated only by golf courses and an occasional shopping plaza done in stucco" (Guterson 1992: 55). Though Guterson went on to criticize the homogenized community as bland and sterile, the same could be said for all master-planned communities, and what he sees as bland, residents describe as safe and secure.

Guterson also calls into question the development's reputation for communal ambiance, noting that the most prominent architectural features in Green Valley are the walls dividing the various tracts, mandated by American Nevada, which also specifies materials, colors, and size. He states that they are "the first thing a visitor notices ... their message is subliminal and at the same time explicit; controlled access is as much metaphor as reality ... both coming and going are made difficult" (1992: 58).

American Nevada rejected the idea of establishing a single town government elected by residents in favor of promoting home-owner associations for each of the villages and also creating a community association with advisory powers. Over the years, however, neither the local homeowners' groups nor the community association have been able to attract a significant level of resident participation.

Although most families bought homes in Green Valley to escape the kind of urban pathologies associated with the seamier side of Las Vegas, like suburbanites elsewhere they have not been completely successful in avoiding crime and criminal influences. Home robberies and rapes were reported in the late 1980s, though in far fewer numbers than in other parts of the Las Vegas area. In 1991, however, a Green Valley bank robbery turned into a shoot-out on public streets between police and robbers armed with assault rifles, and a grisly triple murder was featured on the television series *Unsolved Mysteries* (Guterson 1992: 60).

Green Valley's location in the industrial city of Henderson brought with it another problem, the threat of serious air pollution from heavy industry production at Henderson's chemical plants. The Titanium Metals Corporation of America (TIMET), for example, stored liquid acid in 19 open evaporation ponds during the 1970s and 1980s. When the weather began warming each spring, these ponds, along with industrial chemical by-products such as ammonia chloride from other facilities, created what locals called the "Henderson Cloud," an irritating layer of smog that hung over the area. As early as 1981, residents complained to the Clark County commission that they "'can't see across the street' when the dense cloud hovers over the valley," and that "each hour about 250 lbs. of chlorine and about 100 lbs. of other chlorides seep into the air from the Titanium plant" (*Las Vegas Sun* 1981:1). Health officials studying the problem in the 1980s indicated that, while chemical emissions could be controlled, ozone and nitrous oxide-related photochemical smog was a problem that, as in Los Angeles, would not go away. A major explosion at the Pepcon Chemical Plant in May 1988 was a stark reminder to Green Valley residents of their proximity to the industrial complex, as windows were blown out, garage doors were knocked off track, and some houses experienced serious structural damage. The Pepcon plant has since relocated out of the state, but a number of chemical releases and fires at the TIMET plant complex have alarmed residents.

Although proximity to the airport is a major selling point to Green Valley homebuyers, some also experience excessive airplane noise since parts of the community are located in the final approach path for the east–west runway at McCarran Airport: "one after another flew airplanes only seconds from touching down at nearby McCarran International Airport. ... Low enough that the rivets in their wings could be discerned, the planes descended at sixty-second intervals, ferrying fresh loads of gamblers into port" (Guterson 1992: 60).

Despite these concerns, the community remains popular and continues to attract new families. A major part of this continued success is the legacy of Fine's early vision, namely, the way Green Valley was promoted for its quality of life. To its residents the address connotes an upscale, family-oriented community called Green Valley, not the gambling and tourist mecca 15 miles to the northwest. Though nearly two decades passed while the first 4,000 acres were developed in Green Valley, the more recent 4,500-acre Green Valley Ranch addition was settled much more quickly due to continued population growth as well as having a developed infrastructure in place, including Interstate Highway 215, providing access to Interstate Highway 15, the Strip, and the southwest part of the valley.

Mark Fine's career as Green Valley's master planner ended in 1990, about the time that the Green Valley Ranch portion of the project was in initial development. Fine's marriage to Hank Greenspun's daughter dissolved and, as American Nevada was a Greenspun family operation, it was time for him to explore other options. Fine's departure was merely a transition, however, as his influence as Las Vegas' premier private planner of residential communities would continue with an even bigger project, known as Summerlin. This 22,500-acre community located along the western edge of the valley is six times the size of the original Green Valley.

Since Fine left, Green Valley has undergone several transformations in the 1990s. During his tenure, for example, gambling establishments were not allowed: "Hank [Greenspun] was never in the gambling business, I was never in the gambling business" (Fine 1997). He used the Conditions, Covenants and Restrictions (CC&Rs) to prevent casinos in Green Valley, because "the whole idea of Green Valley was that it is supposed to be *different* from Las Vegas" (Fine 1997). The new operators of American Nevada, however, allowed several small casinos to be built in the area, as well as the Sunset Station, a large casino-hotel which opened in 1997. The integrity of the community as an address separate from the image of Las Vegas and its gaming ambiance thus has been breached.

American Nevada departed from Fine's vision in a second way with the founding of Green Valley Ranch in the 1990s as a separate community on the remaining undeveloped acreage. According to Fine, the idea of Green Valley included not only its separation from Las Vegas, but also its symbolizing an affordable master-planned community. Green Valley Ranch, in contrast, was developed as a more exclusive, and more costly, project. The master-planning concept there includes a community-wide homeowners' association (HOA) that requires dues to pay for added amenities to make home sales more attractive. American Nevada also departed from the original formula by establishing a Special Improvement District (SID) to fund infrastructure. Bonds for the SID were secured through assessments on the property that homeowners must pay over several years. Green Valley Ranch nearly doubled the SID fees imposed by the Summerlin community, perhaps going beyond the point of diminishing returns, as inflated housing prices and the additional costs for prospective home-buyers hurt home sales.

Ironically, the very decision to avoid SIDs and expensive community associations may ultimately be a liability in Green Valley. Rapid growth in Las Vegas to a large extent is unforgiving of older areas, as residents abandon established neighborhoods by trading-up to newly constructed housing. New homes are no longer being built in Green

Valley. Lacking the massive infrastructure support supplied by SIDs, and the well-financed upkeep and architectural restrictions that community-association dues or neighborhood-association fees provide, Green Valley could decline as it ages. It will be interesting to see if the area can withstand competition from newer developments in the future.

## Summerlin

The second major master-planned community in Las Vegas comprises an area nearly three times the size of Green Valley and Green Valley Ranch combined. Located along the western rim of the Las Vegas Valley approximately twelve miles from downtown Las Vegas, the Summerlin site sits on a 22,500-acre plot of land acquired in the 1950s by Howard Hughes. Five miles across and eight miles in length, it ranks nationally as one of the largest single-owned developments adjacent to a major metropolitan area.

The eccentric Hughes acquired the property through a land exchange with the federal government just as the Korean War began. The land was classified as arid and "disposable" by the Bureau of Land Management. Hughes planned to build a research laboratory for his Hughes Aircraft Company, which was outgrowing its Culver City, California, facilities because of its increased federal defense contracts for electronic weapons systems. Although his business advisors pressured him to expand the Culver City location instead, Hughes liked the Nevada site because of its proximity to Nellis Air Force Base and the area's excellent flying weather. He persuaded the government to sell him the large tract of land at rock-bottom prices, for as little as $2.50 an acre, as part of a land exchange for environmentally sensitive land he owned in California. Hughes also planned to move his massive wooden aircraft, the Hercules Flying Boat, also known as the Spruce Goose, to the wide open spaces of the Nevada desert. An avid pilot, Hughes owned TWA for 27 years and later purchased what became Hughes Airwest.

Hughes never developed the immense tract of land but he did move to Las Vegas in the late 1960s and became the largest private property owner in Nevada.* As mentioned in chapter 2, this was a time when mob influence in the casinos was giving way to an influx of more legitimate corporate owners, and Hughes played a major role in this

*Hughes' extensive real-estate holdings in Arizona and California also made him one of the largest landowners in the United States at the time.

shift. The eccentric billionaire purchased the Desert Inn when his long-term residency on its top floor was jeopardized because the resort wanted the suites for high-roller customers. Hughes then purchased several more casino properties including the Sands, the Frontier, the Castaways, the Silver Slipper, and the Landmark. In addition to gaming properties, Hughes also bought mining operations, airport facilities, the Warm Springs and Spring Mountain Ranches, and thousands of acres of undeveloped land. Hughes' eccentricities were exposed when he purchased a television station, KLAS-TV, from Hank Greenspun for $3.5 million, just so he could personally select its late-night programming. When the station signed off the air for the evening, the former movie director and producer would call and have a favorite movie, such as *Ice Station Zebra,* broadcast. Hughes thus used the television station as his own personal projection room, though late shift workers in Las Vegas with a similar taste in movies also were unintended beneficiaries.

In 1973 Hughes named his southern Nevada business empire the Summa Corporation, and its primary operating arm, Howard Hughes Properties. The long dormant Summerlin site passed intact to Summa Corporation in 1985. By then, Las Vegas was a growing city and the once-isolated chunk of vacant desert west of the city was considered prime for development.

In 1988, after three years of design, the masterplan for the property, modeled after the Irvine Ranch in southern California, was announced. The 39-square-mile Summerlin community was named after Hughes' grandmother. A $74-million, Special Improvement District (SID) was created in December 1989 to fund infrastructure development, including the Summerlin Parkway that connects the site to US Highway 95, the expressway leading around the center of Las Vegas to the eastern end of the valley. The SID bonds were secured as a property assessment or lien, so every home and business owner in Summerlin North must pay a levy, based upon acreage, until the improvement district is paid off in 2009. When the Parkway opened, in 1989, it was called the "road to nowhere," a palm-tree-lined highway leading west from Highway 95 at Rainbow Boulevard to a vast expanse of empty desert and the foothills of the La Madre Mountains and Calico Hills. At the time, the four-mile-long Summerlin Parkway, sporting Nevada's first tri-level freeway interchange, led to not one home or business.

By 1989, more than 1 million dollars had been spent by Summa and the Del Webb Corporation on infrastructure for the first 3,000 acres to be developed, including 30 miles of underground utilities – water and sewer lines, power lines, natural-gas lines, telephone and cable lines.

**Figure 5.2** Summerlin

Despite initial progress, Summa suffered a serious setback that same year when the federal government placed the Mojave desert tortoise on the endangered-species list. Construction at Summerlin, in fact on most residential development in the valley, was halted for approximately a year while the environmental issue was negotiated. Summa took on the costly mandated task of moving tortoises from their property to a temporary holding area and, along with other developers, contributed to the construction of a permanent sanctuary.

Although the building ban was lifted the next year, little development had taken place on Summa's gigantic property. The Hughes Corporation possessed limited experience in land development and in 1990 brought Mark Fine to Summerlin. At first, Fine proposed a joint venture with American Nevada, as he wanted to retain a hand in Green Valley's growth and also to be part of a larger project. Summa rejected the joint venture proposal, but, being frustrated with the lack of progress by the people that were heading the development project, asked Fine to take over the Summerlin presidency: "They came back and said, 'we don't want a joint venture but what would it take for you to run this project for us?'" (Fine 1997). Fine jumped at the opportunity to develop a community that was well capitalized, unlike his long-term financial struggle in the Green Valley venture. Fine became the fourth Summerlin president, and the first to oversee actual development. His reputation and connections were an excellent fit for the infrastructure and capital that Summa supplied.

Fine also knew from his Green Valley experience that Summa's corporate style and elaborate restrictions alienated prospective builders, a problem he knew he could overcome because of his prior close working relationship with builders. His first task, then, was to make Summa more builder-friendly: "I was the perfect person for the job. I had a relationship with the builders. I knew what worked. I knew what didn't work" (Fine 1997).

Following Hughes' death in 1976, Summa was busy divesting itself of gaming properties and developing commercial properties such as the Fashion Show Mall on the Strip and a mixed-use business complex, Hughes Center, located east of the Strip between Spring Mountain and Flamingo Roads. Fine's experience developing Green Valley and his local business contacts thus made him all the more valuable to the company as it initiated residential development.

Fine's predecessors had made plans for an elaborate homeowners' association (HOA) with multiple amenities in Summerlin. His experience with affordable housing suggested that, while the amenities were attractive, their cost to residents through a pricey homeowners' association would deter prospective homebuyers, so he scaled back the HOA plans considerably to open the site for more affordable housing: "You can't afford to price anything at a level that's going to alienate the market. My goal was to go out and grab the biggest market share that I could possibly grab in the shortest time. I saw that I had to build in every market segment. I had to do entry-level, I had to do executive, I had to do luxury – I had to do every single market where there was an opportunity to sell homes" (Fine 1997). In short, Fine worked out a full market-segmentation plan for Summa and curtailed the corporate red tape in order to make the project more builder-friendly.

A Special Improvement District (SID) paid for by a lien on home buyer property was created to finance infrastructure. Even with reduced homeowner-association fees to maintain amenities, the cost of housing in Summerlin was greater than in competing locations and builders were hesitant to commit to the project as the SID was a revolutionary concept in Las Vegas. Home-owner association (HOA) fees were initially set at $300 per year, land prices ran 5 to 10 percent higher, and developers would have to pass on the added costs to homebuyers with SID semi-annual billings of approximately $200. These additional expenses had to be overcome by making the property a highly desirable commodity. Californians, used to the similar concept of Mello Roos, were thrilled at the comparatively low housing prices and they comprised a large part of the Las Vegas homebuying market in the early 1990s. While Summa was successful selling to those abandoning the Golden State, home sales in Summerlin were not satisfactorily penetrating the local market, as Las Vegas homebuyers were initially put off by the additional expenses. An educational program was thus created to inform sales people, builders, and home buyers that the SID would allow the developer to take money that would have gone into the normal land improvements of water, sewer, and streets, and instead spend it on parks, open areas, and landscaping. The SID actually became a sales tool and was later copied by Green Valley Ranch, though with less success. The upscale nature of two smaller master-planned communities in the area, the Lakes and Desert Shores, along with local homebuilders' enthusiasm, provided the needed boost, and within four years Summerlin went from selling no property in 1990 to selling $70-million worth in 1994.

Image is everything in real-estate sales and the first property to sell in Summerlin was the Del Webb retirement community, Sun City. As a result, Summerlin became synonymous in the minds of many with elderly people and retirement. A major marketing campaign had to be launched in the early 1990s to redefine Summerlin as a community with a lifestyle suited for families and young professionals. Television and print ads emphasized the development's adjacency to the mountains, and a low-density, environmentally friendly lifestyle where 20 percent of the land was dedicated to open space to protect and preserve the environment.

The Summerlin master-planned community was based upon three diverse village concepts. The *primary village* includes a wide variety of housing, lots of parks, open space, and schools. This type of community offers limited amenities to control the upper end of selling prices and supply a base of affordable housing. Examples of these developments within Summerlin are the Hills, Pueblo, Trails, and Crossing Villages.

The second village concept in Summerlin is the *recreational village*. This is exemplified by the Hills South Village, built around the Tournament Players Club (TPC) golf course, and the Canyons Village, with its TPC at the Canyons course. Home sales prices in the Hills South Village are higher because the TPC is a private golf course, whereas the TPC at the Canyons is public. Two nationally televised tournaments, the PGA Tour's Las Vegas International and its Senior Classic, provide major media exposure to highlight the upscale aspects of the community.

The third type of village in Summerlin, the *retirement village*, is represented by the Del Webb Corporation's Sun City, an age-restricted community. Del Webb operates other Sun City retirement communities in Arizona, California, Hilton Head, South Carolina, and Georgetown, Texas, and has purchased land for others in Florida and Chicago. In its first phase, Sun City Summerlin built 3,000 homes with commercial centers along the periphery, a golf course, and a $6-million private recreation center. The "active adult lifestyle" concept was a hot commodity in the late 1980s and the homes sold so rapidly that developer Del Webb exercised its option on a several-hundred-acre second phase in 1991. The entire Sun City community now comprises 2,530 acres in Summerlin, including three 18-hole golf courses and four major community centers. The centers offer a variety of recreational amenities – swimming and therapy pools, tennis and racketball courts, miniature golf, multipurpose rooms, arts and crafts rooms, and other social areas. The newest center also has a professional theater and a championship softball diamond. Overall, Sun City boasts more than seventy resident-run hobby and recreational clubs. The community is also a model of safety, sporting its own all-volunteer, resident-operated, security patrol, armed with cellular phones.

With more than 7,700 homes and a population of 14,000 when sales closed in 1998, Sun City Summerlin was the first area in the city of Las Vegas where golf carts were authorized street vehicles. In 1997, *New Choices Magazine* named the development one of the top 20 retirement communities in the United States for the sixth consecutive year.

Del Webb and the Hughes Corporation had a cordial and long-term business relationship. However, once Del Webb was no longer buying land to develop Sun City, the former partners became embroiled in a highly publicized dispute over land usage, land exchanges with the federal government, and development in the Las Vegas Valley. The two companies, who constituted separate interests rather than a joint conspiracy of rentiers pursuing growth together (see chapter 1), took their conflict all the way to the Federal Government's Bureau of Land Management. This type of dispute, not uncommon in Las Vegas, is typical of the trend in American urban development where major owners of capital alternately cooperate and compete with one another in pursuing profits.

Up to 1991, not counting Sun City, only 150 homes had been sold in Summerlin. However, the philosophy of developing infrastructure at the leading edge continued. Summerlin's first village park, the 6.7-acre Hills Park, was dedicated to the city of Las Vegas in 1991. Others followed, along with schools and a library, helping provide

Summerlin with a community milieu. That same year, estimates of the time to complete the development and of the ultimate population of Summerlin were reduced. The original plan, released in 1988, called for the development of thirty villages around a central business core or town center, over a 50-year time period. In 1991, the building period was adjusted to 20+ years in order to take advantage of Las Vegas' rapid growth and its strong economy. Population estimates were also revised downward, from 250,000 residents to 150,000, because, according to Fine: "Two-hundred thousand people is a pretty ambitious program. We don't want those kinds of numbers jammed into a community of this quality" (*Las Vegas Review-Journal* 1991: 1K).

At the time Fine made that statement only 120 homes had been sold and a mere two dozen families comprised Summerlin's non-Sun City population. By 1993, however, after aggressive marketing and a large influx of Californians to the area, Summerlin was the fastest selling master-planned community in the United States. Even with extensive infrastructure planning and pre-placement, however, it was experiencing growing pains. Some were similar to the problems Fine faced in developing Green Valley. One of the most complicated of these was securing new public schools, which are a major attraction for new communities, but which are determined primarily by political decisions. According to Fine, in a new community "you don't have schools – you must manufacture them. The school district tells you when you are ready for a school, you don't tell them when you are ready for schools. Once you have schools, you have the big 'missing link' to further development. You can't get by until you have schools" (Fine 1997).

By 1993, the first elementary and middle schools constructed in Summerlin were running on double sessions, making the community less attractive to prospective buyers with families. Summa contributed heavily to a campaign run by the school district in 1994 to pass a two-part, $905-million school bond issue that was needed not only in the western valley for Summerlin, but also to meet the needs of other rapidly growing areas throughout the county, including Green Valley. The bond issue was perceived by many Las Vegans as a way to make existing residents pay to construct schools in new areas of the community for newcomers, while schools in the older areas were neglected. In any event, taxes and public indebtedness of any kind were anathema to the local public (see chapters 8 and 9). This made meeting the needs of growth extremely problematic for all planned communities in the region. As the push of population pressure accelerated during the 1990s, homebuilders had to contend with an emergent growth-control movement among some segments of the local population that seriously affected the ability to raise funds for new school construction. Many felt that developers making billions of dollars in profits should provide land for schools and parks demanded by their homebuyers, the "make growth pay for growth argument" (see chapter 8). In this way, the local political agenda began to change to deal with resident issues.

Also, seniors in Sun City were emerging as a local political force and they opposed the bond issue. As a result, the first half of the bond issue, which involved a rollover of $605 million in bonds issued in 1988, and thus no increase in taxes, was approved. However, voters rejected the $300-million new bond. The part of the bond that did pass, however, authorized three schools for Summerlin, two elementary and one middle school. Summerlin, overseen on the corporate side for years by Hughes Corporation president and CEO John Goolsby, again put its political knowhow and money behind a 1996 school-bond issue. The $643-million bond narrowly passed, and along with the earlier bond, funded Clark County School District's construction of 32 new schools to help keep up with Las Vegas' explosive growth in the 1990s, which required a new school per month.

Water availability is another crucial issue for development in the entire Las Vegas Valley. More than half the water consumed in the desert community is used on residential outdoor landscaping. Summerlin was coming on line at a time when the topic was once again a hot local issue. In February 1991, the Clark County Water District temporarily suspended issuing water commitments for new development and revoked hundreds of "will serve" letters, which guarantee water rights for development, until a new water-use policy was developed.

Given this political climate, Summerlin had to project an image of minimal environmental intrusion. Consequently, it became the first master-planned community in Las Vegas to encourage water-efficient, environmentally sensitive landscaping. The community banned mulberry trees, pollinating olive trees, hybrid bermuda grass, and other high-water-use foliage in its initial Covenants, Conditions, and Restrictions (CC&Rs). Hybrid bermuda was banned because it turns brown in the winter, green grass being a year-round requirement in Summerlin, at least for homeowners, as it remains part of the landscape at the TPC golf course and a soccer field in the Crossings.

Four landscape micro-environments were adapted for the Summerlin community. The *oasis* type includes lush grass and trees, reflected in traditional parks. The second, the *desert garden* or *xeriscape*, utilizes a low-volume drip-irrigation system that uses less than half the water required for the sprinklers needed to maintain the oasis landscape. A third, *enhanced desert landscaping*, reflects the native Mojave Desert surroundings, supplemented by more plants and rock formations. The fourth landscape environment is the original *native desert* style, where land is left in its natural state. Summerlin Parkway, the community's main thoroughfare, is landscaped with drought-tolerant plants such as mesquite, palo verde, and shrubs, interspersed with gravel mulch and red rock outcrops. Dense pine-tree groves near the west end of the parkway are illuminated at night and medians throughout the community are decorated with flowering desert plants.

During the first several years, Summerlin gained an elitist image. The first development phase was based on market segmentation, as mentioned above, but it was initially restricted to the middle and luxury-home buyer. Construction began on two villages, the Hills, with just above entry-level tract homes ranging from $115,000 to $260,000 in 1991 prices, and the Hills South, a golf course community with tract homes starting at $200,000 and custom-home sites where land parcels alone cost several times that amount.

Adding to the area's elitist image was the fact that no multi-family condominiums or apartments were built. Although market mix was an important part of the development plan for Summerlin, the initial homes were mid-level at a time when the Las Vegas real-estate market was being driven by entry-level buyers, with 70 percent of new homes selling for less than $120,000. In order to fully penetrate this market, and to pre-empt possible government intervention, incentives were created in the next Summerlin village to incorporate entry-level and multi-family housing. The Pueblo Village was similar to Silver Springs in Green Valley, but without the latter's custom homes. Local government oversight was also involved. Summerlin North was located within the borders of the city of Las Vegas, requiring regulatory approval by the city council. In this endeavor, however, the size and clout of Summa Corporation aided Fine. As he states: "You've got to realize that Summa gives a lot of money to politicians. We knew everybody at both the city and the county [whose help was needed]" (Fine 1997).

Fine knew that reduced land prices alone would not compel builders to construct 1,000-square-foot-entry-level houses when they could build more expensive, and more profitable, 1,500-square-foot dwellings on the same sized lot, so he offered a rebate to homebuilders for selling smaller and less expensive homes in the Pueblo Village. For example, $4,000 was paid to builders for every home sold between 1,000 and 1,050 square feet and $3,000 for every house under 1,200 square feet. Land prices were thus reduced on properties where smaller homes were built in an effort to reach down in the market and thereby remove the threat of governmental oversight and charges of blocking out less affluent people from the new development.

On this last issue, Fine's problem at Summerlin was the opposite of the one he faced at Green Valley, i.e., to remove the elitist image. The first condominiums were built in Summerlin in the Pueblo Village, but the first rental apartments, located near the commercial area of the town center, were not available until 1997.

Summerlin will be developed in three major phases over more than two decades. The first, now nearing completion, has been unofficially dubbed Summerlin North. Its eight villages comprise 7,500 acres that were annexed into the city of Las Vegas. In the 1980s, developers of two adjacent, upscale master-planned communities, the Lakes and Desert Shores, also chose to annex their property to the city, thus increasing appreciably the boundaries and population of Las Vegas proper.

The Lakes and Desert Shores communities were built around water features that were banned in Las Vegas by the time Summerlin came on line. The 1,300-acre Lakes community, with more than 5,000 homes, was the first master-planned residential project in the far western area of the Las Vegas Valley. It features a 30-acre body of water as the centerpiece for several upscale neighborhoods and advertised the availability of "boating" in the desert. While this seems bizarre given its locale, it was precisely this kind of fantasy element that appealed to potential customers, many of whom came from areas in the country with an adequate supply of water and a recreational lifestyle that included water sports. Of course, this elaborate use of water resources, along with the area's numerous golf courses and the ostentation of casino water displays, is environmentally unsound (see chapter 8).

Desert Shores also covers more than 1,000 acres and features four smaller lakes and a beach club. Both developments were part of the original desert land sold by Summa to local developers in order to help finance the initial infrastructure of Summerlin; the Lakes property to the Collins Brothers and Desert Shores to Hal Ober. The price, of course, was considerably higher than the one charged by the Bureau of Land Management when it sold this "disposable" land to Howard Hughes in the 1950s.

The two future phases of Summerlin did not fall within the purview of any governmental entity and in the 1995 Nevada Legislature, Clark County and the city of Las Vegas waged a highly publicized battle over which jurisdiction would serve the future taxpayers of Summerlin South. The dispute illustrates the often divisive competition between city and county government in the area. The city, antici-pating the development and a continued relationship with Howard Hughes Corporation, had built a $3-million sewer line to serve the area. Hughes Corporation, however, played them off against the county to see who would offer the best deal in terms of services and minimal governmental regulation. Clark County won the first round in Summerlin South, but less than two years later, the city of Las Vegas also claimed victory when Hughes announced that Summerlin West would provide 40,000 new taxpaying homes for the city, justifying their prior infrastructure investment (see chapter 8 for an extended discussion of this city/county conflict).

*Summerlin South* will comprise 6,100 acres stretching several miles south of Charleston to Sunset Road. The property was so far west in the Las Vegas Valley it was not included in the county's land-use guide and was not zoned. Ordinarily, the land would not have been considered suitable for development because it lacked access to sewer and water lines and other basic county services such as fire and police protection. The remoteness of the land and Hughes Corporation's desire to speed up the zoning process spurred a county–Hughes Corporation partnership to create an unincorporated town. After winning its battle with the city in the state legislature, the county approved a final development contract in February 1996, although some county commissioners expressed concern that the process had been rushed. The contract included a proposed 18,000 homes in twelve villages, three gaming sites, restaurants, commercial property, schools, parks, and golf courses. Hughes Corporation agreed to donate $22.7-million worth of land (285 acres) for the beltway, a gov-ernment center, a fire station, and a park. They also agreed to spend $4 million on roads leading into the community, which opened sales in 1997. The first private school in Summerlin South, Faith Lutheran Junior and Senior High School, opened in early 1998, just as the first homes in the community were being occupied.

*Summerlin West* comprises 8,300 acres, approximately the size of Green Valley and Green Valley Ranch combined, and was annexed into the city of Las Vegas in 1997. The city approved a plan for 20,250 homes, two casinos, five golf courses, a satellite government center, a community sports park, and 5.8 million square feet of commercial and office space. Casino-resorts were allowed but were limited to a height of five stories and to 750 rooms. Annexation of the community increased the size of the city of Las Vegas by 10 percent and will sig-nificantly increase the city's tax base. The city and Hughes Corporation agreed to split the cost of two fire stations, with the company donating land for both stations and construction costs for one station, while the city agreed to pay $1 million to build the second fire station. The Regional Transportation Commission was expected to pay $11 million over seven years to expand Summerlin Parkway and incorporate it as part of a beltway that will soon encircle the Las Vegas Valley.

By the 1990s several organized interests had emerged in the Las Vegas area that held conflicting views concerning future patterns of growth in the valley. All of them played a role in shaping the development of Summerlin, the nation's largest master-planned community. These interests also contributed to the process of normalization by influencing local politics. We have already mentioned the conflict between the county and the city over jurisdictional control of Summerlin. A second critical area of conflict involves the building of casinos in residential areas, with casinos authorized for both Summerlin South and West. A third political issue is public concern over growth management, heightened by the rise of an emergent environmental movement in the area. In the case of Summerlin West, the extreme western edge of the project is adjacent to the Red Rock Canyon National Conservation Area, whose park area is a major natural attraction in the region, enjoyed by both tourists and locals. Environmental groups raised an outcry over the proposed development boundaries, which they claimed, encroached upon the ecologically sensitive scenic area. In response, Hughes Corporation worked with the Bureau of Land Management (BLM) in the 1980s to help solidify the boundaries of the Conservation Area by exchanging 5,000 acres of land. This accommodation satisfied environmental interests and political conflict between the corporation and the ecologically-minded members of the local population was avoided.

In 1994, after four years at the helm of Summerlin, Mark Fine left the Hughes Corporation on terms he described as, "not necessarily with good feelings" (Fine 1997), claiming that his entrepreneurial style clashed with the corporate image as conceived by the company's president. Nevertheless, both sides parted after achieving success. Fine was widely acknowledged as the leading master planner in the region, having developed both Green Valley and Summerlin, the two major master-planned communities in Las Vegas, and both communities ranked in the Top Ten nationally for sales at the time of his departure. For its part, the newly renamed Hughes Corporation continued developing and selling in Summerlin at a record pace, with the community ranked as America's best-selling master-planned community from 1992–1994 by Arthur Anderson Real Estate Services Group, and as America's best-selling master-planned community for five of the six years between 1993 and 1998 by Robert Charles Lesser & Co.

Summerlin also received the Pacific Coast Builders Conference Best New Town Land Plan Award in 1993.

The company developing Summerlin renamed itself the Howard Hughes Corporation in August 1994, in an effort to capitalize upon the name recognition of its founder. No longer involved with casinos, helicopters, airlines, or motion picture companies, the newly named corporation's sole focus is on real estate and it is one of the leading real-estate investment and development firms in the southwest.

Two years later, the Hughes Corporation holdings were acquired by the Rouse Corporation, a nationally known master-planning company that developed Columbia, Maryland, and the Baltimore Inner Harbor complex. The merger/acquisition resulted from a recapitalization process initiated in early 1995 by Hughes' Board of Directors, chaired by William Lummis, a cousin of Howard Hughes. Purchase price of the Las Vegas and southern California commercial and residential operation was $520 million.

## Summerlin and Green Valley Compared

Summerlin and Green Valley are among the most desirable addresses for single-family home owners in the Las Vegas Valley. One major difference between the two, however, is that Summerlin requires a community-association fee in each of its three areas, as does Green Valley Ranch. The Summerlin Community Association provides landscaping and trails, maintains common areas, and supervises Summerlin's Covenants, Conditions, and Restrictions (CC&Rs) code, which specifies the types of modifications homeowners can make to their properties and structures. The Association sponsors special events at the community pool, an all-day Fourth of July party with a parade and concert, a springtime egg hunt, and a Christmas holiday lighting ceremony. Originally developed by a public relations firm contracted by Summerlin, the events were designed to generate publicity for the fledgling community and have since become popular traditions in the community. Because it remains a growing community with a large area of yet to be developed land, marketing and sales promotions remain a part of Summerlin life. Green Valley, on the other hand, is already built out, so it is no longer the subject of intense media advertising, although it retains its reputation for promoting family values.

Other extra amenities that help distinguish the Summerlin lifestyle also come at a price. The average homeowner there pays $400 per year in SID billings, $300 per year to the Summerlin Association, and many individual neighborhoods have their own additional association fees.

Also, higher land prices are built into home-sales costs. For these reasons, even affordable housing in Summerlin carries maintenance costs that are not part of the living costs in places like Green Valley, although there are similar extra costs in Green Valley Ranch. Thus Green Valley remains a place for more affordable homes.

Another difference between the two developments is environmental quality. The topography of the Las Vegas Valley resembles a tilted bowl surrounded by mountains on three sides with the high end against the mountains to the west where Summerlin sits and the low end to the southeast toward Lake Mead. The average elevation in Green Valley in the southeast sector of the valley is 1,740 to 2,100 feet, while Summerlin on the higher west end boasts an average elevation of 2,500 to 3,100 feet above sea level and will go even higher as it develops further into the foothills. The most obvious landmark in the Las Vegas Valley, the 1,049-foot-high Stratosphere Tower, is 70 feet lower than the highest point in Summerlin's Arbors village, according to a UNLV geology professor (*Las Vegas Review-Journal* 1997).

Promoters claim that because of its higher altitude, Summerlin enjoys lower temperatures in the summer, cleaner air, and more rainfall. The National Weather Service reports that the temperature drops approximately 3.5 degrees Fahrenheit for every 1,000-foot increase in elevation, so during the blistering heat of the Las Vegas summer, this drop-off can make a significant difference. Las Vegas receives an average rainfall of four inches per year, while the Red Rock foothills adjacent to Summerlin average between six and ten inches annually, which along with cooler temperatures also creates a greater density and diversity of naturally occurring plant life. According to a BLM park ranger stationed at the Red Rock Visitors' Center: "Because of Summerlin's proximity to the Spring Mountains, it probably receives between six and eight inches per year – so it's easy to understand why desert plants thrive in this area" (*Las Vegas Review-Journal* 1996).

Summerlin has cleaner air, according to Michael Taylor, director of the Clark County air pollution control division: "Carbon monoxide emissions tend to settle in the lower areas of the valley, and the prevailing southwesterly winds in the Las Vegas Valley continually keep the air in the Summerlin area swept out" (*Las Vegas Review-Journal* 1996: 1M).

Because it is so much larger, Summerlin's master plan, in contrast to Green Valley, called for an aggressive approach to attract business and commercial development. In this sense it resembles the "New Towns" built elsewhere in the nation during the 1970s, which incorporated a mix of residential and employment opportunities for new residents. Raytheon Services of Nevada moved its 300 employees to Summerlin in 1992, Household Credit Services, with 1,300 employees, opened a credit-card processing facility in the Crossing Business Center, an 80-acre business park, and Williams Sonata relocated its catalog-sales regional headquarters in the community. By 1997, Summerlin had nine fully occupied office buildings, totaling 220,000 square feet, and five additional buildings comprising 280,000 square feet under construction. The Summerlin Medical Center, a full-service hospital featuring all private patient rooms, opened in 1998, and an existing retail center was joined by the first of two supermarket-anchored village centers in 1997. Until then, the only available grocery shopping was located on the fringes of the community. By mid-1998, more than 3,000 people were employed in the community's business parks, medical facilities, and shopping centers, while Summerlin had 35,000 residents.

Summerlin thus offers prospective residents a total lifestyle package, as one can live, work, recreate, shop, and learn without leaving the community. While master-planned communities have been criticized as being insular for isolating themselves from the surrounding community, that is exactly what many homebuyers want. Although some may not wish to move into a community where they can have a lien placed on their home for installing a patio cover or satellite dish without approval from an Architectural Review Committee, many homebuyers are attracted to the master-planned communities of Green Valley and Summerlin, not just for their beautifully landscaped parks and walking trails but because they want protection from neighbors who might disassemble a car in their driveway or pile junk around their house. These "neighborhood nightmares," featured regularly in the *Las Vegas Sun*, can go on for years, even decades, because of slow-moving city or county code enforcement. In short, they seek services and protection they can no longer expect from municipal government. Thus, while some may criticize them as sterile, master-planned communities continue to be a great success in the Las Vegas region, where developers continue to build and sell thousands of homes per year.

## Effects of Mass Residential Development on Regional Land Use

Growth is taking place all across the Las Vegas Valley, not just in Green Valley and Summerlin. North Las Vegas, an incorporated municipality directly north of the city of Las Vegas, has, through a combination of lower land costs and a series of BLM land sales, had tens of thousands of new homes built within its borders since the

1980s. Bounded on the east by Interstate 15 leading to Salt Lake City, and the new section of highway 95 in the northwest, one section of North Las Vegas has been designated the "Golden Triangle," and it is currently the site of a major section of affordable housing mainly built *without* the amenities characteristic of master-planned developments.

North Las Vegas has long had a reputation as a rowdy blue-collar town, going back to its early days as a haven for bootleggers during Prohibition, just out of the reach of Las Vegas police. During the Depression the area known as "North Town" became "Hoovertown," a tent city for those migrating to southern Nevada to work at the Dam, while a decade later minority workers at the Magnesium Plant escaped the racism of Las Vegas by settling in the unincorporated area. The area was incorporated as the city of North Las Vegas in 1946. The opening of Nellis Air Force Base brought bars and "girlie joints" although "for a time North Las Vegas was off limits to the airmen" (McKinnon 1989: 20A). In the 1950s the city's College Park area was one of the valley's early planned communities, and in the 1960s, a series of land annexations expanded its boundaries, taking it from 8 to nearly 32 square miles. Later, gang activity, shootings, and other forms of crime came to characterize the city until the 1990s, when lower land prices brought developers and thousands of new homeowners.

While some large master-planned areas, like Pardee's Eldorado, exist in North Las Vegas, home construction in the area is mostly characterized by comparatively smaller projects, many of which are built by large developers seeking lower land prices. There are also a significant number of older single-family housing, apartment, and condominium complexes. As discussed earlier, more affordable housing is needed for the exploding population of comparatively low-wage service workers who have been drawn to the area by the phenomenal increase in hotel-casino construction. These service workers have simply been priced out of the market in many areas – places such as Summerlin and Green Valley – and, in response, smaller construction companies have also been building in the Golden Triangle. By July 1998, North Las Vegas, growing by nearly 15 percent in one year, passed the 100,000 population milestone.

Henderson, southeast of Las Vegas, has also become a booming site for homebuilders, and more affordable housing. Growth began in the 1940s with the construction of prefab, redwood-sided homes for war-materials plant workers at the Basic Townsite. Streets were designed to twist and turn and dead-end as part of a plan to deter enemy bombers from finding the plants. The area was incorporated as the city of Henderson in 1953. Like North Las Vegas, Henderson had an established core population of approximately 25,000 in the early

1980s. However, as Green Valley developed, builders also constructed homes in the older adjacent areas of Henderson outside the master-planning scheme, expanding its population to more than 160,000. It became the fastest growing medium-sized city in the US until 1997–8, when its growth rate was surpassed by North Las Vegas. Approximately nine new developments are added to Henderson each month (Packer 1998b). In 1998, more than a dozen new communities were being developed there, many of them master-planned but affordable, including Seven Hills, Sun City MacDonald Ranch, and Anthem. The state demographer estimates that by 2000 Henderson will surpass Reno as Nevada's second largest city.

Fast paced growth is filling in the open spaces throughout the Las Vegas Valley, enveloping older custom homes with new housing tracts and commercial development. These older homes constituted the suburbias of 20 to 25 years ago and many of their residents have paid off mortgages there in preparation for their retirement years. Consequently, as rapid growth in the region matures, the Las Vegas area has taken on the look of other expanding metropolises in the nation. From an aerial view there are sections with upscale master planning, older suburban housing being swallowed up by newer building, and uneven development on a regional scale produced by the common practice of clustering housing according to price.

## Uneven Development

Elsewhere in the nation cities that experienced massive suburban development on the periphery suffered a decline of their urban cores. Reams of writing from the 1960s and 1970s document this "urban crisis" and the need for government funding to halt the decay of inner cities as a consequence of population and resource flight to the suburbs. As the most graphic illustration of a more general pattern of growth in our society called "uneven development" (Gottdiener 1994a), this phenomenon is the spatial result of the heightening of economic inequality tied to segregation in housing. Because of the sharp contrast between the new and the old in residential construction, investment in new locations tends to drain resources from older areas within the same metropolitan region, making slums and depressed areas of a city the unseemly "other side" of its upscale projects.

Las Vegas is again a typical American city in this regard. Instead of a shift of population, its patterns of change are a consequence of the differential drift of newcomers to separate parts of the region. Affluent, middle-class newcomers have been, and continue to be, attracted to the new communities because they are willing and able to pay a premium home price in order to reside in a safe environment that is protected by community planning codes. The retired affluent also can afford to buy homes in places like the two Sun City developments on the outskirts of the valley, which provide them with similar community amenities. At the same time, many older areas of the region are experiencing noticeable decline.

In short, the middle class and wealthier newcomers have drifted to Green Valley, Summerlin, and other new communities outside the older sections of the region. In contrast, less affluent newcomers have taken up residence mostly in the established neighborhoods and the lower-priced new communities. Housing costs even in the older sections of the region, however, filter people by income, because people can only purchase what they can afford and because communities are constructed in clusters according to price. This phenomenon, a common feature of suburbias throughout the nation, has important implications for the reproduction of class relations in Las Vegas neighborhoods. Interestingly, this is not so much the case for race in Las Vegas, largely because the in-migrating population selects neighborhoods based on their own price structure. As with everything else in the entertainment capital of the world, money, not skin color, is the deciding factor in uneven regional development.

There are a number of well-established upscale neighborhoods in Las Vegas, located in areas that could be described as the "inner city" core, that have defied the trend of decline. "Rancho Circle" and the "Scotch 80s," the latter where Steve Wynn lived until recently and where many long-time community leaders and other powerful Las Vegans still reside, both are located in or near the inner city of Las Vegas. For the most part, in these neighborhoods property values have been maintained and home prices are far out of reach to most Las Vegans, with many houses priced from half a million dollars and up. These older neighborhoods exhibit a sense of character and tradition, representing a connection with the old Las Vegas' sprawling residential lifestyle, where huge single-story homes sit on large lots framed by mature landscaping.

Driving across Las Vegas along Oakey Boulevard reveals a number of other sprawling, well maintained, lovely older homes and neighborhoods on both the west and east sides. Their occupants are mostly long-time residents who want to preserve their lifestyle, staying in their family homes and maintaining their large yards and mature landscaping. Some upscale professionals have also purchased homes in the neighborhoods where they grew up, around 6th Street near downtown, and carefully converted them into residential-style law offices chosen for their convenient proximity to the courts. Advertising agencies and insurance offices have also participated in this commercial neighborhood preservation of the old Las Vegas. Thus, while it is easy for a newcomer or visitor to miss the small-town character that Las Vegas once had, it still has great meaning for native Las Vegans who grew up there in the 1940s, 1950s, and 1960s. These persons lived in the downtown residential area, and most of them went to the same high school, Las Vegas High, including a US Senator, the governor of Nevada, and many other prominent local leaders.

Many of the remaining areas of the inner city and those adjacent to the Strip corridor, however, have experienced decline. Dope dealers, pimps, prostitutes, and derelicts, along with minimum-wage workers, have moved into depressed properties that are poorly maintained, forming an inner-city core of blight characteristic of other metropolitan areas. The notorious 89109 zip code area is the site of high-density apartments mostly occupied by low-paid service workers and the elderly, but it is also a place of crime and blight. Many of the most troublesome blocks are just a few minutes away from the glitzy Strip, providing a vivid contrast that most tourists never see. Like other cities, graphic contrasts due to inequity abound. This same area is also the site of the handsomely refurbished Flamingo Library, the expanded and remodeled Boulevard Mall, a glitzy "restaurant row" and multi-million-dollar high-rise condos.

An equally problematic outcome of the process of uneven regional development is the deterioration of the urban-core commercial district downtown, as businesses and affluent residents flee to new suburban neighborhoods. Supermarkets, drug stores and other retail outlets have abandoned older neighborhoods, even though the need is still there and most were still making money. People living and working around the older business centers, many of them elderly, have not moved away, but they have fallen further down the socio-economic scale *relative* to the mass of more affluent newcomers. Many long-time business owners within the urban core have thus decided that they would rather seek higher profit margins in newer more upscale neighborhoods than invest the time and money needed to rehabilitate aging facilities. In this way, along with the clustering of housing according to price, real-estate investment also causes socio-spatial inequality.

Businesses are lured away by the generous arrangements offered by developers eager to attract services to their planned sites. For example, only a decade ago, the shopping complex at Decatur Boulevard and Vegas Drive bustled with business activity. The northwest Las Vegas center served the area's upper-middle-class neighborhoods, including homes along the municipal golf course, half-acre

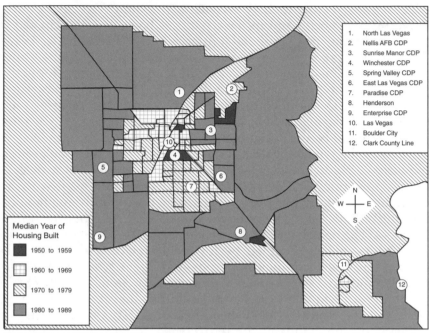

1. North Las Vegas
2. Nellis AFB CDP
3. Sunrise Manor CDP
4. Winchester CDP
5. Spring Valley CDP
6. East Las Vegas CDP
7. Paradise CDP
8. Henderson
9. Enterprise CDP
10. Las Vegas
11. Boulder City
12. Clark County Line

Median Year of
Housing Built

■ 1950 to 1959
▦ 1960 to 1969
▨ 1970 to 1979
▩ 1980 to 1989

Redrawn from an original supplied courtesy of City of Las Vegas Dept. of Planning and Development. Data collected in the 1990 US Census

**Map 1**   Median year of housing built in Clark County, NV, 1950–90

equestrian estates, the once-upscale Stonehaven development, the Twin Lakes neighborhood, and the nearby sprawling estate of Siegfried and Roy. In those days the anchor tenant was Wonder World, a large multipurpose store that sold family clothing and sundries, and the complex also included a dry cleaners, a supermarket, two drug-stores, and a sporting goods outlet. All of these businesses have since moved elsewhere. Now all that remains of the once thriving shopping complex are abandoned hulks of buildings and a massive parking lot with weeds springing up through cracks in the asphalt. Investment has been attracted to the new developments even though both the buildings and the local market demand were sound.

More recently, a few blocks south, at Decatur and Washington Boulevards, a busy Albertson's grocery store closed, abandoning the surrounding lower-middle class neighborhoods populated by long-time residents, including many senior citizens (see chapter 4). At the same time, Albertson's, along with other local supermarkets and drug-store chains, are aggressively expanding into the newer areas of Las Vegas. This drift of business has created political tensions as old-

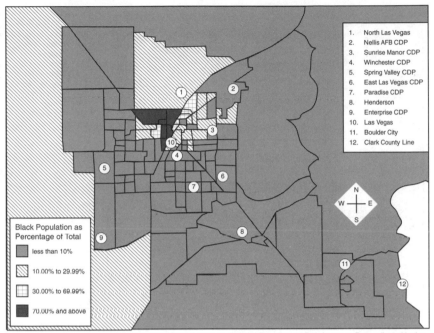

Black Population as
Percentage of Total

less than 10%

10.00% to 29.99%

30.00% to 69.99%

70.00% and above

1. North Las Vegas
2. Nellis AFB CDP
3. Sunrise Manor CDP
4. Winchester CDP
5. Spring Valley CDP
6. East Las Vegas CDP
7. Paradise CDP
8. Henderson
9. Enterprise CDP
10. Las Vegas
11. Boulder City
12. Clark County Line

Redrawn from an original supplied courtesy of City of Las Vegas Dept. of Planning and Development. Data collected in the 1990 US Census

**Map 2**   Percentage of black population in Clark County, NV, 1990

time residents become upset over losing their ability to shop close to their homes, angry that they now must drive miles to purchase groceries or fill a prescription. Such socio-spatial inequity produces a marked decline of quality of life in the community, further affecting home investment in the inner-city areas.

The uneven socio-spatial development of the Las Vegas region can be illustrated by the accompanying maps. Map 1 shows the median year of housing built from 1950 to 1990. The oldest housing is located in the original growth centers of the region: around Nellis Air Force Base in North Las Vegas, downtown adjacent to the central city, in East Las Vegas, at the southern end of the City of Henderson, and in the center of Boulder City. Map 2 shows the same region indicating the percentage of black population for 1990. The highest concentrations are in the older sections of downtown and North Las Vegas. Both the Summerlin area to the northwest and the Green Valley area to the southeast have the lowest concentration of African-Americans in the region. Map 3 shows the regional distribution of the Hispanic population for 1990. It differs somewhat from Map 2. Hispanics are more

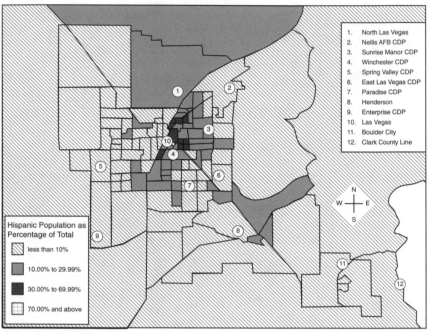

1.  North Las Vegas
2.  Nellis AFB CDP
3.  Sunrise Manor CDP
4.  Winchester CDP
5.  Spring Valley CDP
6.  East Las Vegas CDP
7.  Paradise CDP
8.  Henderson
9.  Enterprise CDP
10. Las Vegas
11. Boulder City
12. Clark County Line

Hispanic Population as
Percentage of Total

less than 10%

10.00% to 29.99%

30.00% to 69.99%

70.00% and above

Redrawn from an original supplied courtesy of City of Las Vegas Dept. of Planning and Development. Data collected in the
1990 US Census

**Map 3**   Percentage of Hispanic population in Clark County, NV, 1990

spread out than are African-Americans. Yet the highest concentration
is in the older sections of the city of Las Vegas. Boulder City has virtually no Hispanics and hence, no significant minority population at
all. Map 4 illustrates class differences in the region. It plots the distribution of population according to median household income for 1990.
The most affluent areas, with households having an income of $40,000
or more, are also in the newest sections of the region, especially
Summerlin in the northwest and Green Valley in the southeast. The
poorest households are concentrated in the central area of the city of
Las Vegas. This area overlaps with the concentration of African-
Americans, Hispanics, and older housing in the region. The final illustration of uneven socio-spatial development is Map 5 which shows
the distribution of people with Bachelor Degrees in the region and
indicates the distribution of professionals. The highest concentrations
are in the new master-planned developments of Summerlin on the
western side of the region and the Green Valley area near Henderson.
Boulder City also contains a large percentage of educated and, therefore, professional people. Residents living in the oldest sections of the

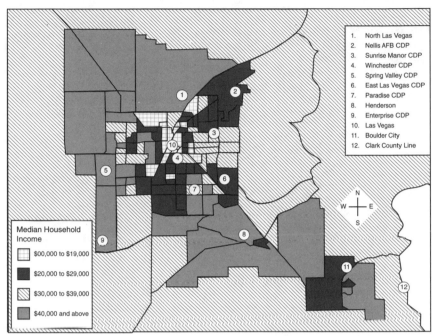

1. North Las Vegas
2. Nellis AFB CDP
3. Sunrise Manor CDP
4. Winchester CDP
5. Spring Valley CDP
6. East Las Vegas CDP
7. Paradise CDP
8. Henderson
9. Enterprise CDP
10. Las Vegas
11. Boulder City
12. Clark County Line

Median Household Income

$00,000 to $19,000

$20,000 to $29,000

$30,000 to $39,000

$40,000 and above

Redrawn from an original supplied courtesy of City of Las Vegas Dept. of Planning and Development. Data collected in the 1990 US Census

**Map 4** Median household income in Clark County, NV, 1990

city of Las Vegas and Henderson, in contrast, have the smallest representation of educated people.

## Fragmented Communal Identities

Class and minority segregation are common results of urban growth in the United States, but this social fact is also manifested as a spatial feature of metropolitan regions. As we have seen, locationally distinct uneven development plagues the Las Vegas region, as rapid growth and the differential drift of new residents with resources has made social and income segregation worse. The construction of new, upscale communities has also spurred the spatial drift of commercial businesses and services such as health-care facilities to the more affluent areas, creating inequality, blight, and inner-city deprivation.

A further effect of the physical and spatial patterns of uneven distribution is cognitive and involves the mental image of local communities. People's conception of where they live and allegiance to their

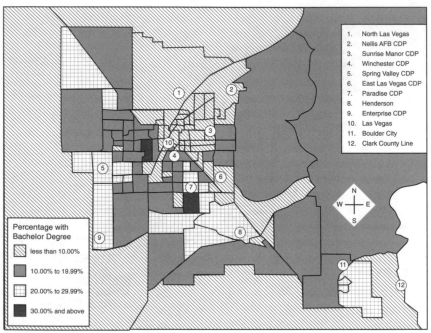

1.   North Las Vegas
2.   Nellis AFB CDP
3.   Sunrise Manor CDP
4.   Winchester CDP
5.   Spring Valley CDP
6.   East Las Vegas CDP
7.   Paradise CDP
8.   Henderson
9.   Enterprise CDP
10.   Las Vegas
11.   Boulder City
12.   Clark County Line

Percentage with
Bachelor Degree

less than 10.00%

10.00% to 19.99%

20.00% to 29.99%

30.00% and above

Redrawn from an original supplied courtesy of City of Las Vegas Dept. of Planning and Development. Data collected in the 1990 US Census

**Map 5**   Percentage of population holding Bachelor Degrees in Clark County, NV, 1990

neighborhoods has become increasingly fragmented as the entire region underwent rapid suburban development. Thus, construction of highly differentiated communities within the Las Vegas region has replaced a general, unifying Las Vegas identity with more localized conceptions, such as: "I live in Summerlin," or "Green Valley," or "Eldorado," or "The Lakes," or "Desert Shores." Many of the planned developments actively promote this separation from the Las Vegas regional identity, as we have seen in the case of Green Valley. With continuing suburban development, residents will continue to derive their locational identities more from their particular area of the region rather than from the Las Vegas region as a whole. This has already led to a social fragmentation that seems to be getting more extreme. Commercial and public development of suburban communities also abets this process of fragmentation. Green Valley residents, for example, no longer have to travel across the valley to shop at the Meadows Mall, or to the Strip casinos to gamble, or to downtown Las Vegas movie theaters for entertainment. The same is true for residents in Summerlin, North Las Vegas, and Henderson. Subsequent commercial development also makes it possible for many residents to find employment near their homes, leading to more fragmentation. Together, residential and commercial distinctions produce increasing fragmentation of the region and this, in turn, leads to political splits that are locationally based, as well as entirely separate cognitive maps localized to neighborhood or community rather than a regional identity.

In chapter 8 we will examine the way in which the process of uneven development is further manifested in a series of local disputes that have transformed the nature of politics in the valley. These cases produce deeply felt concerns that translate into political issues associated with daily life. Residential needs define the new, emerging agenda of local politics, driving its dynamics and replacing, or at least rivaling, the traditional, historical focus on the exclusive needs of business by local government. This conflict is a classic theme of American urban history, but it is new to Las Vegas, which was run as a company town for so many years. Now gambling and tourist interests can no longer rest easy with the success of their growth, because that very success has rapidly expanded the permanent population of residents as its workforce. Local residents have local needs that are manifested in political interests and an agenda that deals with quality-of-life concerns, not business expansion. It is this contradiction that lies at the core of the normalization process in Las Vegas.

# 6 The Normalization Process II: The Production of Civic Culture by the Public Sector

In the previous chapter we described how influential planners and real-estate developers, though less well known than their counterparts in the gaming industry, helped create a mass market for residential homes throughout the Las Vegas Valley. Although success in this area has not been achieved without costs, specifically problems associated with uneven development and regional, sprawling growth, many residents, particularly in the newer areas, express a strong sense of identification with their neighborhoods. In this chapter we focus on the public sector's contribution to civic culture as public officials and residents together struggle to improve the city's quality of life.

Ironically, much of the impetus for the development of civic culture in Las Vegas resulted from controversies generated by what some long-term residents saw as favoritism received by the newer communities from public officials, not only in regard to highway and new school construction, but also in the allocation of civic amenities such as libraries and parks. Master community developers thus have indirectly spurred the growth of civic culture throughout the valley as a whole, but not without controversy and political conflict.

## Libraries as Community Cultural Centers

A major contribution to Las Vegas' civic culture may be attributed to the Clark County Library District. While municipal library services elsewhere in the nation have been sharply curtailed, with entire libraries closed in many cases, library facilities and services in the Las Vegas Valley have expanded dramatically over the last two decades. The Clark County Library District is governed by a ten-member board of trustees, with the Las Vegas city council and the Clark County commission each appointing five members to four-year terms. The library director is the designated fiscal agent of the board and is appointed by, and serves at the pleasure of, the board of trustees. The board establishes policies, while the director is the functional administrator and implements the board's policies.

Charles Hunsberger was director of the Clark County Library District for twenty-one years, from 1971 until 1992, when he retired under a cloud of controversy. Prior to that he had been director of the Monroe County library system, centered in Bloomington, Indiana, a region with an aggressive style of administration. The city of Columbus, Indiana, had launched a campaign in the late 1960s and early 1970s to promote the locale through the construction of signature public buildings by famous architects. Hunsberger followed Columbus's lead, inviting Perkins and Wills of Chicago to design a distinctive library building in Bloomington. From this experience Hunsberger became convinced of the importance of libraries for enriching the community environment, especially if they stood out as examples of signature architecture.

The administrator was also influenced by another view of the role of the library, described in an article in the *American Libraries Journal* as: "a controlled environment, a refuge that should be free from distracting stimuli – one of the last sanctuaries in our aggressive, noise-saturated world" (Rizzo 1992: 322). This same article goes on to argue that libraries are more than just spaces for study, mentioning nine other functions, many of which directly enrich community resources and contribute to the development of a civic culture. Among these are the library's role as an information center and center for the distribution of data; a museum and art gallery whose task is the preservation as well as exhibition of important cultural works; a drop-in-center for all ages, including children, that promotes an educational experience in a supervised, safe milieu; a place for classrooms; a public lecture hall; a civic events center; a recital hall; and finally, a part of the community. This last aspect is amplified in the article as follows:

> Whether public or academic, a library is part of a community. For a city or town, it is an important arm of the municipality – one that serves all age groups and presents the friendly face of government. Libraries are one of the few non-retail anchors in a community and are increasingly used as such in downtown redevelopment projects. The town library can also reflect a community's view of itself and of education. As a public statement of community values, it affects real estate prices and is an important instrument of public policy and community identity. (Rizzo 1992: 324)

It was these ideas that guided Charles Hunsberger's two-decade tenure in Las Vegas.

When he arrived in Las Vegas in 1971, Hunsberger found a rapidly growing region with a population of 275,000. While a large county library was opened that year on East Flamingo Road near Maryland Parkway, just a few blocks from the university (UNLV), resources for libraries in general were limited in the area and spread across the city and county governments. Hunsberger's first task, therefore, was to arrange for the consolidation of library funding and services. As he states:

> I spent a lot of time in politics with the mayor and with the city council and everybody and at the close of that year [1971] we had put together by contract the two library systems. ... By contract I brought them together because there was so much fear that they didn't want to lose control of the tax base because it was during the time of revenue sharing and whoever levied the taxes got the bigger portion of revenue sharing funds.   (Hunsberger 1997)

In the early 1970s, local municipalities were encouraged to develop capital-spending projects under federally sponsored revenue-sharing programs and an assistant city manager who had befriended Hunsberger suggested that the library district submit a project proposal. The city wanted a general-purpose, community center library to rival the county building on East Flamingo. The proposed complex would contain a theater and several multiple-use rooms in an expansive space, and Hunsberger also envisioned a signature public building for the city by commissioning a well-known architect. The library proposal was submitted and approved by the city but it was assigned a low priority, so Hunsberger and the assistant city manager worked together to move it higher up on the list. The project was eventually accepted, but construction had to be approved by the state legislature before work could begin (see figure 6.1).

With city backing, the library district approached the 1977 legislature, proposing a bill to fund $750,000 of the project. Some state senators, however, attacked the plan as violating the legislature's conservative spending goals and the bill was defeated. The appeal to state legislators, however, was not in vain, as several expressed their personal support for the project and suggested that the proposal be reintroduced at the next legislative session in two years time.

By 1979, rapid growth in the Las Vegas area had created more demand for its services so the library district opted for an expanded plan, requesting approval for a statewide bond issue that would provide $10 million in matching funds for local library support. The bond referendum was voted down by a slim margin, with most of the opposition coming from the state's rural counties who viewed it as a "Las Vegas issue." In 1981, the legislation was introduced again, at the

**Figure 6.1** Flamingo Library

urging of Las Vegas representatives, and it finally passed, having been debated in three separate sessions of the state legislature over a six-year time span.

With a $10-million bonding authority and more projects on the drawing board, the library district decided to formalize its consolidation contract. No less significantly, the state legislative act granted official taxing power to the merged city and county districts. Prior to that time the city and county libraries worked together under one administration but remained separate taxation districts. The consolidation bill also included a proposed redrawing of the tax base, calculated on the basis of recent growth in the region, giving the district a 39 percent increase in funding. As a result, the district was able to propose the construction of at least six libraries for the Las Vegas region. Hunsberger's library district also became a model of regional consolidation for the rest of the fragmented area.

Under the bill, funding for the libraries was simplified so that the district did not have to approach the county and city each year with a budget request, as the level of funding was a fixed percentage of the tax base. Because the region was growing rapidly, the budget for the library district thus rose each year automatically as the tax base increased. As Hunsberger noted: "I never had to negotiate how much money I got, I negotiated the tax base. So, I never had to go back to the city council or the mayor or anybody and say how much money are you going to give me? ... This gave us the financial independence to grow with the community" (Hunsberger 1997).

One major planned project was a central district library to be called the Las Vegas Library. Hunsberger envisioned it as a community center, part library and part theater/public-lecture-hall space. The library section would hold the major collection of books in the region, and hence was conceived as a large space. A national competition was held for the design and attracted some of the best known architects in the country. The local architecture community insisted that outsiders could not be used because they didn't have a license to practice in the state, so interested non-Nevada-based architects such as Michael Graves, Dean of Architecture at Princeton University, and the internationally known Antoine Predock, took the state's certification exam. The project was awarded to Predock, a premier designer of southwestern architecture.

Hunsberger wanted a departure from the mold of casino-style architecture that characterized Las Vegas: "I travel to Europe at least once a year and tour architecture and visit libraries. The buildings that last, the things that are worth seeing, are the cathedrals, the churches and the old civic buildings that stand in the heart of almost every European city. And so if you want to define your culture and your people and your communities, you want to do it with the architecture of your civic buildings" (Hunsberger 1997).

When Antoine Predock was awarded the project, he and Hunsberger spent time walking around the desert so the architect could get a feeling for the area. The resulting design set the tone for several other projects that would follow in the next round of construction and ultimately make Las Vegas nationally famous as a site of southwestern-style architecture, although this fact remains little known among tourists today. For example, several years later the county decided to build a new government center downtown. In the architectural competition Predock came in second, but "the architect who beat him had to outdo him in the southwestern style sense. So what you've got is a continual expansion of the Predock idea. ... They have enlarged and expanded it. ... They could have done anything, but they chose the same stone, they chose the colors, they chose the form. It's a wonderful development for a continuation of a theme" (Hunsberger 1997).

Hunsberger added, however, that the city never went to the voters to ask for the money to construct the new civic projects: "They were afraid to because they lost so many bond issues that they just kept putting money away and putting money away and finally said, 'we've got enough money if we do this and we do that,' and so they built it without ever going to the voters and that made the voters a little bit uneasy" (Hunsberger 1997).

The projected size of the Las Vegas Library presented a location problem, however. The district needed an administrative center, but with cultural amenities, such as a theater, attached to the building, the proposed structure would exceed 100,000 square feet. Hunsberger worked closely with then Las Vegas Mayor Bill Briere to find an adequate site. The city of Las Vegas was at the time experiencing blight and abandonment in the downtown area north of City Hall and wanted to redevelop the district with a "cultural quarter" between Cashman Field and City Hall. The mayor at first suggested Cashman Center as the site for the library, but Hunsberger wanted land across the street and asked the city to donate the property. In exchange, the mayor suggested that the library district financially underwrite part of the cost to construct Cashman Field to house a Triple-A minor-league baseball team; Hunsberger agreed to spend library funds on lights for the baseball field to get the land deal. Unusual deals such as this one between public administrators from separate arms of local government were typical of the way business was conducted in those days.

The Las Vegas Library was completed in June 1990, an architectural masterpiece that immediately called attention to the city, although local residents hesitated to use the facility in a part of town known largely for plasma banks and as a hangout for the homeless. The 104,000-square-foot multipurpose building features an impressive red-brick, rolling style characteristic of southwestern architecture. In addition to housing a large collection of books, the library also contains a state-of-the-art theater facility used by the local community for plays and other cultural activities.

Other libraries built during this time include the 23,700-square-foot Sunrise Library, opened in October 1987, in the northeast part of the valley, designed by the Architronics firm. When the district proposed the Sunrise project, they included plans to house a public radio station as another kind of cultural amenity that would also enrich the community. Hunsberger had hired the general manager of a radio station in Kentucky, Lamar Marchese, who developed plans for a fully equipped, top-of-the-line station while working full-time as a library employee. The library board, however, rejected the plan for the radio station as too costly and as lying outside the purview of the library district, arguing that the money would be more properly used to build another branch library. Hunsberger here encountered resistance to his plans from his bosses on the library board and the Sunrise facility was constructed without the radio station. For the first time, the issue of appropriate spending of library-district funds was raised, a source of contention that would eventually lead to Hunsberger's downfall. Marchese later secured federal funding and established the public radio station separate from the library district. Located for years on Boulder Highway, the local–national public radio affiliate KNPR moved to newly constructed facilities on the West Charleston campus of the Community College of Southern Nevada in 1998.

Hunsberger also met with Green Valley developer Mark Fine, to discuss placement of a library in the master-planned community. The multipurpose building opened as the Green Valley Library in February 1988. Designed by Barbara Flammang, the library was an impressive contribution to the emerging civic culture in that area, as it was integrated into the Green Valley master plan and became part of the civic-center complex at the entrance to the community.

The announcement of the Green Valley Library project, however, created a furor. Early Las Vegas had ghettoized its black population in the section known as the Westside, although today less than 12 percent of the Las Vegas African-American population lives there. In the late 1980s, leaders of the Westside community were appalled to learn that the library district planned a Green Valley project, while their older, more established area had no library. Their spokespersons rightly charged that the newer area was being favored in the siting of library facilities. The district responded to these complaints by planning construction of a library to serve the inner-city black community and in January of 1989, one year after the Green Valley facility opened, West Las Vegas welcomed its own library. The 12,200-square-foot building was designed by Arturo Cambiero and is located between US Highway 95-North and the border with North Las Vegas.

Similar problems arose when the manager of the unincorporated Whitney Township, formerly East Las Vegas, also complained that a library was built in the Green Valley area rather than in his older township. The town manager sued Hunsberger personally for "mishandling the libraries," charging him with building cultural centers instead of libraries. Once again, in the face of organized protest, the library district responded by agreeing to build a new library in Whitney Township as well. Hence, the discourse of discontent with Hunsberger's directorship was further fleshed out by these adversarial protests.

Another more inadvertent effect of the construction of a library in

Green Valley affected final plans for the Las Vegas Library, constructed two years later. Although original plans were already quite ambitious for the central structure, something else was added to the initial design when Hunsberger, in the course of a conversation with Hank Greenspun's daughter-in-law about the Green Valley Library, mentioned that he had just returned from visiting his grandchildren in Indianapolis. He noted that every time he made the trip they would ask him to take them to the city's children's museum, and he would wish out loud that Las Vegas had a similar museum for children. Robin Greenspun then informed Hunsberger that she was a member of a politically active women's club which had been pushing for years to create just such a children's museum. Hunsberger suggested that they join forces.

As a result, the central Las Vegas Library added an adjunct wing, the Lied Discovery Children's Museum, in addition to the large theater complex. Hunsberger brought in some of the best designers for the project, including Jeff Birch from the Minneapolis Children's Museum. According to Hunsberger:

> We had already established the idea when we built the first library in the city of Las Vegas with their money that every library would bring something to the community that would enhance the cultural aspect and the cultural life of the community. Because there weren't theaters and there wasn't anything to begin with. (Hunsberger 1997)

In 1990, when the main library building opened to national accolades because of the Predock design, the library district decided that it was a propitious time to make plans for the next bond issue. Continued rapid growth in the region created the need for more than the six libraries supported by the original bond. The plan was to divide the region into sub-districts of 50,000 population and to build a library for each. The district predicted that by 1995 they would need a much larger budget to maintain the existing structures and services while adding the additional buildings: "By the time we put it on the bond issue in 1991, we asked for seventy million for construction and ten million for books. We'd learned that you can't open libraries and not have any books on the shelves and keep people happy. They expect a library full of books" (Hunsberger 1997). Many older municipalities across the country have had to divert funding for books, computers, software, and videos into maintenance and overhead costs, and the need for new library construction in Las Vegas presented a similar dilemma.

In the spring of 1991 the library district, with considerable *chutzpah*, proposed an $80-million bond issue. City primary elections held in

May traditionally have low voter turnout and pundits predicted that the district's proposal would be soundly rejected by tax-sensitive voters. Before the election, Hunsberger had architects build models of the proposed libraries that would be constructed with the bond money. Many voters who saw the scale of the models balked at the high price-tags for the taxpayer-funded buildings, so Hunsberger spent $20,000 to hire a national polling service to analyze voter sentiment in order to target appeals for generating citizen support for the large bond issue. The analysis estimated that only 50 percent of the voters would approve it, an estimate that proved quite accurate, as the measure was carried in the late election-night hours by a slim 1,100-vote margin.

Despite the victory, a growing backlash was brewing among the citizens of Clark County and the city against what many saw as lavish government spending for projects to be concentrated in the newer areas at the expense of older neighborhoods. One project, the West Charleston Library, actually involved moving an existing facility serving the established, lower-middle-income Charleston Heights neighborhood further west to a newer area. Voters wanted libraries but they wanted them in their own neighborhoods and they wanted to see some fiscal conservatism. The *Las Vegas Review-Journal*, the largest newspaper in the state, editorialized that the vote was so close because voters opposed massive cultural centers being built with public funds they wanted spent on libraries and books. Considering the rapid growth of the region, increased government spending was a necessity in developing civic life in the area, yet there existed a strong political culture opposed to government spending (see chapter 8). What is remarkable about Hunsberger is that he was able to operate successfully within this prohibitive conservative milieu for a time.

Differences over library construction eventually split the region's population into a number of ideological camps regarding the issue of government spending. The controversy, sparked by Hunsberger's plans and a decline in spending on library books, stimulated civic action among residents who were at least motivated to make their opinions known. Four distinct group ideologies emerged among participants in the debate. These might be termed: the "create cultural centers at any cost"; the "buildings versus books"; the "build it in my neighborhood first"; and the "no new taxes" perspectives. These orientations which emerged in the library spending debate served to make the local political culture more complex. Perhaps that is its lasting contribution to the region.

The "create cultural centers at any cost" group was comprised of residents, some new, some old, who believed that the metropolitan area had to spend in order to meet the needs of growth. It was precisely Hunsberger's grandiose vision of public architecture and the nurturing of cultural activities, they believed, that would help separate the milieu of permanent residency from the glitzy environment of casino gambling, tourism, and the seamier aspects of those activities long associated with the name "Las Vegas." In contrast, the "buildings vs books" proponents strongly supported libraries and other cultural centers and conceded the need for some public construction and expansion of services to accommodate growth, but viewed the major commissions doled out by the library district under Hunsberger as profligate and excessive. They feared that maintenance and operating costs of the larger structures would, in future years, consume available funding, precluding spending on books and other library materials. Later event proved that this particular group's fears were at least partially warranted.

The "build it in my neighborhood first" group became politically involved because they watched many of the new facilities being designated for the newer, more affluent communities in the region. They viewed the relocation of the library service in the Charleston Heights area as particularly egregious and questioned the subsidization of this kind of move by taxpayers. More than a dozen of the libraries were, in fact, built in new areas, three within a few miles of each other in the upscale, western part of the town, while other, older areas had no libraries within several miles. Finally, the "no new taxes" group was the most resistant, again comprised of both long-time residents as well as newcomers. This group was opposed to increased government spending, either in the form of new taxes or of bonded indebtedness, again viewing the major architectural commissions granted by the library district under Hunsberger as excessive. It is this group that characterizes best the traditional conservative political culture of Las Vegas. The powerful senior-citizen community was split on this issue. Ironically while seniors as a whole tend to vote against school and other bond issues, the more upscale among them supported the library bond because they utilize libraries.

In short, the library's ambitious building plans drew residents into a vigorous public debate and stimulated them to formulate distinct positions on the role of government in the rapidly growing region, an important aspect of the normalization process. These very same four ideologies continue to voice their concerns in the public area as new projects that require bond-debt financing are announced by city and county governments.

Despite the controversy, with the $80-million bond issue in place the district proceeded to build seven new library branches, remodeled an existing library, and constructed a theater addition, each designed with signature architecture providing valuable cultural facilities to the community. The first was the West Charleston Library, which opened in January 1993 on a four-acre site donated by the Community College of Southern Nevada adjacent to one of its campuses. It replaced the smaller Charleston Heights Library and Performing Arts Center, located on Brush Street in a older neighborhood. The 38,900-square-foot structure was designed by Welles-Pugsley Architects and contains a 289-seat lecture hall, an art gallery, two conference rooms, study and word-processing rooms, and a Young People's Library featuring a slate of after-school programs. The library also includes the only public medical and health-sciences collection in southern Nevada.

In August of that same year the second library opened a few miles west, in Summerlin. The 40,165-square-foot building was designed by Robert A. Fielden and won the award for the Best Public Special Use Facility at the 1994 Pacific Coast Builder's Conference. Its architectural features include a tent-shaped skylight, exterior copper-hued metallic accents, and square clerestory windows. The designer used drought-resistant landscaping and indigenous building materials, with exterior colors reflective of the exposed rock striations in the neighboring Spring Mountain Range. The structure also contains a heavily utilized auditorium, an art gallery, a used-bookstore, conference and study rooms, and a Young People's Library section. Exterior courtyards were designed to accommodate additional community activities outdoors.

The Rainbow Library, the third to open that year, is located on a ten-acre site donated by the city in the rapidly growing northwest section. The 28,000-square-foot structure was designed by HSA Architects, a local firm, and contains a 160-seat hall with meeting, study, and conference rooms. The library grounds contain a 500-seat amphitheater for community events, and the landscaping features drought-resistant plants and water-saving technology. The interior design references the "built environment" of Las Vegas more than any other library, especially by using neon signs, a distinctive touch: "Through an entrance of pastel portals to the massive skylight cone above the circulation desk, Rainbow Library's neon signs guide patrons to library services. ... Architects Patrick J. Klenk and Wayne P. Schreiner incorporated playful geometric designs throughout the library's functional spaces" (Las Vegas–Clark County Library District undated: 10).

Following construction of the Whitney Library and one in Laughlin, a small town located 100 miles south of Las Vegas, the next two projects were sited in older areas of town, one a redesign and the second a theater addition. In 1994 the district unveiled another nationally recognized accomplishment, the redesigned Clark County Library, located on Flamingo Road near Maryland Parkway. The 120,000-square-foot "neoclassical functional masterpiece" was designed by Michael Graves and the local Las Vegas firm of JMA Architecture Studios. Its terracotta-colored façade has three-story-high pillars at the main entrance, with a courtyard and parking at the rear. Inside, the library contains a special grants and foundation collection, an expanded audiovisual section, and a reading room for national and international newspapers, periodicals, and trade journals. It also contains a 399-seat theater to accommodate community-theater and music productions, with an elegant lobby that also doubles as an art gallery for rotating exhibits.

In 1994 the African-American community of West Las Vegas filed another protest with the library district. Although the community had a new branch library, the group objected to the other libraries having better amenities, especially theaters. Stung by charges that their library was more than adequate to support the limited usage it experienced, the community staged a protest. Westside residents were asked to sign up for library cards and check out stacks of books. Some books were hauled out of the library in shopping carts and the protest nearly emptied the library shelves. Faced with charges of racism, the district decided to construct a theater addition to the original 12,200-square-foot structure. Further complaints that the stage at the Summerlin library was a few feet wider led to a mid-construction redesign that cost more than $1 million, adding an orchestra pit and a dressing room. A year later the facility, designed by Michael Vlaovich, opened to the public, featuring a 299-seat theater with an orchestra pit, fly tower, and proscenium stage.

An eighth project, the Enterprise Library, opened in April 1996 on Las Vegas Boulevard South. The 26,000-square-foot structure was designed by Domingo Cambeiro Corporation and contains a special collection of building and trades information materials. It also features a large conference room with a kitchen to facilitate gatherings of up to 100 persons and a smaller conference room for 30 people, a media room with public computer access, an art gallery, a used-bookstore, and quiet study areas. The once isolated Enterprise area is no longer so, as the library now sits between two outlet malls and a sprawling development of moderately priced apartments and homes.

The final project built by the library district with 1991 bond-issue funds was the 122,000-square-foot West Sahara Library, designed by Tate and Snyder Architects and Meyer, Scherer and Rockcastle, Ltd, of Minnesota. It opened in 1997, a year later and over budget (see figure 6.2). The West Sahara Library serves the Lakes, Peccole Ranch, and

**Figure 6.2**   West Sahara Library

Summerlin South. The structure includes a 150-seat multipurpose room, conference and study rooms, an art gallery, and a micro-computer center, and is fronted on one side by an entrance that leads patrons to an outdoor entry plaza with a unique spiral sunken garden and sculpted landscaping. The architectural style has been criticized as resembling an airplane hangar on steroids and many patrons are put off by the long entry to the building and its huge lobby. Also, children entering the library must walk up a flight of stairs to find their section, but the largest library in the district offers spectacular views of the mountains and the surrounding community. It is a prime example of postmodern civic-building construction that adds to Las Vegas' luster as a notable place of signature public architecture.

## Political Backlash

As we have seen, when the library bond issue passed in 1991, the district took full advantage of the $80-million budget, constructing seven new libraries, one major refurbishment, and a theater addition between 1992 and 1997. Such rapid and large-scale spending on facilities was unprecedented for the local government, and many citizens took notice. Even before the bond issue was passed, Hunsberger ran into problems with the West Las Vegas community and Whitney township over the priorities of the district's agenda, which seemed to favor the newer communities over theirs. The district did its best to placate political interests, as mentioned above, first by constructing a branch in West Las Vegas, then by expanding its six-year-old facilities to include a large, up-to-date theater complex. When the Whitney Ranch development was built, a library was constructed in that area, though other, older neighborhoods that did not protest did not get libraries. Many people, including some on the library board of trustees, also questioned Hunsberger's practice of spending library monies on public radio and other non-library cultural programs, alleging at the time that the library district had one of the lowest book-to-patron ratios in the country. Consequently, when the new bond issue was proposed, the library district's spending activities were closely scrutinized by area residents.

Following the vote, which passed by a slim majority, the *Las Vegas-Review Journal* published an editorial claiming that the result did not give the library district a "mandate" to spend the $80 million on "big cultural center libraries." The Clark County Commission requested that two new members, both fiscal conservatives, be added to the library board, and openly criticized Hunsberger's spending priorities. In addition, the Clark County Parks and Recreation Department argued that theater facilities were their domain and should be financed and run only by them. This refrain was picked up by the new library board members, producing a split within the group. Closely watched by the newspaper, editorials continued to appear on a regular basis questioning the library district's construction projects.

Several more board members in 1992 joined the chorus of those criticizing the district's plans. Their principal concerns were directed toward what they saw as Hunsberger's lavish spending policies and his targeting of library funds for other cultural areas. Newspaper editorials called for a return to the traditional view of the library as a place for books, opposing his view of the multipurpose function of libraries as community activity centers. Other segments of the community also expressed alarm at the potential maintenance costs of the showcase buildings, especially their projected air-conditioning expenses, which were addressed only in the design of the West Charleston Library. In the other libraries, vaulted ceilings gave the interiors a shape that was costly to climatically control and, in some, created disturbing echo-like distortions.

For Hunsberger, 1992 was a difficult year. Dissidents called for a special audit of the library district's activities and some employees complained about his personal relationship with his assistant director. Also, charges of racial bias within the district's offices were filed, though they were subsequently dismissed. Then, the county commission objected to the inclusion of a museum in the plans for the West Sahara Library. Hunsberger claimed that the plans had already been approved, but the county fought the case, aided by editorials in the *Review-Journal*. When Hunsberger requested a special ruling on the legality of the project from the Nevada Attorney General, he was vindicated and the construction proceeded as planned. Nevertheless, after surviving a general audit of his activities and fighting off the county commission's challenge, Hunsberger decided to quit the directorship after 21 years, one year before his contract expired and his planned retirement: "I had used up so much of my energy. Politics is calling in your chips. I had used up so much that I said 'I am not going to continue to sit here and take this crap.' I said, 'buy me out and I'll leave' to the library board. They bought me out and I left" (Hunsberger 1997).

Hunsberger was successful in his dealings with local politicians in the 1970s, but was less effective with the more formal government that followed. One public official stated, "he just didn't know how to work the structure." Armed with the $80-million bond and a mission to create libraries, many perceived his attitude as arrogant, and he made personal mistakes that overlapped with his administrative position. In the end, few people stepped forward to defend Hunsberger's policies: "The attacks were so massive that the people in the county commission who supported me didn't come forward and help" (Hunsberger 1997). However shortsighted, objection to ambitious government or public-sector spending is deeply embedded in the local political culture, as many residents want their taxpayer dollars spent on basic services, not on elaborate cultural centers or "castles for public servants," as the Clark County government center was called when it opened in 1995. Even those in the community who generally supported library expansion were concerned about the future maintenance and operating costs of the signature buildings. Yet, the fact remains that no other urban area in the nation has spent hundreds of millions of dollars to add fifteen new libraries in the last two decades. When visitors come to Las Vegas to marvel at the themed casinos on the Strip, they often overlook the equally impressive public architecture of Las Vegas, such as the libraries, designed by some of the stellar architects of the nation and containing some of the very best examples of southwestern architecture anywhere in America.

It is doubtful that similar such projects will appear in the future, despite Las Vegas' continuing robust population growth. In 1998 the library district budget exceeded $28 million with 500 employees at twelve branches, requiring a far greater public contribution to keep facilities stocked, staffed, and maintained. Bond issues that passed easily in the 1980s have faced tougher scrutiny by taxpayers in the 1990s. Thus, with a combination of timing and public support, something unique was accomplished as the showcase buildings of the Clark County Library District provide Las Vegas with cultural landmarks that are as impressive as the magnificent architectural statements possessed of older, more established cities. However, we believe the main contribution was the creation of community cultural centers that not only supply a much needed focus for the sprawling metropolitan area, but also provide residents with a sanctuary, a place to go, that not only celebrates the very best values of Western civilization but is the very antithesis of the commercial, pay-as-you-go casino environments that dominate and define the Las Vegas experience for the rest of the world.

## Local Political Culture and Normalization

The March 1998 issue of *George* magazine lists Las Vegas as one of the "ten most corrupt cities" in the United States, renewing the old charge that the city is a "company town" because the interests of casino gambling dominate its political agenda. Obviously, casino gambling and the tourist industry are the life blood of the local economy and city government must service the needs of the gambling industry as a matter of survival. Yet in recent years, an increasing number of concerns originating from the neighborhoods of permanent residents also have surfaced in a process of normalization. Despite its "business first" approach, the fact that municipal government has had to respond to these concerns suggests that a community-based civic culture has begun to emerge in Las Vegas.

The oldest neighborhoods in the region, such as those located near the original settlement downtown, are an incongruous mixture of rundown areas around the Glitter Gulch casino district, and some upscale residential areas, such as the *"Scotch 80s"* neighborhood of custom homes. In the more prosperous older areas, few residents felt the need over the years for special homeowner or community associations to represent their interests, as many of them were influential individuals who enjoyed political clout, often with a direct line to the mayor's office. Now these same established areas suffer because they lack a sense of place as the surrounding region declines and many of the powerful citizens who once lived there have moved out. Residents there have increasingly found their voice to express local concerns.

By contrast, in the newer master-planned communities, people purchase homes as much for a pre-packaged sense of place as they do for the actual housing. Yet, once taking up residence, many of these new arrivals have encountered not only the common problems with defects in housing and infrastructure construction, but also concerns involving the quality of community life. Residents who have moved into a new area to experience the quiet streets of suburbia, for example, suddenly find themselves living on a noisy, dangerous cut-through route that is the quickest way for commuters to get to the highway taking them to work. Others may have moved into a development across the way from vacant desert, only to discover a year later that a new 24-hour shopping center/supermarket complex, a pocket casino, or a bar with video poker is being built there.

Another common objection of area residents, sometimes manifested in the form of sporadic protests to City Hall, concerns the proposed opening of commercial facilities that sell alcohol in their neighborhoods. In the early 1990s thousands of people protested over the building of bars near their residential areas and almost an equal number have protested against the opening of convenience stores, though the overwhelming majority of these commercial-zoning applications were approved by the city council, reflecting their "pro-business" bias (Havas 1992). The major source of contention for Las Vegas' residents is the tendency of the city council and county commission to support developers who had purchased residentially zoned land but later wished to convert the zoning category to commercial use. These land-use changes have played havoc with the emergent civic culture of many new communities, leaving citizens feeling betrayed. They also indicate the hard edge of pro-business sentiment, which remains a vestige of Las Vegas life.

## Public-Sector Support for Neighborhoods

As population growth has continued, concerns among residents about their quality of life also have increased. People in both old and new developments have contacted City Hall to protest about new commercial projects being built in their areas. In response, the Las Vegas city political leadership, in October 1995, began a "neighborhood initiative." Initially, the mayor's office, as well as individual city council members, simply made themselves available to residents wanting to know more about the way growth would impact their areas. They took advantage of the need for better communication with organized homeowner associations, to stimulate their formation in neighborhoods that didn't have them. The initiative proved so successful that, in April 1996, the city formalized the effort by creating a Department of Neighborhood Services.

The department has several charges, including code enforcement – concerned with junk cars on lawns, graffiti, run-down properties, and the like – and the pursuit of federal block grants to support redevelopment for both residential housing and commercial businesses. The groundwork to organize resident associations in the city was established by compiling a list of homeowner associations, which, when developer applications came in to City Hall, were notified of plans that would affect their neighborhoods. Later the department expanded this process by requesting that organized residential groups define their own neighborhood boundaries and register with the city.

Council-ward boundaries were not used as target areas because the department believed that the four city wards were too large in area. Instead, neighborhood self-identification by residents was used because the department felt that the latter would be more reflective of community networks, and because wards were prone to redistricting as the population grew, according to Sharon Segerblom, Director of Neighborhood Services (1998).

In this way, the Department of Neighborhood Services has helped produce a sense of place for residents of Las Vegas by assisting them with organizing into self-identified neighborhoods, many of them for the first time. Another way the department provides support is by holding workshops in organizing, leadership, and board formation. Neighborhood Services also works closely with the individual council members' offices to register newly formed associations as well as working with a national organization, the Local Initiative Support Corporation (LISC), whose goal is to help blighted areas organize "community development corporations" that can apply for federal aid.

Also as part of the Neighborhood Services initiative, the city employed four professional planners to work with neighborhood resident associations. They organize informational seminars on a variety of topics pertinent to the neighborhoods, and hold workshops four times a year, for all associations in the city, on how to communicate effectively with local government. Importantly, all residents of a neighborhood can participate in the process whether they own or rent. The associations registered with the city can schedule clean-up drives with the assistance of city crews and they are notified when develop-

ers apply for zoning changes or building permits in their neighborhood (Cardinal 1998). In less than three years, the department helped
organize more than 150 different neighborhood associations to
encourage resident involvement in this manner.

One issue of concern to residents in the older central city areas of
Wards One and Three involves their aging infrastructure and their relative lack of resources for parks and other programs in comparison
with the wealthier, rapidly growing suburban Wards, Two and Four.
Overall, the valley's five parks-and-recreation departments together
maintain 148 parks, offering a variety of facilities including swimming
pools, baseball and soccer fields, and basketball, tennis and volleyball
courts (Metropolitan Research Association 1998: 22). It is true,
however, that the newest and most elaborate of these are located in the
newer, rapidly growing sections of the valley, especially in the northwest and southeast.

Churches and other faith-based (religious) institutions have not
been particularly active in neighborhood organizations in Las Vegas.
Despite the area's reputation as "sin city," however, the Las Vegas
Valley has a vibrant religious community, with more than 400
churches, synagogues, mosques, and temples (Carns 1998). Also,
approximately 80% of local residents express some sort of religious
affiliation (Metropolitan Research Association 1998: 7), with 25%
claiming they attend services weekly and another 25% monthly
(Carns 1998). Gauging the contribution of religious organizations to
community development, however, is difficult as most concentrate on
serving their own constituencies, although some, such as Catholic
Charities of Southern Nevada, provide a variety of services to non-
members.

Following the successful organizing efforts of the Department of
Neighborhood Services, the city council moved to incorporate the for-
mally registered groups within its overall planning process, passing a
"neighborhood planning" resolution in 1998 to initiate a citizen-
based, grassroots approach to improvement projects. Each community association was urged to draft a plan that would address its local
land-use needs: issues of revitalization, such as the rehabilitation of
housing; transportation infrastructure needs; and other resource
requirements, such as cultural activities or parks. That same year the
department also began a program to encourage children to respect
their neighborhoods. Thus, in just a few short years, the Department
of Neighborhood Services has already compiled a remarkable legacy
in the Las Vegas Valley. Working actively with a mandate for organizing ordinary citizens, it has helped bring a sense of place to many
communities and, with the help of both citizens and planners, has

been able to formalize physical boundaries for these neighborhoods according to the definitions of the people who live there.

## Learning in Las Vegas: Public-Sector Support for Education

### Primary and Secondary Education

There is no more important aspect of public infrastructure for many residents than the availability of quality public education for their children. Yet, in a rapidly growing region like Las Vegas, supplying an adequate level of these facilities is a daunting task. In 1997–8 the Clark County School District was the tenth largest in the nation and had 219 schools and 10,943 full-time teachers serving 192,344 pupils, up 7.5% from the previous year. In 1998–9, it became the ninth largest with a 6.8% increase to 203,777 pupils – close to double the number of ten years earlier – and had opened nine new schools. The district has been experiencing average annual increases of more than 6% since 1994, making it the fastest growing in the nation (see table 6.1).

**Table 6.1** Clark County school enrollment and increases, 1994–2007

| 1994 | 1995 | 1996 | 1997 | 1998 | 2007 (projected) |
|------|------|------|------|------|------------------|
| 156,348 | 166,788 | 178,896 | 192,344 | 203,777 | 330,023 |
| 6.7% | 7.3% | 7.5% | 6.8% | | |

The district's 1998–9 operating budget is $954 million, which includes the opening of five new elementary schools and three middle schools, with 90% of the money going to salaries. Student-to-teacher ratios were 16:1 for the first and second grades, 19:1 for the third grade, 30:1 for the fourth and fifth grades, 25:1 for the sixth grade, and 30:1 for all grades from the seventh to the twelfth. Since kindergarten is optional in Nevada, the student-to-teacher ratio there is high, at 52:1.

With the growth of new communities in the 1980s, new players entering the real-estate sector as mass developers of suburban housing brought pressure on the school district to construct new schools in their areas. For this reason, as in the case of other infrastructure needs, the expansion of school facilities and their siting became a hot political issue in the region. In response, following an independent audit by the Bechtel Corporation, the school district formulated a less-biased planning procedure for establishing new schools. While it has thus far been largely successful in avoiding charges of favoritism, many of the area's schools remain overcrowded.

Planning for future educational needs relies first on accurately determining the capacity of the school system. "Program capacity" is calculated for each existing school on the basis of the number of its classrooms, its operating schedule, instructional offerings, and student-to-teacher ratio, as well as a count of each school's enrollment. Projecting new capacity also requires an additional, complicated calculation, estimating the number of "new development students." This last piece of data is based on a count of new single and multiple family dwellings being built in each school's area, multiplied by a figure estimated as the effective "student yield" for dwelling units in the Las Vegas region. Excess or inadequate supply is then calculated by subtracting the sum of existing students and projected new students from the estimated total program capacity.

Deficits in the program capacity for developing areas provide the primary rationale for the construction of new schools. The school district, however, also takes into account a number of "non-quantifiable data" before a final determination is made. First, they determine if adjusting school-zone boundaries or schedules might help; secondly, they consider the racial and ethnic diversity of the population and any effects a new school might have on that diversity; thirdly, they consider the need for special educational programs in the area; fourthly, they consider the availability of vacant land; and fifthly, they take into account relevant environmental factors. Once all these factors have been figured in, the district inaugurates plans for new facility construction. Exact data on new developments are obtained by the school board's demographers using Geographical Information Systems (GIS) maps derived from space-satellite technology, the most accurate way of maintaining up-to-date knowledge of new construction in the rapidly growing area.

Once it has been determined that a new school needs to be constructed, the available land must be identified, as site sizes are 10 acres for elementary schools, 20 acres for middle schools, and 40 acres for high schools. The school board draws from a number of sources to finance construction. While 64% of the district's annual operating budget ($954 million in 1998–9) comes from local sources, such as sales, property and motor vehicle taxes, and approximately

32% comes from the state, the bulk of new construction is covered by floating bond issues for education. Residents of Clark County have approved most of the recent bond measures, although in 1994 a $300-million bond, requiring new taxes on top of a $605-million rollover bond issue, was rejected. In 1996, a $643-million bond was passed to cover the construction of 16 new schools, the modernization of 130 others, and the addition of 95 new programs at existing schools.

Most recently, a ten-year property-bond issue was passed in November 1998 that will provide the district with a whopping $2.5 billion in construction funds, to be supplemented by an estimated $1 billion from real-estate transfer tax and hotel-room taxes over the next decade. With the $3.5 billion, the school district plans to build 50 elementary schools, 22 middle schools, and 16 high schools. Also, $854 million of the total is budgeted for renovations of existing schools over a ten-year period. The school district expects an additional 150,000 students over that period and now has the funding in place to build schools to accommodate them.

In sum, the Clark County School District has functioned as a great engine for the production of public-school infrastructure by utilizing limited tax resources and helping to secure the passage of education bonds. School after school has been built and thousands of certified teachers have been hired. Despite the relative accuracy of its projections and the district's sophisticated demographic expertise, however, school resources were strained until the 1998 bond. Clark County School District planners had to play the same infrastructure game of "catch up" as their colleagues in other local public agencies. Unlike other school systems in the country, this burden of keeping pace with rapid growth is, perhaps, the principal challenge of the district. Yet, as the region matures, problems that plague other locales in the nation are also emerging to haunt the already strained Clark County school system.

One of the most compelling of these issues involves the recent change in the ethnic mix of the school population, especially due to the increased in-migration of Hispanic families to the region. During the 1995 school year the ethnic breakdown of the district was 62.8% white, 17.6% Hispanic, 13.8% black, and 5.8% "other." Only two years later, however, the Hispanic population's proportion had increased to 23.3%, while whites declined to 56.3%. It is unknown how much of this is due to a flight to private schools, which are growing in number around the valley, but it mirrors the changes experienced by the Los Angeles school system and requires new thinking regarding the education of large numbers of students for whom English is their second language, a change that will no doubt place additional strains on the system in the future.

The future of bond issues is also uncertain. The area is home to an increasing number of senior citizens, who are nationally known to resist funding for public education when it affects their taxes, although elderly Clark County voters have been largely supportive of school-bond issues thus far. Many live on fixed incomes, however, and are wary of any threat to their rate of property taxation, one of the primary sources of funding for the county school district. Anti-tax sentiment is also spreading across a broader spectrum of Las Vegas' residents, reflecting a national trend that started with Proposition 13 in California in 1978. In short, the future may bring increased resistance to bonded indebtedness and tax increases as means to support the much-needed expansion of school facilities in the valley. California's elementary-school systems, for example, have been hamstrung for years with poor budget support as a consequence of the Proposition 13 tax revolt. As the declining quality of instruction has negatively affected education, ways of funding schools have had to be renegotiated. The same sort of conflict is a likely scenario for Las Vegas in the near future.

Finally, many jobs in the area remain intimately tied to the gaming industry. Although Nevada law requires all casino employees to be aged twenty-one to work, most casino jobs do not require a high school diploma. This indirectly acts as a disincentive for many local teenagers to further their educational careers, as jobs at casinos, such as parking valet and waitress, can earn as much as $30,000 a year, a high salary for lower-level workers. The end result is that the Clark County School District has one of the highest high school drop-out rates in the nation. During the 1996–7 school year, for example, 10.8 percent of students in grades 9 to 12 dropped out. While we do not know the exact reasons for their departure, it is claimed that a significant proportion of them find jobs in the area that pay enough for them to abandon school. This alarming situation has only recently become a topic of discussion in the Las Vegas area. The local United Way, for example, has approached casino owners regarding this problem, urging them to support high school equivalency diploma studies as part of their employee benefits. The organization's reasoning is that, if these corporations, however inadvertently, are attracting former drop-outs with adequate salaries, they might help alleviate the drop-out problem once they hire them as employees.

## Community College of Southern Nevada (CCSN)

The rapid growth of the Las Vegas Valley is also reflected in the growth in the local community-college system, which has four separate campuses, one of which it shares with a new high school in the affluent northwestern portion of the valley. CCSN started out in 1971 in a donated building in the downtown area before moving a few years later into its own building in North Las Vegas. Then known as Clark County Community College, the school survived numerous controversies over its budget, staff, and product. Its enrollment, faculty, and physical plant increased significantly, however, in the 1980s and early 1990s. The institution now has three main campuses – the original Cheyenne campus in North Las Vegas; a West Charleston campus, site of a nationally respected dental-hygiene program and the local–national public radio affiliate (KNPR), as well as three large classroom and office buildings, with a fourth on the way; and a Henderson campus, with two buildings and a third under construction. In 1998, in a unique partnership with the school district, the two-year college opened a $5-million classroom and computer lab in Summerlin on the new Palo Verde High School campus, with offices for ten full-time faculty and six employees. High school students use the 33,000-square-foot building in the morning and early afternoon, while the community college uses the center and adjacent high school building to hold 120 classes in the late afternoons and evenings. A second $5-million joint-use center opened in January 1999 on the campus of Western High School.

Upon his arrival in 1994 from Santa Monica College in California, president Richard Moore accelerated CCSN's growth, though not without controversy. Facilities on each campus were expanded, while Moore's aggressive marketing campaign brought more students and his extensive lobbying of legislators and community leaders enhanced public and private funding. By 1998, CCSN had more than 26,000 full-time and part-time students enrolled. Moore hopes to receive approval in the 1999 state legislative session to add enough faculty to double the number of staff members since his arrival. His quest for publicity and, at times, reckless spending, however, have alienated many faculty and raised eyebrows throughout the community. For example, a sleek, eye-grabbing class schedule included comments seen as denigrating UNLV, earning Moore a reprimand from the Board of Regents. Buildings on the West Charleston campus were painted orange and purple, seen as vibrant and eyecatching by some, but as tacky and gaudy to others. At the Cheyenne campus, 26 palm trees were illuminated at a cost of $1,000 each, another $17,000 was spent to string lights along the exterior of the theater, and a $19,000 information booth was built for a two-building campus. More important, perhaps was that Moore's spending created a budgetary crisis at CCSN, requiring sweeping cuts. The fact remains, however, that enrollment has increased dramatically, new buildings are being constructed, the number and quality of faculty has increased, and new programs are being added. In 1998, classes to train ultrasound technicians and ophthalmic dispensing were added to a roster that offers associates degrees and certification programs in 11 health-care fields, including physical therapy, occupational therapy, cardio-respiratory therapy, pharmacy, and toxicology. Between 1992 and 1998, enrollment in the health-care programs nearly doubled, although "the college's health care programs are expensive to operate because of equipment needs and small teacher-to-student ratios. The programs eat up $3.1 million of the college's $52 million annual budget" (Patton 1998b).

## University of Nevada, Las Vegas (UNLV)

The southern Nevada community also boasts a flourishing university in the University of Nevada, Las Vegas. Established as the southern branch of the Nevada university system by the legislature in 1957 under the name Southern Regional Division of the University of Nevada, the fledgling institution was located on a 335-acre campus alongside the unpaved Maryland Parkway, southeast of town. Its first degrees were awarded in 1964 and the next year its name was changed to Nevada Southern University, although many called it "Tumbleweed Tech," even after it officially became the University of Nevada, Las Vegas, in 1969.

In 1984, Robert Maxson became UNLV's president and immediately recognized that a strong university could play a major role in the rapidly developing community by helping to diversify its economy and altering its "sin city" image: "There is not a single first-rate city in America, not a world class city in this country, that does not have a first rate university in it. The university provides the intellectual base for this city and, by definition, you'll never become a great city if we don't become a great university" (quoted in Collins 1987: 2). Maxson achieved his goal of making it fashionable for the community to financially support the university and sustained incredible growth by raising more than $20 million from the community in the first three years of his tenure. At that time, UNLV offered 50 undergraduate and 40 graduate programs and was one of the nation's fastest growing universities. University and Las Vegas-community growth came at a time when many other higher institutions of learning were suffering cutbacks, and UNLV attracted a number of distinguished scholars to its faculty as a result. In 1987 the university began offering doctoral programs, and overall enrollment increased 17 per cent to 13,000 students. Today there are more than 21,000 students at UNLV with 3,347 enrolled in one of the school's 51 masters or 17 doctoral programs.

UNLV is perhaps best known nationally for its College of Hotel Administration, recognized worldwide for the quality of its management training in the hospitality industry. The program began in 1967 at the request of the Nevada Resort Association and enjoys an excellent collaborative relationship with the Las Vegas resort industry, where students serve management traineeships at some of the world's largest hotels.

Less well known is the fact that UNLV has a strong liberal-arts core curriculum that all undergraduates must complete. With an outstanding young faculty recruited from the finest educational institutions in the nation, the university offers a first-class education.

The university has become a focal point for research in the local community, with the Center for Business and Economic Research serving as an important liaison between the southern Nevada business community and academia, compiling statistics that monitor the area's economy, including the annual *Las Vegas Perspective* community profile. Also, the Sociology Department houses the Howard Cannon Center for Survey Research, which conducts surveys on a variety of social and economic issues, using state-of-the-art computerized telephone-survey equipment.

UNLV has become an important cultural center as well for the local community, providing a variety of speaker series and musical and theater productions. One of these, the Charles Vanda Master's Series, features outstanding musical groups and individual performers from around the world. In addition, the entire campus is designated as an arboretum for the study and display of southwestern plant life. The university landscaper, along with master gardeners from the University of Nevada Cooperative Extension, maintain and conduct educational tours to acquaint new residents with the types of flora that can survive the region's desert climate.

A growing on-campus community life has developed as UNLV has been transformed from a commuter campus to a full-service academic setting. The university has built a number of dormitories, but still can house only 1,100 with thousands more on waiting lists. UNLV is attracting a larger number of students from other states, especially California where the higher costs of out-of-state tuition are balanced by the fact that they can get a degree at UNLV in four years that might take five or six years at overcrowded California universities.

Campus community life was enhanced in 1983 when the 18,000-seat Thomas and Mack Center opened to house the basketball team. The UNLV basketball program achieved national stature and top ranking in the 1980s and won the National Collegiate Athletic Association Championship in 1990 under controversial, but successful, basketball coach Jerry Tarkanian. Shortly after Tarkanian departed, university president Maxson was forced to step down, as some members of the community never forgave him for the departure of their beloved coach. The Thomas and Mack Center also brings a number of locals to the campus for basketball games, special events, concerts, and the National Finals Rodeo.

The university's explosive growth in the 1980s has continued on an unprecedented scale throughout the 1990s: "I cannot imagine too many places in the country where they can talk about 12 new buildings, 14 new programs, growth at 5 percent a year, 112 new faculty, the kind of energy and creativity and spirit of can-do here" (Patton 1998c: 1B), UNLV president Carol Harter proclaimed as she welcomed the new faculty in fall 1998. A long-awaited Architecture Building was inaugurated and a new law school opened its doors in a temporary facility, while construction began on a new library, a new Music Building, an International Gaming Institute, and a Professional Development Center for education majors. With a number of new undergraduate and graduate programs also starting up, the university continues to expand both quantitatively and qualitatively, expecting to receive authorization from the state legislature to add 99 new faculty for the 1999–2000 academic year.

Higher education continues to be a bargain in Nevada, as a prominent local journalist and former governor emphasized recently, pointing out that for a student carrying a full 15 semester hours, the total cost at CCSN is approximately $950 to cover estimated tuition, books, and lab fees for each semester. Similarly, at UNLV, tuition for a full-course load is $1,596 for tuition and another $500 for books and supplies: "The great advantage we have in Clark County is the vast array of educational opportunities available for us no matter what hours we work or what subject matter interests us. College credits are awaiting us and so are degrees, and they aren't out of our reach financially. ... None of us lives very far from either a UNLV or CCSN classroom, and new classes are being presented every semester" (O'Callaghan 1998).

The state legislature has responded to higher educational demands from the community, increasing "state funding by 30 percent since 1996. No other state except for California has received even a 20 percent boost in that time" (Patton 1998a). Despite the largest boost in funding in the state's history, however, demands on the university and community-college system are growing, with an estimated 134 percent increase in high school graduates in Nevada expected between 1996 and 2012. It should also be noted that nearly one-third of the students in the system are part-time and over 30 years old.

Given the region's anti-tax culture, its ideology of limited government (see chapters 8 and 9), and its resulting reliance on bonded indebtedness as a primary financing tool, it seems all the more remarkable that Southern Nevadans have managed to construct hundreds of schools, a flourishing university and community college, architecturally impressive library/cultural centers, new city and county buildings, and other public-service facilities so essential to the development of a thriving metropolitan area. While some of these accomplishments resulted from the actions of a few visionaries, others were built amazingly rapidly out of sheer necessity. Overall, however, the community's response to its public-sector needs has in turn created new opportunities for employment that have attracted professional middle-class individuals and families to the area, who then have further enriched the civic life of Las Vegas. While serious problems have also emerged, largely as a consequence of that same rapid growth, the quality of life for most Clark County residents remains high. In the next chapter we shall examine some of the benefits and costs of living permanently in one of the nation's most popular tourist destinations.

# 7 Living in Las Vegas

Las Vegas is in many respects like any other metropolitan community. Most people live in homes, go to work, raise families, pay mortgages, celebrate holidays, shop for groceries, take vacations, and mow their lawns. In other ways, however, Las Vegas is unlike any other place on the planet: part gambling and entertainment mecca, part postindustrial Sunbelt metropolis, part Old West frontier town, and part glorious desert setting.

The pastiche that is Las Vegas includes multi-colored castles, 30 million tourists a year, the Statute of Liberty and the Eiffel Tower, water- and snow-skiing on the same day, Egyptian pyramids and sphinxes, grocery shopping at 3 a.m., Venetian canals, pirate battles, more than 70,000 new residents a year, the Brooklyn Bridge, no identifiable town center, Alpine resorts, traffic congestion, and the Stratosphere Tower looming over the landscape like a 110-story phallic symbol. The souvenir industry peddles second-order simulacra, replicas of Las Vegas copies of landmarks from other cities and countries: "Get your model Statue of Liberty from New York-New York! Just like the one in New York."

Yet Las Vegas also is a place where most people work eight hours a day, though not necessarily 9 to 5, and lead lives typical of any southwestern city, rarely going near a Strip casino unless they want an inexpensive meal or are entertaining visiting friends or relatives who expect them to play tour guide. Las Vegas is also a place where one can earn a living as a professional gambler, a topless showgirl, a valet-parking attendant, a magician, or a blackjack dealer. As in any other resort area, when you live in Las Vegas, everyone wants to visit. Guests, however, are often disappointed to find that residents don't live on the Strip or, in many cases, even within ten or fifteen miles of the neon and glitter.

## The Unusual as Usual, or Normalization of the Odd

### It's a Dry Heat

Las Vegas sits in the Mojave Desert, where summer temperatures can top 110 degrees Fahrenheit. Drivers find that merely getting into their cars exposes them to temperatures approaching a life-threatening 150 degrees. The uninitiated experience the relentless brutality of the sun when they reach for a seat belt and burn their hands on the metal buckle. Any metal object in a vehicle is a potential scorching hazard, from door handles to uncovered steering wheels. Then the car may not start. Auto batteries have extremely short life spans in the arid desert air and many Las Vegans brag if they get more than two years out of an 84-month battery. Operating a vehicle on streets melting in the 106-degree desert sun presents other challenges. When Las Vegas has a series of days where the temperature consistently tops 110 degrees, as happened in the summer of 1994, broken-down vehicles dot the landscape as radiators overheat, hoses break, and humans dependent upon air conditioning are forced out onto the sizzling pavement.

An oft-heard refrain is "it's a dry heat." With summer humidity levels usually less than 10%, that is true, as Las Vegans begin grumbling about humidity when it hits double-digit levels above 12%. And, with more homes and developments come more lawns, lakes, and golf courses, making the humidity creep upward. A breeze at temperatures above 100 degrees, however, has less of a cooling feeling than the effect of a blow dryer. Long-time desert dwellers like to believe they take on the characteristics of a lizard, with less heat sensitivity but no tolerance for humidity.

## At Your Service

Las Vegas also seems to be the valet-parking capital of the world. At casinos, restaurants, and even shopping malls, men and women with VALET emblazoned in large letters across the backs of their shirts, dart about with the speed of desert cottontails. For them, time is money. They hustle to park cars in the reserved valet-parking areas and, on the return trip, deliver cars to waiting drivers who tip them for the service. These energetic workers provide a tremendous convenience for those in a rush, who have no problem handing over their car keys. Although they pay minimum wages, the competition is heavy for these often lucrative jobs, as they are supplemented by significant tip or "toke" income that can amount to tens of thousands of dollars a year.

## That's Entertainment

Las Vegas residents are also treated to a wide variety of entertainment attractions, even without leaving their own back yards. Several times a year fantastic fireworks displays, on a scale surpassing those of Fourth of July festivities in most communities, erupt in the night sky, celebrating the opening of a new casino, or a refurbishment, expansion, or anniversary of an older resort. Or perhaps it's Chinese New Year or a major boxing match is in town. For these reasons and more, fireworks are a fairly regular part of the Las Vegas skyline. The traditional aerial pyrotechnic displays have been augmented recently by lasers, as the glittering lights of Las Vegas now extend toward the heavens. One of the most interesting outdoor entertainment spectacles unique to Las Vegas came with the filming of *Honeymoon in Vegas*. For a week, night after night at dusk, Las Vegans could look to the sky in the direction of the Strip and see strange, lighted objects falling from the heavens, backgrounded by a colorful desert sunset, as the precision-parachuting "Flying Elvi" team floated towards ground-zero at a major Strip resort. It was raining Elvis!

A walk in a local park, such as Angel Park on the western side of the valley, can present its own version of the Las Vegas postmodern experience. Traversing the walking path to enjoy the panoramic vistas of the golf course, the Spring Mountains, and expansive desert, one can encounter a variety of activities beyond the conventional scenes of competitors on the tennis courts, families barbecuing, or children playing on swings and slides. A couple might be exchanging wedding vows on the lawn in a fairy-tale-like setting, with the bride in long white gown, groom and wedding party in tuxedos, bridesmaids dressed like pastel confections, a minister, and even a singer with a full-size battery-powered keyboard. Further down the same expanse of lawn might be a group of tai chi practitioners slowly moving in a choreographed ballet. A short distance away might be two armies of fully armored knights practicing their jousting and sword techniques as their chain metal rattles and their swords clink. Las Vegans take it all in as part of a normal stroll in the park.

## Art – From Van Gogh to Dice Clocks, or Show Me the Monet

There is little subtlety and fewer limits in Las Vegas when it comes to art. The category of what passes for art covers the entire range from the masters to dice clocks. Caesars Palace sports a larger than life-sized version of Michaelangelo's statue of David and numerous marble Roman fountains, and the most extensive art collection in the state is located not in a museum but in a resort-casino. The $300-million Bellagio art collection includes originals by Monet, Matisse, Van Gogh, Renoir, and Picasso, provoking a series of quips such as "Picasso, the blackjack period." This private collection vividly contrasts with the sea of kitsch art flooding the green-felt jungles of most casinos, but it also comes at a price to the public, as admission fees are charged to view the exhibit.

Artistic entertainment in Las Vegas offers a similarly extreme range of opportunities for locals and tourists alike, from Pavarotti and Andrea Bocelli to Elvis and female impersonators. A particularly strange contrast is found in the community where classically trained musicians earn their living playing behind Wayne Newton or Engelbert Humperdinck. To satisfy their artistic souls, many also play in the local symphonies or teach music to children at the Nevada School of the Arts, providing the community with an unusually high number of professionally-trained musicians.

The quality of Las Vegas culture, however, is found in its pastiche and juxtapositions. Casinos and community venues together implode artistic periods and forms of entertainment, and sustain the complete range of pop culture from Country stars to high culture to just plain kitsch. The same can be said for Las Vegas' architecture. It is not "a style," but the implosion of styles borrowed from virtually every historical period and Hollywood fantasy that characterizes the aesthetic dimension of the built environment. These juxtapositions of the built environment, as one outrageously themed casino contrasts with others around it, are the stimuli that created a pedestrian street culture on the Strip (see Gottdiener 1997). The visual contrasts of the casino exteriors have produced a new urban fabric in Las Vegas and are now a spectacular sight in their own right, best enjoyed on foot.

## The Culture of Growth: Build It and They Will Come

Rapid growth and constant change have become a way of life in the Las Vegas Valley. Residents joke that the state bird is the construction crane, as dozens of the multi-story metal machines hulk over the skyline. Each hour, two acres of land are developed and two new homes are built. Statistically, those homes are purchased by the nine people who move to the valley in that same hour. Homes are often sold before they are built and the desert southwest has become a land of homes constructed, from foundation to occupancy, in 90 days. Las Vegas is the only city in the country to have new telephone books issued every six months, and property tax rolls are updated twice a year to avoid losing revenue. In the last half of fiscal year 1996 alone, $4 billion in taxable value was added. Street maps change daily with hundreds of new streets added each year. To keep up with growth, the

Clark County School District would have to build a new school every month, a new classroom every day.

The annual steady stream of 60,000 to 80,000 new residents expands the Las Vegas Valley each year by the volume of a medium-sized city. Living in Las Vegas is thus like living on a constantly changing and moving stage. A homebuyer can purchase a home on a dirt road at what appears to be the edge of civilization and within a year face busy six-lane streets filled with cars. Buildings appear almost overnight, new home developments sprout miraculously and roads are constantly under construction: "We're basically going to tear up every street in this valley and either widen it or improve it. If you see any roads on that map not marked for construction, let us know and we'll take care of it," quipped Lee Gibson, director of regional transportation for the Southern Nevada Planning Authority. The *Review-Journal* opinion page sardonically titled the quote, "Who would Notice a Difference?" (February 5, 1998).

## Traffic: Life In the Construction Lane

Surveys of Las Vegas residents consistently produce the same answer to the question, "What is the worst problem in Las Vegas?" It is traffic. Growth has overwhelmed the area's highway and street infrastructure and efforts in the struggle to keep up create construction projects that cause more delays. The spaghetti-bowl interchange was built in the 1960s when Clark County had an approximate population of 200,000. No one could have predicted that the population would explode to 1.3 million thirty years later. By 1990, traffic volume south and east of the interchange totaled 135,000 and 120,000 vehicles daily, respectively. A multi-phase reconstruction that will cost more than $300 million has begun, but it will take years to complete, while hundreds of thousands of cars pass through the construction zone daily.

One of the more unusual experiences in Las Vegas traffic comes when traveling northbound on Interstate 15 during rush hour. Heading into the notorious spaghetti bowl, two lanes of traffic merge left onto the freeway at Charleston Boulevard. At the same time, a substantial number of vehicles already on the highway merge to the right to access the US Highway 93–95 expressway, giving one the feeling of being shuffled inside a deck of cards. In rush hour, the term "expressway" is a misnomer as a wall of vehicles exiting to US Highway 95 westbound creates a non-moving barricade in the second of five lanes of heavy traffic, while vehicles whiz by on both sides at high speeds.

## Public Transportation

Transportation is a major issue for a growing number of residents, including the elderly. As in many other southwestern cities, Las Vegans have an unusual attachment to, and dependence upon, their personal vehicles. Prior to the 1990s, public transportation was not much of a priority in southern Nevada. However, recently the community has actively worked to improve public transportation, which for years existed in its best form primarily for tourists on the Strip; Citizens' Area Transit (CAT) buses now cover most of the metropolitan area, including Boulder City. Established routes have been expanded and other routes are added regularly as new neighborhoods are built. Seniors are eligible for half-price fares on the CAT bus system, which also provides para-transit services for personalized pick-up and drop-off for the disabled and the elderly, to encourage their use.

## Death Penalty for Crossing Outside a Crosswalk (and Sometimes Inside It)

Traffic congestion in Las Vegas, as elsewhere, produces less than courteous drivers. It also creates impatient pedestrians. The mix is lethal for more than 100 pedestrians each year in Las Vegas, as the one crime in Clark County that is punishable by an on-the-spot death penalty is jaywalking. On a regular basis, tourists and local pedestrians are mowed down and, if they are not within a crosswalk, the driver is seldom charged. This creates a curiously cavalier attitude toward pedestrians as police officers at the scene say, "(s)he was outside a crosswalk," in a tone that implies the death was deserved. On the Strip, tourists don't want to walk to the corner to cross in a crosswalk – hardly an automatic guarantee of safety, anyway. They merge across the street and cling to medians. Some don't survive. Also, there are few crosswalks in most residential areas, except near schools. Local residents getting off buses can't find crosswalks or won't walk to a corner if their destination is just across the street from the bus stop, thus placing themselves in similar peril.

## Change is Evolution

In Las Vegas everything used to be something else. Long-time residents still refer to the Palace Station as the Bingo Palace, to Hoover Dam as Boulder Dam, to Las Vegas Boulevard as the Boulevard rather than the Strip, and to local restaurants by their name from three to five incarnations ago.

And then there are the casino evolutions. Bally's used to be the MGM at the Strip and Flamingo Road. Now the MGM Grand is a newer casino at the Strip and Tropicana Boulevard, which itself replaced the Marina Hotel and Tropicana Golf Course. The legendary Sands, home of the Rat Pack, was blown up to make way for the Venetian. The Dunes was imploded to lend its grounds, including a now defunct 18-hole golf course, to the Bellagio. The Landmark, which once dominated the Las Vegas skyline, was blown up to create a parking lot for the Convention Center. The Hacienda was demolished to make way for Mandalay Bay. Even resorts that maintain their original names have to change and evolve constantly. At Caesars Palace, a former parking lot and Formula One racetrack became the Forum Shops. At the Flamingo Hilton, resort operators decided that Bugsy Siegel's rose garden would attract more visitors as a penguin habitat, in the desert. The *Cirque du Soleil* Circus big-top tent has been replaced by the Treasure Island high-rise parking garage. Other resorts are similarly in the process of growing vertically as well as horizontally.

### Only Partially a 24-Hour Town

Casinos are not the only establishments to remain open 24 hours a day in Las Vegas. Many grocery stores, drug-stores, gas stations and bars also are open all day and all night, as are some service industries, such as dry cleaners located in the apartment neighborhoods within a few blocks of the Strip. However, many suburban residential parts of the Las Vegas Valley are more like Anywhere, USA, where restaurants, dry cleaners, malls, professional services, and car dealers close at the end of the day. In these neighborhoods, the sidewalks roll up at dusk. On the Strip and in Glitter Gulch the night-time is no frontier but an already colonized time-zone that affords tourists with a departure from the ordinary routine of daily living. People in casinos can carve out any part of the 24-hour cycle they wish to live. In this sense, Las Vegas means freedom from objective time.

### Ring in the New Year – at 9 p.m.

New Year's Eve is a unique time-warped celebration in Las Vegas. For years the fireworks display and celebration in downtown's Glitter Gulch was held at 9 p.m. in order to be televised in the Eastern time-zone. Las Vegas now holds two separate New Year's celebrations, one on the Strip and one downtown. Both schedule the major fireworks and revelry for the national cameras at 9 p.m. and again at midnight. In 1996, the battle for the title of most popular place to spend New Year's Eve became a declared war between Las Vegas and New York's Times Square, with the former's celebrated implosion of the Hacienda Hotel. The crowd of revelers on the Strip topped 200,000 and a massive fireworks display lit up the skies both before and after the forty-second implosion. The pyrotechnic event received live national television coverage, just as the fireworks at the Union Plaza in downtown Las Vegas had in previous years.

The battle was highlighted three days later when New York-New York opened on the Strip. The mayors of Las Vegas and New York engaged in a friendly, media-hyped argument over who had the largest New Year's crowd and event status. The Las Vegas mayor was confident of victory as the community's 98,000 hotel rooms boasted near total occupancy and tourists spent $56 million, not counting gaming revenues, and the six-lane Las Vegas Strip was transformed into a pedestrian mall for eight hours, from 6 p.m. to 2 a.m., for New Year's revelry. Emphasizing the normalization of the odd, Las Vegas gets to welcome the New Year twice, with a full-scale, nationally televised dress rehearsal at 9 p.m. and a midnight celebration, sort of an early and late show.

## White Tigers and Dolphins in the Desert

Another less than normal circumstance in Las Vegas-world is the sponsored presence of non-indigenous species of animals, as habitats have been created for dolphins and penguins in the southern Nevada desert. When Steve Wynn was seeking a federal permit to house dolphins on the Las Vegas Strip, he flew the Superintendent of the Clark County School District to Washington on the Mirage corporate jet. The school administrator, whose salary was then being supplemented by Mirage contributions, testified that the exhibit would be educational for the children of Clark County, though one wonders if these school children now believe that the Las Vegas Strip in the Mojave Desert is a natural habitat for dolphins. At the Flamingo Hilton, a renovation eliminated Bugsy Siegel's rose garden, replacing it with a group of penguins, a species more normally associated with an Antarctic climate than with cactus and sand. The white tigers that appear and disappear nightly in the Mirage showroom are not even a naturally occurring species, but a genetically manufactured breed. Siegfried and Roy's claim of salvation and preservation is thus not just saving a species, they have actually created one. Only in Las Vegas!

## The "est" Philosophy: New*est* Bigg*est*, Fast*est*, Costli*est*, Loud*est*, Tall*est*

Visitors and locals alike have a very short attention span as far as what constitutes a must-see attraction in Las Vegas. When the Mirage opened with a large-scale, full-volume exploding volcano, locals and tourists would plan their schedules around the show times to gather and watch the volcano erupt. A few years later, when the Treasure Island pirate ship fired its cannons, those same locals and tourists could be observed rushing past the exploding volcano with barely a glance, to get in position to watch the pirate battle. Similarly, the moat and castles of Excalibur were quickly surpassed as the Sphinx and pyramid of Luxor arose next door. Older resorts struggle to compete in the highly themed world of the mega-resorts and they either change, upgrade with the times, or are imploded. The motion-sensor rides at the Excalibur were outpaced by the high-tech "Star Trek" at the Hilton and "Atlantis" at the Forum Shops. The "world's highest roller coaster" atop the Stratosphere was outdone by the New York-New York roller coaster that loops through the casino and across the Brooklyn Bridge. Titles of "world's largest sign" and "world's largest hotel" move constantly along the gaming corridor.

## Trick or Treat

October 31 is a state holiday in Las Vegas. While better known as Halloween to the national populace, the holiday is Admissions Day in Nevada. Even school children, who get the day off, seldom know that October 31, 1864, was the day President Abraham Lincoln signed a proclamation designating the territory of less than 40,000 people as the 36th state. The act was part of Lincoln's strategy to bolster the Union during the Civil War. Some find it ironic, or appropriate, that Las Vegas, the land of glitz and neon, and style over substance, is part of a state that gained admittance to the Union on a day celebrated with masks, costumes, and anonymous revelry. In actual fact, Las Vegas was not then a part of Nevada, but was added from Arizona ter-ritory three years later. Reality, however, has never stood in the way of a celebration in Las Vegas. As elsewhere, Halloween has become an adult holiday in Las Vegas, where store and bank clerks wear costumes to work, although a new resident or visitor can find it disconcerting to transact a bank deposit with Dracula or purchase groceries from the Wicked Witch of the East.


## Wedding Chapels and Divorce

Las Vegas is known for its ease of marriage with no wait, no blood test, and a mere $35 license fee. Equally famous are its notorious wedding chapels, and this industry also has seen its share of changes. The Little Church of the West has been relocated several times in its 55-year history to accommodate Las Vegas' growth. The first of its kind, the Little Church is listed on the National Register of Historic Places because of its link to the Nevada wedding industry, which itself became famous in the 1940s and 1950s for its quick and easy ceremonies. The chapel was built in 1943 with the Last Frontier Hotel, just north of Spring Mountain Road, out on the dusty highway to Los Angeles that would eventually become the Strip. Celebrities who married there include Judy Garland, Betty Grable, Mel Torme, Dudley Moore, Robert Goulet, Mickey Rooney, and Zsa Zsa Gabor. It was the first Las Vegas wedding chapel built exclusively for that purpose and is one of the few remaining from that era. The Little Church of the West moved from the grounds of the Last Frontier in 1954 to a site near the old Silver Slipper, now the site of the Fashion Show Mall. In 1979, to make way for the mall, the Church was carefully braced, loaded onto a flatbed truck, and moved to the grounds of the Hacienda in an early-morning procession that shut down Strip traffic. In 1996, the chapel was moved again, to an area of small motels at the south end of the Strip to make way for Mandalay Bay. The rear of the property abuts part of McCarran Airport, where vows are sometimes drowned out by departing flights. Perhaps, then, it is the only structure on the National Registry that changes its location, thereby symbolizing the uniqueness of Las Vegas and its rapid growth.

Las Vegas boasts a host of other wedding chapels, which feature singing Elvises ("the king was married here"), rental wedding dresses and rings, volunteer witnesses, and a drive-through establishment where vows can be exchanged with the ease of ordering a burger and fries.

Divorce is more difficult. For nearly half a century Las Vegas was known for the ease of uncontested divorce, making it a haven for Hollywood stars seeking to terminate a marriage in what was called "the six-week cure." The six-week residency requirement spawned a mini-industry of dude ranches in the 1930s and 1940s, known for their party atmosphere. Uncontested divorces, however, are rare in the 1990s. Nightmare stories emanate from the family court, where couples battle for years over alimony, custody, and child-support issues (Hopkins 1997). One wealthy couple who filed for divorce after a mere three months of marriage were in and out of court trying to get divorced for nine years.

## Landscape – The Desert is Not a Wasteland

Southern Nevada has no sand dunes. Visitors, and some residents, associate palm trees with Las Vegas, but the tropical trees are not native to the area. They are, rather, expensive imports and as difficult to maintain as are the non-indigenous saguaro cacti that increasingly dot the valley. The demand for palm trees is so great that companies across the southwestern United States hire "spotters" to find good trees in people's backyards (Bluethman 1997). These spotters negotiate with the homeowner, paying prices of up to $1,000 to uproot the trees. Canary Island palms are the hardest to acquire and bring the highest price. Once the tree is purchased, uprooted, and transported by truck to Las Vegas, the price can escalate to $4,000. A mid-1990s upgrade of a four-mile stretch of the median in the Strip included 1,000 lights and 1,500 palms at a cost of $15 million. Summerlin Parkway, known locally as the "road to nowhere" when it opened, is lined with these costly trees. The city of Las Vegas' $22-million beautification project, completed in January 1999, also lined Las Vegas Boulevard from Sahara Boulevard through downtown, as well as Fourth Street, with palm trees. The Mirage's lush tropical ambiance includes palm trees outside and preserved palms in the lobby. The interior of McCarran Airport is similarly decorated with metallic palm trees.

## Las Vegas Directions: You Can Get There From Here – Sort Of

Until recently, street addresses were not well marked in Las Vegas, making many business and home addresses difficult to find. Typical Las Vegas directions, often included in business ads, might be, "go past the Winchell's on the corner, just past the restaurant that used to be Carlos Murphy's and it's the three-story building in the next parking lot." In other communities, this would hardly constitute a valid business address.

## The Dark Side of "Gaming"

The definition of compulsive gambling has expanded recently to encompass the stock market, where compulsive investors are now defined as gambling addicts: "By far the most gambling in the world is performed in the stock market," according to the head of the National Council on Problem Gambling (Edwards 1998a). Compulsive gambling has become a significant problem across the nation as financial risk-taking achieves a new level of respectability. Statistics are difficult to obtain on the number of compulsive gamblers, however. One local medical facility that treats them, Charter Behavioral Health System of Nevada, estimates that the problem afflicts 3 to 5 percent of the population. The affliction is recognized by the American Psychiatric Association as an impulse-control disorder, not an addiction, so treatment is not covered by most health insurance plans, though the Gamblers Anonymous 12-step program conducts nearly 50 weekly meetings in Las Vegas, and compulsive gambling often overlaps with other compulsive behaviors, such as alcoholism and credit problems. All gambling problems are not necessarily related to compulsive gambling, however.

Gambling parents sometimes, forget about their offspring in the pursuit of a jackpot, and over the years a number of tragedies have occurred when parents abandoned children to gamble. Two famous cases took place in Stateline, now Primm, Nevada, where two seven-year-old Californian children were killed, in separate incidents years apart, after being left in the arcade by a gambling parent. The murderer of the male child was never caught, though a Californian man was tried and acquitted for the crime. The boy's family sued the casino, even though they had abandoned the youngster in a casino arcade for several hours on Thanksgiving day. In the second case, casino security guards tried to return a young girl to her father several times between 1:30 a.m. and around 4 a.m., before she was murdered in a bathroom by a Californian teenager. Upon learning of his daughter's murder, the father was quoted in a local newspaper as having asked the casino for gambling chips, free beer, and funeral expenses. The girl's family also subsequently sued the casino for their daughter's death. Other tragedies have occurred at casino campgrounds where children have burned to death when left alone in a camper while the parents gambled. These tragic incidents often took place during holiday seasons.

One of the most pathetic sights in Las Vegas is seeing children crying, while their mother throws the family assets into slot machines at the supermarket. It becomes obvious that some have been gambling for a while when their ice cream melts and drips into a puddle beneath their grocery carts.

## Gambling among Local Residents

While it would seem that the majority of Las Vegans gamble regularly, a recent survey indicated that 42% of local residents said they never gambled, 11% said that they used to gamble but no longer do, and only 46.9% reported that they currently gamble (Woo 1998: 4). Of the 46.9% who reported gambling, less than one-fifth reported gambling several times a week or more and another one-fifth reported gambling once a week. Video poker was the preferred game (53.9%), followed by slots (20.4%). The vast majority of Las Vegas residents who gamble prefer casinos catering to locals (72.8%), followed by Strip casinos (13.6%). Reflecting the utilization of local casinos for dining and entertainment options other than gaming, one-fifth to one quarter of Las Vegas residents report visits to local casinos several times a week (21.5%) or once a week (22%), far more often than they report gambling (Woo 1998: 4).

## "Where Locals Go to Play" – Growth of Local Casinos

No major resorts were built on the Strip between 1974 and 1989. During that period, primary growth in the gaming industry came from catering to the burgeoning Las Vegas population although, as the town grew and tourism increased, local residents became less willing to fight the traffic and crowds on the Strip. When tourism slumped, resorts aggressively marketed to locals, but once it picked up again on the Strip, casinos there paid less attention to local residents.

Other off-Strip casinos, however, were built and advertised as places "where locals come to play." One of the first gambling halls of this sort was called "The Casino" when it opened in 1976. The small gambling hall, with one hundred slot machines and six table games, was located just west of the Strip on Sahara Avenue. In 1977, it was renamed the Bingo Palace when the property was restructured to increase its attraction for the local market. The concept of targeting a casino strictly to locals was greeted with skepticism at first, but the success of the Bingo room, a buffet and live Keno at the site proved that the concept could work. In 1984, it was renamed the Palace Station following another expansion and remodeling effort to reflect a railroad theme. The Palace Station became a popular entertainment gathering place for locals, who came to sample the dining options, dance in lounges to live entertainment, and stay or stop by for the late night/early morning breakfast specials.

To meet increasing competition in the growing local-casino market, a 22-story tower was added to the Palace Station, along with a high-rise parking garage in 1990. Existing rooms were refurbished, bringing the total room-count to 1,041, large by "locals" standards. The parent company, Station Casinos, has since grown to four properties, Texas Station, Boulder Station, and the first Green Valley resort-casino, the $198-million Sunset Station, located across from the Galleria Mall. The latter three properties have multiplex movie theaters with 40 screens and another 11 planned.

Other locals-oriented casinos serve as virtual community centers, bringing movie theaters, bowling alleys, dance halls, and a variety of dining options, from inexpensive smorgasbords to intimate gourmet settings, and even skating rinks, into various parts of town. At the intersection of Valley View and Flamingo, the Gold Coast introduced a new concept, the first casino movie theater. For years the only theater showing foreign, subtitled, and art films in Las Vegas, the Gold Coast's two-theater operation, was famous for $1 popcorn and drinks. The constantly changing venue of small independent and foreign films was available only by walking through the casino, creating a bizarre mental pastiche as theater-goers stepped out of a four-hour subtitled movie about the Czechoslovakian revolution into a smoke-filled casino with clanging slot machines. Booking for the Gold Coast theaters is now done by a major film chain, however, so car chases, explosions, and alien invasions have, for the most part, replaced the more thoughtful fare, and the popcorn prices have risen. Las Vegas now has more than 200 movie screens with multiplexes being added all the time and one-fourth of these are located inside casinos.

Across the street from the Gold Coast, the all-suite Rio resort-casino debuted in 1990, inaugurating the expanded multi-option Carnival Buffet, with separate areas for Mexican, Chinese, Italian, and other specialty foods in addition to more traditional buffet fare. The Rio recently has grown to become the thirteenth largest hotel in the world and its just-off-Strip towers have become a familiar part of the Las Vegas skyline. The 2,563-suite resort was undergoing yet another $200-million expansion in 1998 when *Travel & Leisure Magazine* named it the world's top hotel value. The hotel's $79 average room rate was clearly superior to the second-rated hotel, which featured a room-rate of $1,148, while the average room-rate of the top ten resorts was $432. The Rio, with 119,000 square feet of casino space and 14 restaurants, thus has achieved significant status as the first off-Strip megaresort.

The Carnival-themed property was bought by Harrah's Entertainment Inc. in August 1998, for $888 million, making Harrah's a competitor with Hilton for the title of largest gaming company in the world.

The expansion of local casinos into residential neighborhoods became a controversial issue in 1987 when construction began on Arizona Charlie's, an $18-million casino and small hotel located on Decatur Boulevard, in a commercial area near long-established Las Vegas homes and a senior residential center. When Arizona Charlie's opened in April 1988, neighboring homeowners protested, fearing an increase in crime and traffic. In 1991, the protests increased when the casino added three six-story towers. Two years later, angry neighborhood residents went to City Hall to oppose the closing of Evergreen Avenue to allow further expansion, making Arizona Charlie's the archetypal example of the evils of casino encroachment into residential neighborhoods for many.

The city of Las Vegas finally took a stand against neighborhood casinos, refusing to allow construction of a new 100-room property, the Fiesta, proposed to be built at the northern edge of the city. The developers then went across the street to North Las Vegas, a city that has turned down few businesses proposing to build in their once-disrespected and economically strapped town. The builder's action here was reminiscent of the move across Sahara Avenue at Las Vegas Boulevard by the El Rancho, Last Frontier, and Flamingo, to the county-regulated Strip in the 1940s. In 1995, another property, Texas Station, was built next to the Fiesta, bringing badly needed revenues to North Las Vegas in the form of a new casino district in close proximity to thousands of new homes.

## Senior Gamblers

The freedom from time commitments that comes with retirement can also be a burden, as many seniors with lots of free time are bored. Thus, many off-Strip Las Vegas casinos, whose primary customers are local residents, aggressively market to seniors with time to spare. Courtesy buses provide free rides to the casinos, picking up the seniors in their apartment complexes, condominiums and neighborhoods. A typical multi-family complex with a large number of senior residents will have as many as three or four regularly scheduled shuttles to pick up residents and transport them to a variety of local casinos each day. In addition to door-to-door service, seniors also receive coupons for meals, free slot play, and other freebies. One local casino, Arizona Charlie's, runs three shuttle buses which transport between 8,000 and 10,000 people each month and cover nearly every senior community in Las Vegas (Przybys 1998: 1). The riders are willing captives of the casinos for an average of four to eight hours per visit, playing Bingo and slots, meeting friends, socializing, and eating meals at the buffets and coffee shops. One local casino executive has gone so far as to claim that, "Local casinos have become de facto community centers" (Berns 1997b: 2D).

Casinos designed to cater to locals also have slot clubs, where members can earn gifts through points they receive when they gamble. Other benefits may include VIP privileges at buffets, and private parking lots for senior club members. Slot clubs allow casinos to ascertain exactly how much each customer gambles per visit and to track their casino spending over time, as patrons insert their individual slot-club membership cards into the machine each time they gamble in order to receive club credits. Thus, every quarter they drop into a machine is tracked.

Seniors who visit casinos often claim that they spend little money while receiving numerous entertainment, dining, and social benefits. This is difficult to believe, however, given that casinos conduct detailed market analysis of the number of seniors in a neighborhood and the amount each spends per gambling visit, while constantly searching for new ways to expand their marketing to elderly patrons. Needless to say, the bottom-line-conscious resorts would not subsidize the shuttle service if it did not reap profits.

There is, of course, a dark side to the senior gambling scenario. The gathering of official statistics on the problems created by excessive spending of gambling dollars by seniors is discouraged. However, anecdotal evidence suggests that many bored seniors who spend large amounts of their free time in casinos are losing their life savings and even the homes for which they paid cash to shelter them in their retirement years. Others get depressed or experience family problems, including divorce, as a by-product of excessive gambling.

## Las Vegas – Like Living Anywhere Else

In many ways the media hype about Las Vegas is contradicted by the reality of everyday life there. Many locals never go near a casino and barely notice them as they cross the Strip on the Desert Inn super arterial, a cross-town road constructed to avoid congested vehicle and tourist traffic. Most similarly ignore the ever-present slot machines in supermarkets and convenience stores.

## Neighborhoods

The more mundane aspects of life in the town can be seen by taking a walk in its residential neighborhoods, which could be anywhere in the US. In the master-planned parts of town, with their wide sidewalks and tree-lined streets, residents can be seen out walking, pushing a baby carriage, rollerblading or bicycling. Fitness walkers and joggers chug along at their own pace, exchanging pleasantries with home-owners working on gardens and home improvement projects, or washing their cars. In the summer, many beat the heat by exercising in the morning, often at sunrise, the coolest part of the day. At places like Angel Park, which sports a walking path, a serious seniors contingent greets the day and each other, along with younger walkers and joggers trying to get in some exercise before the work-day starts.

With the proliferation of differentiated communities within the Las Vegas Valley, residents now say, "I live in Summerlin" or in any of the other neighborhood communities, rather than identifying with the city as a whole. As each section develops commercially, it becomes even more self-contained as residents no longer have to travel across the valley to shop at a mall or to Strip casinos or movie theaters. They live, shop, eat, recreate, and some are able to work in their own small world within the larger community.

Las Vegas has long been believed to be a city of transients; however, a 1998 survey revealed that this, too, has evolved. Six out of ten Las Vegans reported knowing at least a few of their neighbors by name and another 25% were on a first-name basis with most or all of their neighbors. Furthermore, 71% reported helping a neighbor with a problem, 62.4% had watched their neighbors' property when they were out of town, and 42.3% had borrowed tools or food items from a neighbor (Woo 1998: 7, 22).

## Recreation

Recreational opportunities are also an important community component. Lake Mead offers beaches, fishing and boating from small dinghies, motor boats, and luxury yachts. The 160,000-acre lake covers 3,000 square miles, boasting nearly 600 miles of shoreline. Tour boats with dinner-dance cruises and nature-watch tours cover the lake. On a February day, it can be sunny, maybe 70 degrees Fahrenheit in the valley and 80 degrees at the Lake. People can be water-skiing and see snow-capped mountains in the distance where other Las Vegans are skiing down slopes a mere 45 miles to the west. In addition to snow-

**Figure 7.1**  TPC Canyons Golf Course

skiing at the 8,000-foot level, visitors to Mount Charleston can take a horse-drawn sleigh ride through the forest or simply sit by the fire in a lodge and watch the snow fall. In the hot summer months the mountains provide a cool respite from the heat and hikers can find waterfalls and Native American petroglyphs on the surrounding cliffs.

## Political Activism

Despite rapid growth, levels of political activism in the Las Vegas Valley can be underwhelming. Less than 15% of registered voters turned out in a recent municipal election to elect the city council – the five people who control a $250-million budget and make the most important decisions about their everyday lives. These decisions concern the placement of stores, casinos, billboards, stop signs, and traffic lights in neighborhoods, as well as street maintenance, road cleaning and paving, trash collection schedules, and sewage-treatment services.

Ironically, voters turn out in much larger numbers to elect state and national officials, whose decisions have much less direct impact on their everyday lives. In the November 1998 election, 48% of Clark

County voters went to the polls, surpassing the national average by more than 10%. In the previous non-presidential election year, Nevada turnout was 60%. Perhaps because of growth-related issues, and hard fought campaigns for a number of elected offices, Las Vegas Valley's voters want to have their voice heard.

## Crime

Since its Wild West, shoot-em-up beginnings, through the days when organized crime was a dominant force in the casino industry, criminal activity has been a major element in the Las Vegas image. As the metropolitan community grows towards two million residents, the image remains, even though it no longer matches the reality of everyday life for most people in the valley. For example, the city made national headlines for having the nation's highest crime rate in 1995. This was erroneous, however, as it resulted when the Knight Rider news service's Washington Bureau took FBI crime statistics for Clark County and calculated rates based upon the population of the city of Las Vegas alone. Las Vegas Metropolitan Police Department (LVMPD) (Metro) Sheriff Jerry Keller called attention to the fact that the crime total covered Metro's entire jurisdiction, not merely the city of Las Vegas, so the rate was not 18,354 crimes per 100,000 population but instead 7,303 crimes per 100,000 (FBI 1995.) A subsequent retraction, however, did not scream across the nation's front pages as had the previous story. Las Vegas ranked 40th in crime rate per 100,000 population in 1995, based upon the FBI's Uniform Crime Reports; however, even that rate is misleading as it is calculated solely in terms of the residential population, excluding the more than 30 million tourists who visit Clark County annually. Furthermore, fewer crimes were reported in Metro's jurisdiction in 1997 (58,995) than in 1995 (60,178), despite an increase in population of more than 150,000 new residents (Las Vegas Metropolitan Police Department 1998). That trend continued into 1998: while 85,000 additional residents moved to the valley, the actual number of crimes as well as the percentages decreased dramatically (Puit 1998b). Also, the bulk of those offenses (49,937) were crimes against property. As a result, LVMPD Sheriff Jerry Keller proclaimed recently that, "Las Vegas is the safest it's ever been" (KVBC-TV3, March 12, 1998).

Equally significant in regard to crime is the level of residents' feelings of comfort in their community. A 1998 study conducted at the University of Nevada, Las Vegas, by the Cannon Center for Survey Research found that most Las Vegans (76.9%) feel safe or very safe walking alone at night in their own neighborhoods. The overwhelming majority of those surveyed (96.3%) also reported that they felt very or somewhat safe from crime in their homes at night (Woo 1998: 9).


## Seniors and Crime

As a group, seniors tend to be more fearful of crime, which some researchers have tied to their viewing large amounts of television (Gerbner et al. 1986). Seniors who live in isolation tend to feel particularly threatened by the potential of being a crime victim, but southern Nevada does not have a high crime rate against seniors. For example, in 1996 only 8 of the 168 murder victims in Las Vegas were aged 62 and over (Las Vegas Metropolitan Police Department 1996: 14), perhaps influenced by the fact that Nevada law doubles the penalty for any crime committed against a senior over age 65. As in most other parts of the country, Las Vegas seniors are more likely to become crime victims in their own living rooms via telemarketing scams than as victims of violent crime. Similar to other age groups, seniors most at risk live in low-income areas, whereas those in upscale private communities, such as Sun City, see little crime. In the first ten years, the more than 10,000 residents of Sun City Summerlin have endured only one murder in their area, where volunteer members, armed with cellular phones, patrol their neighborhoods and watch the houses of those on vacation, thus maintaining an enviably low burglary rate by reporting any suspicious activity to the police.


## Suicide

Nevada had the highest suicide rate in the nation in 1994 according to official statistics, at 23.4 per 100,000 residents. Such high rates are in general characteristic of communities with large in-migration and are thus clustered in the western states: Wyoming ranks second with 22.5, closely followed by Alaska 20, Arizona 18.8, Montana 18.5, and New Mexico 18.3 (National Center for Health Statistics 1997: 99).

More recently, the Center for Disease Control and Prevention reports the Nevada suicide rate at 22.2 suicides per 100,000 people, near the top of the list and almost double the national average of 11.8 (Puit 1998a). However, these numbers are inflated by at least 14 percent by non-resident suicides. Without them, the rate would drop into the middle range among the western states. Also, if an individual moves to Las Vegas, rents an apartment, and kills him or herself the next day, that person is categorized as a local resident in the suicide data.

The Clark County Coroner, Ron Flud, ascribes rapid growth and failed relationships as the primary causes of suicides in the valley: "We have a lot of people coming here from all over the world to find their professional life, to find another chance, and some of those people find out when they get here that things may not work out the way they had planned" (Puit 1998a). Similarly, a counselor at the Community Counseling Center describes suicide as a complex problem with multiple causes, pointing out that, in regard to Las Vegas: "People bring their problems here from other places and they think that by making a geographical change, that all of a sudden those problems will go away. They get here and find out that is not so, and it ends up creating a real sense of futility for a lot of people" (Puit 1998a).

## Health Care

The rapidly growing community needs expanded health-care services. Southern Nevada has ten full-service hospitals, with a total bed-count of 2,686. The newest opened in Summerlin in 1997, and the first phase of the next, St Rose Dominican Hospital West, is scheduled to open in 1999. The area also has five hospice programs and four specialty hospitals devoted to psychiatric, long-term, and neurological disorders. However, Nevada ranks 34th nationally in support for public health, 49th in per capita Medicaid spending, and 33rd in access to primary care (United Way of Southern Nevada 1998). Las Vegas, like the state as a whole, has an inordinately high percentage of medically uninsured residents, at 14.7% percent (Nevada State Bureau of Health Planning and Statistics 1998), the majority of whom are employed full-time. Health-care data for children in Nevada are particularly alarming, as approximately 20% have no health insurance. Also, because the state does not fluoridate its water, Nevada schoolchildren suffer from dental problems, with 18% of first graders and 12% of sixth graders in need of some form of urgent dental care (United Way of Southern Nevada 1998).

The region's mental-health services are also grossly underfunded. A 1990 report by the National Alliance for the Mentally Ill called Nevada one of the stingiest states in the nation in expenditures on public services for the poor and mentally ill (Manning 1990), and little has changed since then to alter that grim assessment, although the Las Vegas area is somewhat better served than the rest of the state. The legislature did, however, authorize an expanded budget that included new programs for the state Division of Mental Hygiene and Mental Retardation in its 1998–9 budget. As a result, construction began on a community residential-treatment center in Las Vegas and a $3.8-million crisis center will be proposed as a priority construction project to the 1999 state legislature.

## Homeless in the Land of Plenty

As with the rest of the country, the problem of homelessness is growing in southern Nevada. Many homeless persons come to the desert, attracted by the climate and seeking riches where the streets are paved with gold. A rude awakening comes when temperatures sometimes dip below freezing in the winter or when the temperatures top 110 degrees Fahrenheit in the summer. Many are drawn by the promise of plentiful jobs that require little formal education and skill, yet "a significant portion of these newcomers arrive with insufficient financial resources to re-establish themselves in our community" (United Way of Southern Nevada 1998: 8).

Many of the homeless also are drawn by reports that Las Vegas boasts one of the lowest unemployment rates in the nation, along with the fastest job-creation rate. However, "approximately one-third of the jobs being created are entry level positions paying $6 to $8 per hour" (United Way of Southern Nevada 1998: 8) and it is not uncommon for 1,000 people to apply for 100 jobs when casinos announce that they are hiring. Major expansion projects and the ongoing construction of new resorts, combined with the rapidly growing housing market, have created a booming construction industry. The addition of thousands of new hotel rooms in particular creates thousands of jobs, many for unskilled labor. Also, prospective employees don't have to speak English to make beds, and salaries for maids start at nearly twice the minimum wage. Reality sets in, however, as down-on-their-luck job seekers find it difficult to secure employment without an address or telephone number. Many end up out on the street alongside those who are there by choice or who have problems with mental illness, alcoholism, or drug use. In 1998, 16,000 Southern Nevadans had no permanent address and more than 3,000 had no roof over their heads (United Way of Southern Nevada 1998: 8).

Las Vegas has never been a national leader in helping the homeless, as decades ago, "welfare" was a one-way bus ticket to Los Angeles. More recently the attitude has been, "ignore them and they'll go away." Relatively few shelter beds are available, a mere 1,400 in winter months according to an estimate by the Clark County

Homeless Coalition (United Way of Southern Nevada 1998: 8). The city's main concern has been to keep wandering street people away from the view of tourists enjoying the neon glitz of Glitter Gulch. In Las Vegas, homeless people have been arrested and charged with stealing when found foraging through dumpsters for food, clothing, aluminum cans, or other usable salvage. One bag lady was officially evicted from a dumpster where she spent her nights. Ironically, her green metal home was located behind a vacant office building owned by the former city official and real-estate mogul who requested the "eviction." Clearly, poverty and the plight of the homeless have no part in the dazzling image the gaming mecca wants to project.

## Water in the Desert: Life Force – Death Force

*Floods*   During the summer months, a light rain that might pass as a shower in other parts of the country has catastrophic potential in Las Vegas. An inch of rain can wreak havoc, killing the unwary and destroying millions of dollars in property. Much of the ground in southern Nevada is composed of caliche, a cement-like substance which allows rainwater to roll over it, like the water-repellent feathers of a duck. A little rain in the nearby Spring Mountains thus can translate into a four-foot wall of water rushing across the higher western edge of the valley, gathering speed and volume as it moves towards the lower eastern side, until the rain torrent reaches Lake Mead, the lowest point in the valley. Cars, people, mattresses, and anything else in the way are swept into the rushing waters. A major rainstorm in 1975 sent dozens of cars floating around the Caesars Palace parking lot. The resort built a massive underground water-channel system, alleviating its problem with the Flamingo wash but pushing the hazard across the Strip to the Imperial Palace. To counteract this, the Imperial Palace was built on stilts, but its swimming pool area often collects mud and debris, even during minor summer cloudbursts, and on several occasions cars have floated out of the parking garage. Flood control is being addressed on a regional basis in the valley, but multi-million-dollar storm-drain and flood-basin construction is continually outpaced by population growth. All this in a community with an average annual rainfall of a mere four inches.

Even when flooding is not a problem, the slightest amount of rain wreaks havoc on Las Vegas traffic. Oil deposits build up on roads during months-long periods of dry weather and a few sprinkles of rain bring the oil to the surface, making the roads hazardously slick. Las Vegas drivers, not known for outstanding avoidance of traffic accidents in any event, end up needing an army of tow trucks and Metro officers to disentangle the resulting mess. Also, drivers not used to encountering standing water often miscalculate and cavalierly try to plow their way through, ending up having to be rescued from drowning.

*Water waste*  The fact that the Las Vegas Valley is located on the edge of the Mojave Desert gives one the clue that water might be a scarce commodity. It is, but developers and many homeowners seem to exist in a state of permanent denial. People used to move to Las Vegas for health reasons, to get away from humidity and allergies. However, the area now contains more than thirty 18-hole golf courses, as well as several communities built around artificial lakes. Also, new residents, upon their arrival, waste no time in introducing their native flora into their Las Vegas yards, escalating the local pollen count. New residents seem to desperately want the community and their home to be someplace else, usually the place they left. Up to 40 percent of new residents come from California alone, especially from areas that were transformed from desert as the population grew and clustered against the ocean, with transplanted Phoenicians a distant second. Thus the bulk of new residents come from two areas with problems that southern Nevada seems to be mimicking – declining air quality, traffic congestion, and water shortages.

### Big Skies and Wide Open Spaces

Many who live in the desert love the vast southern Nevada sky, which unleashes a spectacular performance at the beginning and end of each day, with sunrises and sunsets so beautiful they seem unreal. The East Coast and other areas with lots of trees and heavy foliage, on the other hand, can make a Southern Nevadan feel claustrophobic. Perhaps the best displays in the desert appear in the early evening, when the skies are scattered with puffy clouds that transform from pink to orange to a bright red in a matter of minutes. The setting sun creates shadows on the surrounding mountains that give vivid meaning to the phrase, "purple mountains' majesty." The skies over Las Vegas thus provide perhaps the most spectacular show in a town known for glitz and glamour, twice daily, at sunrise and sunset and with no admission fee.

### Land of Duality

The duality of Las Vegas may be seen in the differences between long-time and new residents. Of the 1.25 million Clark County residents, half did not live there ten years ago. Bank and casino employees wear nametags that read: "Mary, Boston." First name and city of origin are often more important defining factors in a community where it seems that everyone is from somewhere else.

The ultimate duality in the growing community lies in its very name. People who use the term "Vegas" either don't live in southern Nevada or are associated with the "player" aspect of gambling or lounge-lizard-style entertainment. The term sends shudders down a local's spine, roughly equivalent to the San Francisco residents' reaction to "Frisco" or San Bernardino residents' reaction to "San Berdoo."

For many old-time Las Vegans, the fact that the region is becoming a major metropolis is not necessarily a good thing, as they want to maintain that small-town feel of knowing everyone. Many of them, for example, wax nostalgically about the days of frontier justice in the community, when jurors were selected from among the derelicts openly consuming alcohol on the Court House lawn. The prosecuting or defense attorney who bought them a bottle usually ended up winning the trial of the day. Still others say they long for the days when the Mob ran the town, claiming that street crime was virtually non-existent given the Mob's no-nonsense, and no civil rights, approach to offenders, a view that was largely shared by local law enforcement of the time.

In the 1970s, Las Vegas still seemed in many ways like a small frontier town. Casual western attire was acceptable in most situations, as were polyester leisure suits in places like City Hall. The Boulevard Mall was joined by the Meadows Mall, but stores at the two shopping centers were distinctly limited in the sartorial variety they offered, so residents made regular pilgrimages to Los Angeles or San Francisco to expand their shopping options. At the time, only 250,000 called Clark County home and less than half a million lived in the state. Las Vegas belied its glitzy façade by being a fairly conservative town, peopled by an odd combination of Mormons who headed west from Utah, Oklahomans and other Southerners who never quite made it to California, and Easterners seeking the warm winters of the Sunbelt. Only later did Californians, fleeing smog, traffic, earthquakes, violent crime, and the high cost of living in the golden state, join retirees in a mass migration to the silver state, helping establish Las Vegas as a retail shopping mecca (see chapter 4).

Since the 1970s, there has been a huge diversification in acceptable attire, reflecting changes nationwide. The corporatization of Las Vegas brought an upscale suit-and-tie crowd to offices across the valley although shorts and tee-shirts have become acceptable garb in showrooms and restaurants. It's nearly impossible to violate a dress code, especially on the Strip, where tourists or locals dressed in sequined gowns and tuxedos can be found alongside the shorts and flip-flops crowd. Also, reflecting changing dress standards nationwide, and partially because of the heat, school children wear shorts to classes and some teachers have been known to do the same.

Another Las Vegas duality can be seen in the political arena. A site identified on maps as Tule Springs since 1869 once housed a famous divorcee dude ranch. When the city handed over the grounds in 1977 to create a state park, Tule Springs was renamed Floyd Lamb State Park in honor of a powerful state senator. It is the only state park in Nevada to be named after an individual. However, a few years later, Senator Lamb was found guilty of taking $23,000 in bribes from an undercover FBI agent and was forced to resign in 1983 after 26 years in the state legislature.

A series of attempts to restore the park's historic name have included petition drives and a Las Vegas city council resolution. But the chairman of the State Assembly Natural Resources committee refused to allow a vote on a bill in 1997 to change back the park's name, because that would be an "insult" to the 83-year-old former senator and convicted felon. On the other hand, the name of powerful, long-time US Senator Howard Cannon was unceremoniously removed from the Reno Airport while he was still alive but involved in no scandal.

## Denial

Denial is another manifestation of the quality of Las Vegas life. The names of streets, apartment complexes, housing communities, and businesses reflect a curious lack of recognition that they are situated in the midst of the desert southwest. Thus, Las Vegas has two residential communities called "the Lakes," and a plethora of nautical, forest, and tropical-paradise themes celebrated in the names of apartments, restaurants, and streets. Nautical names such as Desert Shores, Yacht Harbor Drive, Gull's Landing, Paradise Cove, and Mariner's Bay dot the desert community, located more than 300 miles from the nearest ocean.

When Citicorp located its credit-card operations in Las Vegas, it was attracted by the town's location and low business taxes, but was leery of the "lost wages" reputation, so the company unilaterally changed its address to The Lakes, Nevada and a separate zip code was created.

## Postmodern Pastiche as Urban Culture

Postmodernists employ terms such as fragmentation and pastiche to describe the dizzying, often bizarre contrasts of everyday life or the implosion of diverse cultural influences in contemporary society. Our discussion here of living in Las Vegas certainly seems to fit this characterization, even though other communities also have experienced rapid growth and change. Casino gambling and large themed commercial spaces have spread across the nation as well (Gottdiener 1997). The result is that Las Vegas also may be seen as a unique combination of the exotic and the mundane that increasingly typifies the postmodern urban environment in the nation as a whole. As progressively more downtowns emulate Las Vegas, American urban culture will be characterized more and more by hype, themed environments, glitzy archi-tainment, and perhaps even casino gambling.

# 8 Local Politics and Community Interests

Recent literature on urban affairs yields the overriding conclusion that big-business interests play the tune to which all others must dance. This was not always so obvious, however. During the prosperous 1950s and 1960s, under a succession of liberal, or at least moderate, governments at all levels across the country, unions and community interests were successful at negotiating both the tenor and pace of growth so that resources were channeled towards satisfying social as well as economic needs. One of the major beneficiaries of this "corporate liberal" phase of urban history was the public school system, including higher education, which enjoyed generous government support for the expansion and upgrading of both physical plants and academic programs. Another beneficiary was county and municipal planning, which received federal support for slum clearance, highway construction and housing renovation. It was thus during this period that the interests of big business, while still dominant, were at least moderated by the influence of local citizens and non-business organizations in their quest for the public good.

By the 1970s, with the onset of deindustrialization and fiscal crises percolating through every level of government, community and public needs were largely ignored, and unions faced massive job losses. Many states also enacted tax cuts in a wave of conservatism. As a result, county and municipal governments also suffered cutbacks in revenues, payrolls, and programs. A great wailing of city souls was heard throughout urban America as community resources of all kinds suffered for lack of funding. With local urban economies reeling under the impact of declines in manufacturing, the specter of job loss, and shrinkage of the tax base, politicians responded by catering to business. Henceforth, in most metropolitan regions, the dominance of private-sector interests in defining the public agenda became increasingly prevalent.

In this context, it is tempting to characterize local Las Vegas politics as simply an extreme case of domination by the major industry in town – casino gambling. In fact, area politics has long been stereotyped by the national media in this manner. To be sure, when it comes to Las Vegas, legalized gambling is the "goose that lays the golden egg" and the needs of casino owner/operators have historically shaped the priorities of local government. Yet, it would be a mistake to subscribe to this one-dimensional view today, especially because it is based on an equally erroneous assumption that the gambling industry is a monolithic enterprise. Rather, the major corporate casino interests compete fiercely among themselves for their share of Las Vegas' multi-billion-dollar gambling/tourism profits. Further, as the metropolitan region has increased in population and matured as a place of permanent residence, a number of other local constituencies, both business and community-oriented, together constitute an increasingly complex political environment in the Las Vegas Valley. In this chapter we will provide an examination of this new political scene as further evidence of the normalization process in Las Vegas.

## The Framework of State and Local Politics

Nevada has a bi-cameral structure of governance with a state senate and an assembly. Carson City, in the northern area of the state, is the capitol. Because of its location, northern interests have historically dominated the state legislature. In southern Nevada, Clark County comprises nearly 8,000 square miles and contains more than two-thirds of the state's population, generating more than 70 percent of its revenues as well. While an appearance of political equality has been created as numerical representation has slowly evolved, with 13 of the current 21 state senators representing Clark County and 26 of 42 assembly representatives also from the south, the county's share of political power in the state still lags behind its percentage of population and revenues. One reason for this results from the impact the state capitol's location has on political seniority. Every two years, southern legislators must leave their homes, families, and businesses for at least five months to live in motels more than 300 miles from home. The resulting personal and financial toll means that southern politicians rarely serve the lengthy terms in office required to attain seniority. Thus northern Nevada legislators, who can live at home during the sessions, find it easier to serve longer careers in the legislature – building seniority and the power that comes with it. In addition to the north–south split, the conflict between the more populous urban counties and the economically strapped, rural "cow counties" also plays a significant role in Nevada's politics. The rural counties have historically been a powerful force in state government, as much of the state's land is classified as "frontier" and the vast majority is federally owned.

Traditionally, southern Nevada's power has been manifested more at the federal than the state level, with much federal largesse over the years going to the south (see chapter 1). Today, both United States senators are from Clark County, although its congressional representatives are split between the north and south. While the bulk of Clark County constitutes Nevada's first congressional district, 30 percent of the county, along with the rest of the state, comprise the second congressional district, suggesting that Clark County's voters should have more impact on that district. Also, following the 2000 Census, it is expected that Nevada will obtain a third congressional seat due to its enormous population growth.

In Nevada, the spatial divide between north and south has always been more salient to political debates than party ideology. Historically, Nevada has been ruled by the Democrats. Since the Depression-era administration of Franklin Roosevelt, powerful Nevada Democrats, like Senator Pat McCarran, have played an important role in obtaining federal funds for the state. Although Republican Paul Laxalt enjoyed influence during the Reagan Administration, when he retired he was replaced by a Democrat, Harry Reid. In this sense, Nevada politics parallels that in California, where public officials at the national level have run a well-oiled machine for most of the twentieth century. The interesting difference is that, at least since World War II, California's power has been based on its population, while Nevada and other southwestern states that have received federal support have benefited more from the shrewdness and seniority of their senators and congressmen.

Nevada Democrats, because of the state's frontier heritage and the influence of the gambling industry, have strongly opposed government regulatory intervention, like their Republican counterparts, in Nevada and elsewhere. Senator McCarran set this tone with a hands-off policy, championing localism and opposition to government oversight. Somewhat hypocritically, at the same time, McCarran actively lobbied for every conceivable type of government assistance and program, including nuclear bomb testing, as a means of developing the region's economy. In short, Nevada Democrats traditionally have behaved more like Republicans in actively resisting all forms of federal government regulation. Yet, at the same time, they have aggressively pursued federal funds of all kinds. In this sense Nevada Democrats more closely resemble southern "Dixiecrats," who also displayed a penchant for anti-regulatory sentiments while promoting their own special interests.

At the city and county levels, a distinctive hybrid of structural features also characterizes local politics. Chapter 1 described the way city government was reformed by progressive principles. Yet, despite instituting a professional city-manager type of municipal governance, the city also retains an elected mayor and an elected city council in a ward system. Because of Nevadans' traditional support for limited government, the mayor and city council members are paid to serve only part-time by law, making local politics in southern Nevada appear to be something of an avocation. For example, in 1998, Ward One, the west urban-core area, was represented by a police officer, Michael McDonald; Ward Two, the southwest suburban section, by Arnie Adamsen, who worked for a real-estate title company; while Ward Three, the east-central section that also includes the Westside, had a barber, Gary Reese, as its councilman. The only exception was in Ward Four, the northwest area, where Larry Brown, an ex-baseball player and Harvard graduate, quit a lucrative position as a Water Authority executive to serve full-time when elected in 1997. And an independently wealthy, former auto-dealership and grocery-chain owner, Jan Laverty Jones, served as Mayor, also a part-time position, elected at-large by city voters in all four wards.

A similarly limited government also operates Clark County, which is run by a board of seven commissioners, chosen in separate district elections, with the chair rotated among them. They, too, are paid to serve on a part-time basis. In a community of 1.3 million residents, the bulk of commission business involves running local government and providing services and infrastructure. The tourist industry occupies a major part of the agenda concerning county affairs, as competing casino interests battle regularly for commission approval of expansions, licensing, access roads, parking, and various sorts of other permits. The power of the casino/resort industry also is illustrated by its role in the history of the development of McCarran International Airport (see chapter 2), long supported by the commission despite negative environmental and residential impact, because it brings millions of vacationers to the region.

## Interests and Dominance in the Political Process

While key economic interests have dominated the Las Vegas region throughout its history, there have been a succession of business elites over time, with one group replacing another as a consequence of changing economic fortunes. Ranching in the early 1800s gave way to mining and railroad interests, by the turn of the century, that directed the town's development as a commercial center. Between the 1930s and 1950s, a number of local businessmen dominated the region, although growth was due largely to massive federal government spending, first for dam construction and later for the war effort. By the 1950s, however, casino gambling interests rose to the top and their concerns have largely defined the agenda of city and county politics up to the present time.

As discussed previously, two distinct trends are today changing the face of local politics. First, multinational corporations are gaining increasing control of the casino/resort industry, although there remain a few prominent individual players, such as Steve Wynn and Sheldon Adelson. The large corporate enterprises appear to be less concerned with the day-to-day operations of city and county government than were the individual owners of the past, although there are exceptions, and remaining individual owners continue to be very visible in local politics. Secondly, as metropolitanization has proceeded, massive population growth has fostered the appearance of several non-gaming and non-business interest groups within the permanent resident population. Together these two trends have produced a more typical American local political scene, greatly removed from the outdated, stereotypical view of Las Vegas as a company town. To be sure, the needs of the gambling and tourism industries still come first in the Las Vegas Valley, yet even these are often racked by internal conflicts among themselves and, increasingly, diverse local residential constituencies are making their interests felt – and their needs often differ from those of big business. Consequently, local politics is much more complex and conflictual than in the past.

While a complex political environment characterizes metropolitan regions across the US, not just in Las Vegas, some urban sociologists prefer to reduce this picture to a simplistic clash between business interests, on the one hand, and residents, on the other. This has been conceptualized, for example, as a one-dimensional dichotomy pitting the needs of "use value" against "exchange value" (see Logan and Molotch 1988). Such an argument is disappointing and misleading, as we will show. Not only does it ignore the importance of image and symbols, i.e., "sign value", in the promotion of place, a major force in Las Vegas' history, but it fails to capture the complex way both use value and exchange value cut across interests in both the business and resident communities. The characteristic produced by the process of normalization is, in fact, the richness and shifting nature of local political interests as both business and residents adjust to rapid growth.

## Competing Elites

### Intra-Industry Competition

The aspect of local Las Vegas politics most neglected by outside commentators is the fact that the gambling/tourist industry does not
speak with a singular voice. Rather, the industry is more accurately
described as one composed of various competing factions operating in
the region, as outlined in chapter 1. Many of their battles are waged at
the level of county politics, where Steve Wynn's Mirage Resorts Inc. is
perhaps the dominant player in the field, as the largest property-tax-
payer in the county in 1998. Mirage Resorts runs an efficient political
machine, providing major contributions to local, state, and national
campaigns. The company also boasts a polling facility run by a skilled
political consultant, and a get-out-the-vote phone operation. The
nearly 20,000 Mirage corporation employees are strongly urged to
vote and political candidates supported by Wynn have been allowed
to address resort employees on company time. Wynn's Mirage
Resorts' effectiveness at the city level was demonstrated when it
became the first business in the Las Vegas metropolitan area to permanently occupy and close a busy urban street – Carson Street downtown.

A major Strip competitor is Sheldon Adelson, owner of the Sands
Expo Center, who is building the $2.8-billion Venetian down the road
from the Bellagio. Adelson has forcefully injected himself into the
local political scene, largely as the result of his ongoing battle with the
local Culinary Union over his not pledging to open the Venetian as a
union shop. In 1996, he provided significant financial backing to help
a political neophyte, Metro police officer Lance Malone, unseat long-
time county commissioner Paul Christensen, in an outrageously
expensive contest where a total of $1.44 million was spent by the two
candidates for a part-time position that pays $54,000 a year. As politi-
cal consultant Dan Hart observed: "It has more to do with how much
power they'll have than how much they'll be paid. The influence local
officials have over all sorts of segments of the community and the
economy is significant" (Zapler 1997c). Since the county commission
makes decisions that directly affect the operations of the billion-dollar
resorts on the Strip, the resort giants want to have the ear of county
commissioners in seeking advantages concerning various county
requirements, gaining approval for expansion plans, and influencing
infrastructure decisions that affect their properties. This is backroom
politics of the old style, familiar in many cities run by business elites.

But Adelson only represents himself, and big money is no longer as

**Figure 8.1**   Opening night at the Bellagio, 1998

effective as it once was. In the 1998 elections he spent $2 million in a failed attempt to place three candidates on the county commission. His Committee for Fairness funded a television blitz campaign, viciously attacking two incumbent commissioners and a state assemblyman running for a vacant seat, all of whom he felt favored the Culinary Union. Governor Bob Miller charged that the action mocked the spirit of campaign reform he'd championed in his decade as governor: "In my over 40 years in Nevada, and 25 years in public office, I have never seen a more egregious campaign tactic than I've seen by the so-called Committee for Fairness" (Freiss 1998). Both Wynn and Adelson as the "big players," therefore, have experienced their political failures in the increasingly open local political process.

One issue, in particular, brought the owners of several major resorts into conflict with each other, placing the county commission in the middle. In 1994, when the MGM and Luxor added thousands of hotel rooms at the intersection of Las Vegas Boulevard and Tropicana Avenue, the county built four pedestrian walkways, at a cost of $12 million, to elevate pedestrian traffic above the busy roadways in order to resolve problems of pedestrian safety and traffic flow. Subsequently, when the massive Bellagio project was announced at the congested intersection of Flamingo Road and the Strip, the county sought to build the same type of structure there. What followed was a three-year battle over its design and location among the Bellagio, Caesars Palace, Bally's, the Barbary Coast, and the Flamingo Hilton. Mirage Resorts started the conflict by claiming it didn't want the visual aesthetics of its billion-dollar Bellagio negated by the bridges, suggesting a much costlier tunnel system as an alternative. After the county had spent more than a million taxpayer dollars on design plans for the $28.8-million tunnel, Caesars Palace and Bally's refused to pay the higher price for what they claimed would be a dangerous and difficult-to-maintain system. Mirage Resorts responded by offering to pay the difference for the cost of one tunnel if the others would split the costs of the remaining three walkways.

Finally, in December 1997, Bellagio, Caesars Palace, and Bally's agreed to privately design and build the south and west bridges at the intersection, which were completed by October 1998 when the Bellagio opened. However, even after the Bellagio's debut, the 3,000-room Flamingo Hilton and the 200-room Barbary Coast were still locked in a battle over which of them would front the location where the $8-million north and east bridges touch down.

Another costly battle between two major resort giants was fought for ten years between Harrah's and the adjacent Sands, now the site of the Venetian, over cooperatively building a driveway between their two properties. While a driveway sounds like a small matter, the unresolved issue came within days of halting construction on the $2.8-billion Venetian. Only after years of meetings, negotiations, and litigation between the two resorts and the county was a plan for a $3-million access road between the resorts finally agreed upon.

Yet another major battle, waged in front of the county commission, between two gaming giants, this time Caesars Palace and the Mirage, gained national media coverage. This dispute involved county construction of a much-needed service road to access the back entries to the resorts west of the Strip. In the process, a casino tower expansion, the pedestrian overpass/tunnel project, and a cross-town arterial were held hostage. County commissioner Bruce Woodbury warned attorneys for the two resorts that "what's at stake here is important to the community and is more important than these two properties" (Schweers 1997a). When the county first proposed the frontage road plan, Caesars readily agreed to donate a $500-million section of its property. Caesars later discovered that Mirage Resorts wanted to make a deal with the county to obtain the air rights so that it could build a monorail linking its Mirage resort with the Bellagio, bypassing Caesars Palace in between. Caesars angrily protested against such private use by a competitor over land that it was donating to the county, and wanted to maintain its right of refusal on use of the air rights. Caesars was willing to donate the air rights for a *public* people-mover system, but not for a competitor to construct a *private* transportation system. The county commission retaliated by holding hostage its approval for a 14-story 702-room tower and parking garage at Caesars Palace that would bring $2.6 million in annual room taxes to the county and $1 million in property taxes. The county claimed that it was prepared to spend more than $4 million in taxpayer funds to condemn the Caesars land in a process that could potentially have delayed all the projects for years. The Mirage weighed in with an implied threat that it would not donate land to the county from the old Dunes property to build the Harmon Road connection.

Finally, in June 1998, Caesars agreed only to donate the land. Their tower project was approved and Caesars then agreed to pay $2 million towards the pedestrian overpass. Even after this truce, any further move by the county to transfer air rights to a competitor for private transit development would probably end up in the District Court. The *Wall Street Journal* took notice when Bally's chairman Arthur Goldberg entered the fray with a letter to the county, criticizing its "unseemly, forcible governmental extraction … for the apparent purpose of conveying them to a competitor to use for a private people mover system" (Schweers 1997b). ITT Corporation president Rand Araskog also wrote to the Clark County commission, criticizing the county vote to hold the tower project hostage and bringing further national media focus on the clash of the casino titans, with the county commission in the middle.

The gambling industry presents a much more united front, however, when it comes to state politics, especially concerning proposals to increase legalized gambling taxes. Mirage Resorts chairman Steve Wynn won a major personal victory in the state legislature when he secured a special tax break for the art collection he gathered for Bellagio. The 1997 legislature passed a law exempting part of the 7 percent state sales tax for residents who buy art worth more than $25,000. The measure was introduced and passed just as Wynn began purchasing a $300-million-dollar collection that includes works by Picasso, Van Gogh, Monet, Cézanne, Gauguin, Matisse, and Renoir. It was estimated that Wynn and Mirage Resorts Inc. would save an estimated $15 million in sales taxes in the first year alone, along with an annual property-tax exemption of nearly $3 million (Associated Press 1998). A condition was that the art be publicly displayed for 20 hours a week, 35 weeks a year for free to the public. Characteristically, Wynn immediately challenged the State Tax Commission's ruling refusing to allow him to charge a fee for taxpaying citizens to view the works.

Instead, a $10 per person fee was instituted for viewing the art when the Bellagio opened and Wynn did not file for tax exemption, so that he could charge the public.

Another controversy arose when concessions were awarded for the $197-million D-Gate terminal at McCarran Airport (see chapter 2). In 1998, as the new terminal opened at the airport, the State Ethics Commission investigated four of the seven county commissioners to ascertain whether ethics laws were violated in granting the lucrative concession contracts. A number of the people awarded the highly sought-after contracts for "disadvantaged" businesses were well known in the community, including a former Reagan and Bush communications director who was a partner with the daughter of a former airport director, Bob Broadbent. From a pool of 66 applicants, the 13 successful candidates included all 10 names on a list prepared by commission Chair Yvonne Atkinson Gates. She and fellow-commissioner Lance Malone subsequently were found guilty of violating state ethics laws, Gates on six counts and Malone on three. Gates's long-time friend and political consultant was given two concessions, and a close friend who had done political fundraising for the commissioner was granted two coffee kiosks, expected to earn profits of $500,000 per year (Morrison 1998a). It was the second time County Commission Chair Gates had been found guilty of ethics violations in less than a year. Malone sponsored the names of his wife's long-time friend (who received two business approvals), and his brother's boss. Although the awards process was supposed to be free of political cronyism, making the very creation of a list a violation of the process, the situation was exacerbated when Gates gave the list to the county manager, who then passed it on through the Aviation Director to the master concessionaire in charge of the screening process. The master concessionaire for retail business testified that "he accepted the list from the commissioners and ordered his staff to make sure those names made it as a final recommendation" (Morrison 1998a). No fines were levied, however, because the Ethics Commission could not determine that the actions were willful.

An FBI investigation was subsequently conducted on the airport-contract award process, while the commission decided not to void the contracts because "they faced more liability in revoking the contracts than they would in defending a lawsuit filed by an unsuccessful applicant" (Morrison 1998b). The situation raised several troubling issues in the community, and a prominent local newspaper columnist, a lifelong resident of the community, reflected a widespread sentiment: "It has taken months, but thanks to the Ethics Commission I now remember the true definition of the word disadvantaged. It means, 'Any poor sucker who isn't tight with a county commissioner'" (J. L. Smith 1998b). While this situation is hardly unique to Las Vegas, it paints the entire county commission in a negative light and damages commissioners' public credibility as they engage in the vitally important work of providing services and infrastructure for the rapidly growing community. This and other incidents illustrate the weak nature of limited government, which we will discuss in the next chapter.

## Suburban Interests

The overwhelming majority of the population in Clark County resides in suburban communities of single-family homes, like the American population as a whole. And, like other Americans, residents are concerned about traffic, crime, education, medical care, taxes, and the environment. Many live in communities that have defined themselves in opposition to the Las Vegas casino image, while enjoying the industry's subsidization of their tax benefits. A growing number also oppose the opening of casinos in residential neighborhoods (see chapter 7). Their dissatisfaction with highways, traffic jams, and increasing commute times that have resulted from the rapid population growth has been translated into political pressure to deal with the infrastructure needs of that growth as the number-one priority in the region. This interest is separate from the "business first" ethos traditional for local government and represents a major instance of normalization.

Suburban Las Vegas residents are also concerned about maintaining the value of their property and consequently are seeking greater autonomy from the general population, preferring to break down large county districts into smaller, and therefore more segregated, units. For example, some claim that the Clark County School District, the nation's ninth largest, and a model of regional consolidation, should be broken up into smaller zones servicing individual communities with their own school boards (see below). Thus, as disaggregation and local community home rule increasingly characterize suburban political concerns, they present a challenge to the traditional machine of county politicians. The many issues of concern to local residents will be discussed in the second half of this chapter, as it is this conflict between public versus business needs that constitutes the principal contradiction at the core of the normalization process, as we shall see shortly.

*Seniors*

As discussed in chapter 4, seniors comprise a rapidly growing segment of the region's permanent population. Seniors are a potent political force nationally because they follow issues and have a high voter-turnout rate, and southern Nevada is no exception. In a November 1996 local election, for example, while the average turnout rate for all of Clark County was 56.3 percent, rates for the two precincts in the retirement community of Sun City were 87.9 and 88.5 percent. Additionally, seniors are becoming a potent political force in Las Vegas in terms of sheer demographics. In the same election, 141,565 registered Clark County voters were over age 55, constituting nearly one-third of the total.

One of the reasons for the active involvement of seniors in politics is the fact that many live on fixed incomes. This makes them highly sensitive as a group to public issues that affect tax rates and other forms of municipal indebtedness. Another factor sparking senior involvement in Las Vegas politics is the presence of both public and private programs that have established a number of community senior centers. Many centers are located in lower-income neighborhoods, such as the Las Vegas Senior Center located one block north of City Hall, and the Howard Cannon Senior Center in the east-central section of the city. These centers offer a wide variety of services to the elderly, including a convenient meeting place for the mobilization of political interests, which the general population lacks.

Class differences between the indigenous aging population and the large number of seniors who move to southern Nevada to retire also has potentially significant consequences for the local political process. A large percentage of the long-time resident senior population were employees in the local service sector. Many of them were minimum-hourly-wage employees who relied on tip income and do not have substantial pensions or retirement-program options. For these individuals, retirement is a financial struggle from the start. On the other hand, retirees who relocate to southern Nevada from other areas are usually much wealthier, with average retirement incomes of $30,000 and average estates valued at more than $300,000 (see chapter 4). Many have sold their previous homes and are able to pay cash for their retirement homes in Las Vegas, exemplified by the fact that the majority of homes sold in Sun City were bought with cash. This economic split among Las Vegas retirees has significant implications for the local political process, where long-time residents who might be predisposed to support local bond issues out of a sense of commitment to the community may be forced to vote "no" because of their personal financial situation. Meanwhile, the more affluent newcomers, more able to afford bond issues, might vote against them because they may have few personal ties to the community. This is especially likely to be the case for those who reside in planned communities where many amenities are provided, making them less dependent upon municipal services for parks and other infrastructure.

Clark County seniors' propensity to vote has been supplemented by other forms of political action. Seniors, along with other well-established homeowners, for example, protested against a proposed widening of US Highway 95, which would require the removal of 175 homes, 115 apartments, and 21 businesses. The alternative is to expand the highway over an archeological site of one of the earliest Las Vegas settlements. Many of the homes in the affected area were occupied by seniors who had lived there for decades and who had paid off their mortgages. For them, losing a home would be losing a way of life. The group's vocal protest was aired nationally on NBC's *Today* program on April 7, 1997.

During the 1997 state legislature, the Nevada Seniors Coalition also opposed passage of a proposal to raise the Clark County sales tax by ¼ percent to pay for water and sewage-system expansions. The $1.8-billion expansion of the Water Authority's aging water-delivery system, or "second straw," was designed to provide a more reliable alternative means of delivering water from Lake Mead and to accommodate new growth (see below). The Nevada Senior Coalition's president expressed the group's concerns: "Our position is that growth should pay directly for growth, which is what this expansion is about. Average workers and people on fixed incomes shouldn't have to pay for somebody else's new buildings" (S. Greene 1997d). Another growth-related public-funding issue is schools. A major school bond campaign was run by the Clark County School District (CCSD) in 1994 to pass a two-part, $905-million school-bond issue. The bond issue was perceived by many Las Vegans as a way to make existing residents pay to construct schools in developing areas of the community for newcomers, while older area schools were neglected. Seniors in Sun City were just emerging as a political force and they, too, opposed the bond issue, as did seniors living in older Las Vegas neighborhoods who also would not benefit directly. As a result, the first half of the bond issue, which involved a rollover of $605-million bonds issued in 1988 and thus no increase in taxes, was approved. However, voters rejected the $300-million bond that would have required an increase in taxes. For a later school-bond issue, in 1996, the CCSD paid special attention to seniors, campaigning heavily in Sun City and at senior centers across the valley. The $643-million school bond was passed by a slim margin.

A large population of retirees thus can have a tremendous impact on the social structure of a community. Their tendency to vote against growth-related bond issues in rapidly growing Las Vegas has not, however, applied to library bonds. Most, especially the more affluent recent in-migrants, seem to feel that libraries offer them ongoing services that schools do not. Critics also note that the rapidly growing senior population also has the potential to place a tremendous burden on the local healthcare system and could eventually crush the state budget with rising Medicare, Medicaid, and Social Security expenses.

## The City of Las Vegas versus Clark County

Ever since the 1940s, when the El Rancho Vegas, the Last Frontier, and the Flamingo Hotel opened on Las Vegas Boulevard outside the city limits to avoid city taxes and codes, there has been a split power structure in the Las Vegas Valley, as downtown casino interests did not always have the same goals as the county resorts on the Strip. As the latter area has become increasingly more successful, competition between these two poles of the casino economy has intensified. At the same time, the city of Las Vegas has seen businesses fleeing the inner city for locations in the newer areas, forcing it to fight to retain its economic base.

Tensions between the two geographical bases of local political power thus have been high and many of the city government's efforts to compete with Clark County have caused concern among local taxpayers. As elsewhere, business flight to the suburbs is fought by the city in the form of subsidies to businesses that choose to remain in the downtown area. This form of competition, however, is looked on by some as extortion. For example, in 1997, the city paid dearly, in the form of a $5.7-million-dollar grant to "a downtown bank that threatened to flee to the suburbs unless it got the cash" (Zapler 1997a). Critics called the action a shameful example of corporate welfare, while city officials responded that the action would bring a new $57-million, 13-story class-A office building along with associated businesses with hundreds of employees to the downtown area. They also estimated that the Sun Plaza would bring $450,000 per year in property taxes to city coffers. Nevada State Bank officials cited the $5.7-million figure as the difference in their costs of building downtown rather than in Green Valley or Summerlin. The start of work on the futuristic-looking building took place in 1998, making it the first privately owned major office structure built in the downtown area in seventeen years.

City–county competition extends beyond the gaming and business areas, as the city has aggressively made deals to annex suburban development such as the Lakes, Desert Shores, and Summerlin (see chapter 5). Yet, these arrangements point to the growing crisis of the central business core and the threats it poses to the city's tax base. While this is a dilemma faced by many declining inner cities across the nation, in Las Vegas it primarily takes place in the form of competition between the city and the county. As in many other disputes, this spatial split in the power structure is a major factor in local politics.

### Casino Owners versus Real-Estate Developers

Traditionally, the most influential groups on the local political scene have been the casino owners and other local business operators. In dealing with local government, as seen above, casino interests are often less a unified voice than fierce competitors, as the major corporations and prominent individual owners battle for a larger share of gambling and tourism dollars. Intense struggles between resort giants over approvals for expansions and licensing, access roads, property air rights, and pedestrian overpasses are fought regularly in city council and county commission meetings.

As normalization has progressed, a second political force in the business community has emerged, namely the growing power of residential and commercial real-estate developers in the local economy. Their interests have coincided with those of suburban residents to create a force that is often in opposition to the gambling/tourism industry. As elsewhere, developers rely heavily for their success on local-government decision-makers who control land use. In the city of Las Vegas alone, applications for single-family homebuilding permits surpassed 500 a month in 1998, giving some indication of the pace of growth. The city issued more than 7,000 permits in the first five months of 1998 for single-family homes, apartments, commercial and public buildings, together valued at $490.6 million. More complex are the applications for re-zoning of land parcels, which may require the granting of a variation in the regional land-use scheme. Re-zonings often are based as much on political influence as on the particular merits of the case (Gottdiener 1977). In 1997 alone there were hundreds of re-zonings in the unincorporated areas of Clark County, many in what were previously isolated parcels.

Although developers and casino owners both push for growth, they are often interested in different aspects, leading to political conflict. Casino owners seek to maximize the tourist trade and want local gov-

234 Local Politics and Community Interests

ernment to support the tourist infrastructure, especially its air and surface transportation routes. Real-estate developers, on the other hand, seek government infrastructure improvements for residences, especially water delivery, sewage hookups, spending on education, and re-zonings for commercial development. Funding these public activities often places casino and real-estate developers on separate sides of heated fiscal arguments, framed generally in terms of the persistent controversy over who should bear the costs for rapid growth in the region (see below).

In sum, while it is true that local politics in Las Vegas, like other metropolitan regions, is dominated by business interests, it is by no means the case that these are unified into a single governing elite, nor is it true that business alone shapes the public agenda. As a consequence of massive population growth across Clark County, a number of other political issues and interests have emerged, including the needs of suburban residents, the special perspective of senior citizens, and the growing power of real-estate developers. Even the powerful consortium of casino owners is often split between the downtown operators and those on the Strip, and among those within the Strip. In the next section we shall discuss the major political issues facing the Las Vegas region, emphasizing how these various interests sometimes cooperate and sometimes compete with one another to make public administration in Las Vegas an exceedingly complex task.

## Political Issues in the Rapidly Growing Region

In 1996, "Las Vegas approved more building permits per 1,000 population than any other city in the country" (Timmons 1996: 9) and, as we have seen, the pace of growth has not diminished since then. Over the past thirty years, Las Vegas has undergone a profound transition from a single-industry-dominated, good-old-boy frontier town to one of the largest metropolitan regions in the United States, with a diverse population approaching 1.3 million and an increasingly diversified economy. The ever-increasing permanent resident population of middle-class, suburban home dwellers has greatly complicated the issues of local politics because they are concerned, like citizens elsewhere, with traffic, crime, schools, taxes, and the value of their property. Most prominent in the eyes of many residents are transportation infrastructure problems that produce congested highways and increasing commuting times. There is also a similar concern when quiet suburban streets become major thoroughfares, and with developers transforming space adjacent to homes into shopping centers or, in some cases, neighborhood casinos. These pressing infrastructure concerns over development and quality-of-life issues are further complicated by the question of who will pay for them.

## Infrastructure Crises

As we noted earlier, new developments require streets, water lines, sewer lines, and connecting roads. Communities also need parks, public transportation, cultural centers, and schools. Yet, as one local city planner noted, local government often allows developers to build before adequate public services are in place: "What they do is build, and then we catch up" (Hynes 1997). Summerlin has been an exception, having spent millions on infrastructure before any homes were built. However, even there the infrastructure impact spread beyond the community's boundaries when an additional traffic burden was placed on US Highway 95 as the community developed and others sprouted up around it. Also, as the availability of large parcels of land decreases in the valley, this scale of pre-planning is likely to be done less often. Alternatively, some infrastructure needs are paid for by homebuyers and developers. In 1998, the local Homebuilders Association estimated that homebuyers were paying $25,000 to $30,000 of the purchase price for property improvements, hookups, and impact fees, with water connection costs alone for newly constructed housing tripling from 1996 to 1998. Those who live in communities with Special Improvement Districts (SIDs) pay even more, with all these costs added to the price of a home.

The 1997 State Legislature considered a quarter-cent sales tax increase in Clark County to fund a $1.8-billion proposal by Southern Nevada Water Authority to double the water system capacity in the Las Vegas Valley, known locally as the "second straw" project. Funding the project quickly became a lightning rod for discontent even as construction began, as long-time residents balked at the idea of paying to support projected growth. The Nevada Taxpayers' Association, for example, complained that the county already had plenty of money to pay for infrastructure needs, but was wasting much of it, and the Nevada Seniors' Coalition also opposed passage of the expansion.

The 26-year-old system broke down for the first time in February 1997, while the legislature was considering the funding issue, leaving the area on an emergency back-up system for days. According to the Water Authority's general manager: "At this point, Southern

Nevada's water supply is not secure; 1.2 million people are dependent on one single pipeline with no backup should anything go wrong. Imagine this valley in the month of July, temperatures between 110 and 115 degrees, and there not being any water for three or four days. ... What would this community look like?" (S. Greene 1997b).

The state legislature authorized the ¼ percent increase in the sales tax in Clark County but, fearful of jeopardizing their re-election chances with tax-conscious voters, passed the responsibility to enact the increase on to the Clark County commission, which required a supermajority vote of 5 out of 7 to impose the tax. Three commissioners, two of them up for re-election in 1998, voted to pass along the decision to levy the tax increase to an advisory vote of the people in fall 1998, when 72 percent of the voters approved the increase, making Nevada the only western state to seriously consider funding water projects through a sales tax. Among other rapidly growing western municipalities, Los Angeles is paying for $3.9 billion in water improvements through water-rate hikes, Denver is funding $470 million in upgrades through water rates and connection fees, and the Arizona Department of Water Resources is paying its $2.2-billion share of the Central Arizona Project with ground-water pumping taxes and a property-tax hike.

This water-delivery funding crisis prompted some officials to talk of privatizing the water supply in the region and setting up competition as a mechanism of controlling costs, though others are pessimistic that such a plan would be effective. Although the debate mirrors other struggles over infrastructure needs, when it comes to the water supply, most people believe that increasing the price of water for users would be the strongest conservation tool.

The Las Vegas Valley has other infrastructure needs as well, estimated to total $10 billion over the next decade. County sanitation officials claim that they "need $1.3 billion in new tanks, pipes and treatment processes beginning in 2003 to meet demands of growth and to keep up with increasingly stringent environmental standards" (S. Greene 1997b). Sewage treatment standards in the Las Vegas Valley are especially stringent because effluent empties into Lake Mead, a federally protected body of water, which then flows via the Colorado River across national borders into Mexico (see below).

A 1997 newspaper poll found that 37 percent of residents rate the need for improving roads and transportation infrastructure to relieve traffic congestion as the most important priority for the future (S. Greene 1997b). The state alone has authorized spending $37.5 million on road-construction projects in Clark County in 1998. Also in 1998, the federal government, via the Intermodal Surface

Transportation Efficiency Act (ISTEA), gave Nevada the largest amount ever, $1.1 billion over six years. Nevadans will get back $1.14 for new roads and improvements for every $1 paid into the highway trust fund. The most expensive road-construction project in the state is underway at the Spaghetti Bowl, the name given the bewildering maize of narrow lanes that entwine where Interstate 15 and US Highway 95 intersect. The downtown interchange was built in the 1960s for a population of little more than 200,000, but by 1998, an estimated 310,000 cars traveled through the intersection each day. A multi-phase upgrade begun in the mid-1990s will ultimately cost $200 million and will take several years to complete, while at least four more Spaghetti Bowl projects, totaling almost $100 million, are awaiting funding. Dozens of other road projects, including a beltway around the valley, also are being constructed with Regional Transportation funds.

The ongoing battle over infrastructure in the Las Vegas Valley mirrors the national anti-tax sentiment that began in California with Proposition 13 in 1978, as long-time residents of rapidly growing communities resent having to subsidize growth. While some long-term residents want higher fees on new housing to pay for growth, this ignores the fact that existing residents move within a community to larger homes as families grow or as income level allows and renters of modest means save to purchase their first homes.

The issue of "who pays for growth" also divides developer and tourism-industry interests, despite their common pro-growth orientation. Residential developers prefer sales taxes as a solution because additional housing fees would hurt the construction industry. Also, Nevada has no state income tax, in part because of the revenues paid by gamblers and other tourists through hotel, gaming, and sales taxes. However, the casino/resort owners view additional levies on their own industry, in the form of increased gaming and room taxes, with concern and continue to spend vast resources lobbying the legislature to prevent them. They have an unlikely ally in the senior population, which also opposes the idea of an increase in the sales tax. Consequently, the position that new residents should pay for growth often conflicts with the notion that infrastructure should be funded by tourists in the form of increased gaming, room, and sales taxes.

Controversy over the issues of growth, infrastructure costs, and funding sources was prominently displayed in the 1997 Ward 4 elections, in the burgeoning northwest section of the city. Some residents of the new Summerlin community were appalled to discover that plans were proposed for a casino site adjacent to their multi-million-dollar custom homes on the Tournament Players Club golf course. The

238 Local Politics and Community Interests

incumbent councilman, Matthew Callister, an attorney and former state legislator, was charged with receiving campaign financing from the casino/gambling industry, while the challenger, Water Authority executive Larry Brown, was accused of having "established close ties with Las Vegas developers" because he had previously served on the Planning Commission (Zapler 1997b). While Brown won the election in an upset by a narrow 63-vote margin, the anti-development versus anti-neighborhood gambling-issue framed the candidates' conflict.

Few politicians in any large metropolitan community are able to conduct expensive campaigns without contributions from business, but as elsewhere, capitalists are divided by factions that often compete with each other politically as well as economically. The cost of this campaign for a part-time city council position that pays $35,416 per year was $750,000, with Brown raising $300,000 and Callister $450,000 (Zapler 1997c). The enormous sums spent on local campaigns such as this one and the county commission race discussed earlier are simply indications of the critical importance of local government in Las Vegas for both developers and the casino/gambling industry.

## The Politics of Growth

Concerns about rising infrastructure needs also have led many residents to question the rapid growth that has made Las Vegas the sprawling metropolis it is today. A poll conducted locally in 1997 found that 71 percent of them were unhappy with the county's performance in handling growth; 89 percent of the survey respondents also felt that continued growth at the current pace of six times the national average was too fast, and two-thirds of them felt that growth controls were necessary "to avoid traffic congestion, preserve undeveloped areas and make utilities and other public services more efficient" (S. Greene 1997c). County commissioners somewhat petulantly responded that only one-third of southern Nevada's development takes place within the county's jurisdiction. Nonetheless, the burgeoning growth-control movement of the 1990s led state senator Dina Titus (Democrat – Las Vegas) to propose a moratorium on development that would establish a "ring around the valley." Assembly Bill 490 would have stopped development in areas "north of Grand Teton Drive, east of Hollywood Boulevard, South of Henderson Executive Airport and west of Summerlin." The plan also identified the following growth-control issues: (1) limiting leapfrog development which necessitates infrastructure expansions; (2) promoting infill development on land close to population centers with infrastructure in place; (3) the imposition of impact fees; and (4) the creation of a green belt of open space around the developing area to establish a boundary for growth.

Five of the seven county commissioners opposed the bill, because they opposed government regulation of growth following the dominant political ideology. They claimed that Titus's growth-control plan would "raise property taxes and allow an unconstitutional taking of private land" (S. Greene 1997c). Throughout the state, other opponents of controls echoed the conservative ideological position against active government regulation, and the bill was defeated.

Despite this setback, sentiment in support of growth controls still runs strong among many residents, as advancing sprawl and the infrastructure crisis persist as problems in the valley. A local environmental activist, Jeff van Ee, stated shortly after the failure of the plan: "It's about time somebody put together a road map for growth before things get even more out of control" (S. Greene 1997a). Before the end of the 1997 session, state senator Jon Porter (Republican – Boulder City) proposed the formation of a 21-member Southern Nevada Strategic Planning Authority to study growth controls and to "create a regional debate about growth and then use all the ideas to find the best approach" (McKinnon 1998a). This "study group" was given two years to complete its tasks, but not without opposition. State Assembly woman Chris Giunchigliani (Democrat – Las Vegas) whose own bill to establish a regional planning board also had failed in the 1997 session, stated that it was already too late to merely "study" growth-related problems: "We don't need to study to figure out we have a crisis. I think the public is well aware that we have maxed our infrastructure needs" (S. Greene 1997a). Senator Titus also announced that she was working with the Las Vegas mayor and other sympathetic legislators, like Giunchigliani, to reintroduce a plan for more stringent controls in the 1999 state legislature. In the meantime, the debate continues as some, like North Las Vegas Mayor Michael Montandon, argue that: "Growth poses no problems that the free market – and some well placed infrastructure – can't deal with" (McKinnon 1998a).

In early 1998, the county commission adopted an informal set of growth-management strategies in a move to create the appearance of a master plan, yet public officials maintained their market-oriented, anti-regulatory approach. Commissioner Mary Kincaid was quoted as saying that too much growth management could send the wrong message that "we don't want anyone else to move to Las Vegas." A second commissioner, Lorraine Hunt, agreed, stating: "We don't want to take away the right to build in the middle of nowhere. That's what made Nevada" (McKinnon 1998b).

When discussing growth in the Las Vegas Valley, it is tempting to conclude that all municipalities encourage rapid growth and development, but a notable exception in Clark County is the municipality of Boulder City. Long known as the only city in Nevada that has never legalized gaming, a legacy of its early days as a federally planned community for dam-construction personnel, Boulder City only legalized liquor sales in 1969. Overlooking Lake Mead at the southeast end of the valley, Boulder City is a 200-square-mile city, the largest in land area in Nevada, but with a population of little more than 14,000 residents. An example of its conservatism towards growth and its residents' unusual amount of power is reflected in a law passed in 1996 that requires the city to seek voter approval to sell an acre or more of its land, a significant point since the city owns all but six square miles of land within its boundaries (Packer 1998a). Growth control is thus a way of life in "Clean, Green Boulder City" where no more than 120 housing units can be built each year, including every apartment in a complex, causing developers to bank allocations over a period of years to build multi-family complexes. Residents avidly follow city council meetings and actively participate in decision-making, opposing several projects, including one for a landfill in the Eldorado Valley that would have brought $1 million annually to city coffers. The town actively promotes its wholesome image with Fourth of July parades, picnics, and pancake breakfasts, and the community-based Art in the Park each fall brings tens of thousands to the large park in the center of the historic town while raising money for the local hospital. The town's staunch anti-growth sentiment has a downside however, because of its limited property-tax base, as it continually loses public servants to its wealthier neighbors in Henderson and Las Vegas.

Rapid development expansion and new construction, rather than growth controls, however, continue to characterize the Las Vegas area as a whole, reflecting the region's dominant political culture, which combines anti-tax limitations on public spending with a pro-business, almost "anything goes" approach to growth.

## Downtown Redevelopment and the Fremont Street Experience

The origins of Las Vegas' downtown renovation are in many ways typical of other American cities. Until the 1970s, most of the casino action was located in Glitter Gulch, which provided the signature images representing "Las Vegas" as a cultural icon. In the 1990s, however, with the advent of megaresorts, profits from gambling on the Strip and the amazing increase in tourism there have attracted

**Figure 8.2**   Fremont Street Experience during the day time

business away from Glitter Gulch. Thus, downtown Las Vegas, as elsewhere in the nation, is being competed out of existence by businesses located outside the central core (see chapter 2).

The short history of downtown redevelopment has had its share of political conflicts and clashes among separate interests. In 1986, the Las Vegas city council sold $50 million in bonds to launch redevelopment of the area, seeking out Bob Snow, developer of Church Street Station in Orlando, Florida, to develop a major retail project. Snow's initial plan was an eight-block shopping and gambling mall. That idea vanished, however, when the city failed to invoke eminent domain to obtain the land. Snow, with millions of dollars of his personal wealth and millions more in redevelopment funds, then proposed a single facility, Main Street Station, an emporium devoted mainly to entertainment and dining, with gaming an afterthought. Backed by the city, the project was expected to upgrade an area of deterioration and blight.

Although ten downtown casinos filed an unsuccessful lawsuit in 1990, protesting at the spending of millions of redevelopment dollars to create competition for them, Snow opened Main Street Station in 1991, a turn-of-the-century-style establishment that provided an upscale dining and entertainment experience. It featured an expensive antique collection, spectacular stained glass ceilings, doors and brass grill works from nineteenth-century banks and other historic buildings, and an 1890s snooker table from Windsor Castle. With its location in a rundown area more than a block from Fremont Street, lack of proper marketing of the place as a gambling facility, and food costs more expensive than bargain-hunting locals and tourists wanted to pay, Main Street Station drowned in red ink only ten months after opening.

Another city redevelopment fiasco, not related to tourism, ensued when the city cut a deal with Japanese developer Masao Nangaku to build Minami Tower, a skyscraper office building to be located across from the Federal Courthouse. The city was attempting to re-energize the downtown professional business core and add to its economic base. Nangaku walked away from the Tower project in 1991, leaving a huge hole in the ground that had absorbed millions of the city's redevelopment dollars. Six years later, the city had to spend $300,000 to remove contaminated dirt used to fill the gaping hole for what was going to be the state's tallest building. The city later donated the land to the federal government to construct a $97-million, seven-story courthouse.

The Minami and Main Street Station fiascoes led to a great deal of media criticism and general public skepticism regarding the downtown redevelopment process. An art project that put neon colored tubes shaped like Lego toys on the marble façade of City Hall brought even more public outcry, as did a reflecting pond portion of the project that never worked, adding to the view of downtown redevelopment as a series of failures costing taxpayers millions in business subsidies. In this sense, the city of Las Vegas resembles many other downtowns elsewhere in the nation.

Despite Main Street Station's demise, city political and business leaders knew they had to match the spectacular tourist environment flourishing on the Strip to attract gamblers and other tourists, so they responded next by attempting to duplicate the Strip's themed architainment attractions. In 1994, a consortium of ten casinos joined with the city to construct the Fremont Street Experience, a $70-million sound-and-light show canopy that covered four city blocks of Fremont Street in the heart of Glitter Gulch; $30 million for the project came from public funds and the city pledged to build a parking garage adjacent to the project at a cost of another $23 million. The city also pledged $1 million a year for upkeep and maintenance from its parks-and-recreation budget.

Problems arose almost immediately for the city in the construction of the parking garage. The canopy itself did not require extensive renovations of property, although the famous Vegas Vic sign had to be modified, but the city had no vacant land downtown. After repeated attempts to negotiate land sales, the city exercised its power of eminent domain to condemn a 7,000-square-foot plot containing the typical downtown tableau of bail-bond, pawnshop, and tee-shirt businesses. Several private owners of the land sued, but the city went ahead with construction. By 1997, a 1,500-space, $23-million parking garage designed to provide adequate visitor parking was completed at the far end of the sound-and-light show canopy.

A Clark County judge subsequently ruled that the manner in which the city seized the property violated numerous state and federal statutes. Others complained that the public had already subsidized the privately-owned development and that the city engaged in poor planning. The city's use of eminent domain to support a private-sector project also was disputed, and may become a critical test of its future prospects, as it has used the power of eminent domain 49 times in its nine-year history, but cannot afford the lawsuits to settle the contested claims. Critics of the practice also say that it unfairly favors large casino operators over small businesses and represents a gigantic subsidy of public funds for Glitter Gulch casinos. At the same time, defenders claim that it has restored somewhat the tax base in downtown Las Vegas and has kept other businesses there. A proposed second phase of the Fremont Street Experience was approved by the city council in 1998. The $100-million "Neonopolis @ Fremont Street Experience" will be a 254,000-square-foot retail and entertainment center.

In 1995 a group of citizens filed a suit with the American Civil Liberties Union, claiming that the privately controlled downtown mall violated the constitution by restricting free speech. The casino consortium has broad authority to control activities along the pedestrian mall and under a city ordinance "picketing, rallying, proselytizing, distributing handbills and soliciting donations are all banned unless otherwise permitted by casinos" (Zapler 1998a). According to the consortium's attorneys, however, the pedestrian mall is not a public space, but a commercial and entertainment complex, though this seems to contradict comments by the city's mayor, who has called the mall a "town square" (Zapler 1998a). Thus, while some Las Vegans extol the use of eminent domain and public subsidization of business to improve downtown, others see it as yet another example of local government ignoring the rights of the public in the pursuit of economic revitalization. Nonetheless, in 1998 construction was underway on several other major downtown projects, including a $131-million Regional Justice Center, approved by voters in a September 1996 bond issue, a $78-million County Jail expansion, a $97-million Federal Court House, the 13-story $57-million futuristic Sun Plaza Building, and a $16.5-million Clark Street Associates' office complex. Regardless, the new projects will proceed within the environment of a new political culture, with increasing scrutiny by local resident groups and, therefore, giving an increasing complexity to local public affairs.

## Environmental Concerns

### Nuclear and Chemical Waste

Environmental issues also have played a significant role in Las Vegas' history, pre-dating the period of rapid development. In 1989, the endangered desert tortoise halted development in the valley and delayed the massive Summerlin project for more than a year. More prominent are concerns surrounding the former atomic bomb test site, located 65 miles northwest of Las Vegas in a high desert area approximately the size of Rhode Island. Above-ground testing was conducted in the 1950s and 1960s, followed by underground testing, until a 1992 moratorium halted all testing. Prevailing winds in the area usually blow from west-to-east and lawsuits charging ill effects of radioactive contamination have been filed from areas located downwind, especially in southern Utah.

After testing activity ceased, Congress proposed converting a part of the test site at Yucca Mountain into a national repository for the growing store of nuclear waste. Many area residents were outraged at the prospect of becoming the nation's nuclear waste-dump site while others in the construction industry, who would build the project, as well as several labor unions, supported the nuclear repository. Among many southern Nevadans' fears is the specter of nuclear waste being routed through the community, as major transport highways intersect in its midst at the notorious spaghetti bowl. Tourism officials also fear the negative impact of a nuclear accident on the area's leading industry. With strong lobbying by the Nevada congressional delegation, the governor, and state legislature, Nevadans have thus far been able to stall the federal government's plans for Yucca Mountain, but the issue is not yet settled.

One outcome of the Yucca Mountain controversy was the growth of activist environmental organizations in the region. One such organization, Citizen Alert, has held entertainment fundraising events to fight Congressional plans for the high-level nuclear-waste dump. One of these combined "No-Nukes" rock music and "Honor the Earth" tours while the governor, county commissioners, and the Las Vegas mayor proclaimed "Nevada is not a Wasteland" Day. The high-profile event brought national attention to the anti-nuclear/environmental cause in the region, as have numerous other such functions featuring celebrity participants.

A second long-standing environmental problem is the legacy of magnesium- and titanium-processing chemical plants that were built during World War II in Henderson, located at the southeast end of the valley. Ground water has been contaminated and, for decades, a phenomenon known as the "Henderson Cloud" consisting of a noxious white haze that hung over the lower part of the valley, appeared on windless summer days. The Titanium Metals Corporation of America, or TIMET, which stored liquid acid in 19 open evaporation ponds in violation of the 1971 Federal Clean Air Act, was identified as the major culprit. Other companies implicated in the creation of the air-pollution hazard were the Kerr-McGee Chemical Corporation and the Montrose Chemical Company, which also operated plants in Henderson. During the 1980s, Green Valley builders brought suit against the chemical companies, who had previously been disciplined only with light fines (see chapter 5). Today, the open-air tanks are gone and pollution controls are now more strictly enforced, although several chemical plants still remain in operation.

## Air Quality

Nuclear issues and chemical contamination from the past, however, are not the only concerns. Rapid development and metropolitan-scale automobile commuting have produced additional problems with air quality. People who moved to Las Vegas for the wide open spaces and minimal regulations now live in a valley with serious air quality problems and increasing restrictions. The Las Vegas Valley sits in a bowl, surrounded by mountains on three sides, and ozone levels have risen in recent years.

Ozone is a summertime pollutant produced when the sun reacts with organic gases such as hydrocarbons and nitrogen oxides. Vehicle emissions from cars and other vehicles driven by more than 1.25 million residents and 30 million annual visitors are a major source of the ozone problem. According to National Air Quality Standards, the Las Vegas metropolitan region is in "non-attainment" and quickly approaching "serious non-attainment" for ozone levels. On the other hand, Las Vegas air quality has improved in terms of levels of carbon monoxide and visible particulates (blowing dust). As more of the desert is paved, particulates decrease, except around construction sites, so the Air Pollution Control District has begun fining developers and gravel-pit owners for noncompliance at building sites. The brown haze that can cover the valley in the winter months, however, continues to concern both residents and health officials. As a result, innovations such as bicycle lanes, which frustrated Las Vegas drivers often use as turn lanes, expensive timing systems for traffic signals, oxygenated gasoline, and tougher restrictions on construction sites have become a part of Las Vegas life.

Environmentalists identify the operation of diesel machinery as another major threat to air quality as diesel engines, unregulated by government, are notorious sources of pollution. In addition to the diesel machinery used for new home construction, idling trucks, and construction equipment, there are the massive fleet of Clark County school buses and McCarran International Airport's diesel ground equipment, as well as unregulated air emissions from jet fuel.

At present, the Las Vegas Valley has the fifth worst air quality in the nation, on a par with New York City, and its non-attainment profile resembles that of Los Angeles due to the high level of both particulates and ozone. The community is battling to avoid federal sanctions that would cost it millions of dollars for highway construction and other federal funds, by working to meet air-quality standards despite rapid growth.

Pollution issues have not yet reached the critical mass of public concern that would pose a challenge to the current political agenda, yet neither the tourist industry nor the housing industry can neglect them much longer, as they threaten the city's quality of life. The scary potential exists that tourists might refuse to come to Las Vegas to see dirty skies and suffer through bad traffic, despite their long historical tolerance of sitting for hours in smoke filled casinos. Even more troubling to Las Vegas' business interests than air quality, however, are declining water quality and water resources, which also have become contentious political issues.

## Water Issues

Water is a major political issue in the southwest because it is an arid, desert region. The main water source for Arizona, Nevada, and southern California comes from the Colorado River via Lake Mead, the nation's largest water reservoir, with an estimated 9.2-trillion-gallon capacity, created by the building of the Hoover Dam. This mega-storage function maximizes the resources of the river for the entire region, yet growth in the area is projected to outstrip water allocations. By a long-standing agreement, made in the 1930s when there were far fewer residents there, several western states have rights to a fixed percentage of water volume from the system. Nevada is approaching its limit, so future development of the Las Vegas Valley depends very much on political negotiations among the network of upper and lower basin states serviced by the Colorado River and the ability to secure alternative water sources.

The quality of existing water is another immediate concern. For years Las Vegas' drinking water consistently tested as one of the safest in the nation. However, Colorado River water is hard and many residents don't like the taste of naturally occurring minerals or of chemicals added for purification. New residents often install water softeners, most containing salt, to lessen the impact of the mineral content in the form of soap scum and lime build-up in sinks, showers, toilets, and washing machines. They also install drinking-water filtration systems in their homes and buy gallons of bottled water, refilling them at water filtration stations located throughout the valley.

Several other factors are adversely affecting the Las Vegas Valley's water profile, including extensive pesticide and fertilizer usage; the decline of natural wetlands; and treated effluent from the local municipalities' sewage systems that flow into Lake Mead. Many Las Vegans maintain large green lawns in tribute to their former homesteads in less arid parts of the country. In the desert southwest these lawns can remain green all year round, but they are often heavily fertilized. Also, the threat of insect infestation has created a burgeoning pest-control industry. The massive infusion of pesticides and fertilizers, however, is contaminating the ground water that flows into Lake Mead at the lower end of the valley and threatening the drinking-water supply.

For example, in 1987, diazanon, "a federally approved cockroach killer," and, in 1992, the insecticide malathion, were found in some washes – washes are natural channels, dry most of the time, that divert rain and flood water to Lake Mead (Rogers 1997a). These and other pesticide problems, plus pressures created by population growth, forced Las Vegas to upgrade its sewage-treatment plant in 1992 and, according to the environmental manager for the plant, there have been no problems with insecticide contamination since. However, although three sewage-treatment facilities (Clark County, Las Vegas and North Las Vegas, and Henderson) together process more than 140 million gallons a day, the capacity of the system remains strained due to increased population growth. As a result, the system has undergone extensive upgrades, including $105 million on the county plant in 1996, $54 million to upgrade the filtration system at the city of Las Vegas plant in 1994, and a newly constructed treatment plant in Henderson, also in 1994.

All treated water and ground-water run-off in the valley go into Lake Mead, which is perceived as a serious problem by environmentalists, since Las Vegas' water is obtained directly from the lake. In the past, a vast region of wetlands adjacent to the lake, consisting of reeds and cattails, helped filter much of the pollution out of the run-off. In recent years, however, these wetlands have been depleted by development, resulting in contaminated ground water. Recent studies of streams feeding into Lake Mead have discovered other threats as well. Carp obtained from remaining wetlands, for example, were found to be contaminated by DDT and PCBs, although these have been banned for more than twenty years in the region. In 1990, the county approved a $13.3-million bond issue to restore 2,000 acres of wetlands in an attempt to re-create this vital natural barrier to biological and chemical contaminants.

Despite these significant measures, the quality of water in the region remains a matter of concern. According to a local biologist: "The valley's pollution woes won't be solved until controls are put on pesticides and toxic wastes discharged into the sewer and cleanup of contaminated ground water layers is finished" (Rogers 1997a). Contaminated ground water is perhaps the major threat to water quality as "Lake Mead faces an onslaught of contaminants washing off parking lots, golf courses, lawns, construction sites and a shallow aquifer formed underneath the Las Vegas Valley, as it continues to grow" (Manning 1998). The problem also extends outside of the Las Vegas Valley, as Nevada overall has 56 non-point sources (areas which receive water from Lake Mead but are located some distance away), neighboring California 560, Idaho 960, and Oregon 870, raising the specter of water contamination in these other areas as well.

The industrial past of suburban Henderson is also adversely affecting the area's water quality. For the first time, in 1997, perchlorate, a rocket-fuel ingredient, was discovered in water flowing into Lake Mead. Major rocket-fuel manufacturing was done at Pepcon from 1958 to 1988, when the plant was destroyed by a series of deadly explosions. Also, the Kerr-McGee plant is phasing out the manufacture of ammonium perchlorate in its Basic Magnesium Inc. (BMI) complex on Clark County land near Henderson. However, the plant lies upstream from the Las Vegas wash, a major run-off channel that feeds into Lake Mead only six miles from the drinking-water intakes. When perchlorate was detected at high levels in wells at the plant site, a Kerr-McGee company spokesman told a newspaper reporter that: "He was not surprised that perchlorate was detected in ground water beneath the plant because the plant has been in operation for about 50 years, the first 25 years of which was a period of unregulated disposal practices" (Rogers 1997b). There are presently no federal standards regarding acceptable levels of perchlorate in water, but California has temporarily set 18 parts per billion as the level to trigger remedial action, while water samples in the Las Vegas wash registered perchlorate levels as high as 1,680 parts per billion.

The perchlorate problem is only one aspect of the more general threat posed by contaminated ground water around the chemical plants as toxic clean-up sites are numerous and remain relatively neglected, despite the availability of federal funding for clean-up. The state has tried to pressure companies to deal with this issue, but legal sanctions are weak. The quality of Lake Mead water thus remains a concern not only for Las Vegas but for other contiguous states as well, as growth in the region continues unabated.

## Disappearing Open Space

Both the quantity and quality of open space in communities in the Las Vegas Valley vary from one area to another. The master-planned communities have landscaped roads and parks, with Summerlin in particular allocating at least 20 per cent of its 22,000 acres to open space. In many other areas, however, open public space is disappearing under the impact of rapid regional growth, as development encroaches upon the mountains, Lake Mead, and desert washes. Furthermore, although the Las Vegas Valley has 148 parks, many older communities are underserved. According to a local activist: "The core of Las Vegas is being developed to such an extent that little space is available for parks or open space" (Zapler 1997d). The national average of open space for every 1,000 residents is 4 to 6 acres, but in Clark County, the figure is between 1.9 and 5.7 acres, the amount varying, "depending on whether land designated as open space – but which has not been converted into parks – is included in the calculations" (Zapler 1997d). Thus, the Las Vegas region remains below the national norm for open spaces.

As parks are an important component of the quality of life, citizens have lobbied to increase park funding and resources for park acquisition, but have been forced to seek financing from public bonds. Both government budgets and the use of bonds to fund public projects, however, are limited severely by the public's reluctance to incur debt and the prevailing conservative ideology of local government. In May 1993, for example, Clark County residents voted down a bond measure that would have provided $125 million for new parks and would have cost the average homeowner $45 annually. In contrast, however, Henderson voters approved parks-bond issues in 1993 and again in 1997. The issue is also being addressed in Las Vegas, which in 1997 passed a zoning code requiring that 15 percent of the acreage in the city's new development tracts be allocated for open space. At that time the city had $6 million worth of parks projects under construction in the northwest sector alone.

The construction of the beltway, a 52-mile highway that will encircle most of the valley, provides an opportunity for additional open space and recreational areas – though almost exclusively servicing middle-class suburban residents. The county plans to spend $10 million to construct a bicycle and walking trail alongside the entire loop. The first four-mile stretch of trail was completed in 1998, but the trail system will probably not be finished until work on the beltway is completed in 2003. Eight miles of the beltway will intersect or abut upscale Summerlin and the developer has "dedicated space and paid for design work for a well-landscaped trail system along that leg" (Zapler 1998c).

Under pressure from local residents, in 1998 the Southern Nevada Strategic Planning Authority agreed to set a parks standard of 2.5 acres per 1,000 residents. Two valley communities already meet or exceed the standard, Henderson with 2.5 acres of parks per 1,000, and the growth-controlled Boulder City with 4.75 acres (McKinnon

1998d). When considering park acreage in the valley, nearby recreational areas such as Red Rock Canyon, Lake Mead, and Mount Charleston are not included, yet each offers amenities not found in other cities that might offer more parks. However, valley growth is having an impact on these areas as well. More than 1.2 million people visited Red Rock Canyon National Conservation Area in 1997 and the 195,000-acre scenic area is rapidly becoming an urban park, though the BLM has attempted to lessen the effects of human intrusion: "Trails are more clearly marked, mountain bikes and horses are restricted from popular hiking areas and every so often, when the parking lots are full and traffic is heavy, rangers simply close the gates to the loop for a few hours" (McKinnon 1998e). A $5-per-vehicle or $20 season pass was instituted in late 1997 but the fee has not discouraged visitors, though it has helped cut down on vandalism.

## The Need for Regional Cooperation

Given the complex and interrelated nature of the challenges that the area must meet, it is clear that the Las Vegas Valley is hampered in many ways by the excessive fragmentation of a large county bureaucracy and four municipal governments. One way to deal with this problem, employed in many metropolitan regions around the country, is to consolidate them into one governmental entity. The first efforts towards consolidation in the Las Vegas Valley since the 1946 attempt by the city to annex the Strip came in 1973 when the Las Vegas and Clark County Police Departments were merged. In 1975, the state legislature expanded the city of Las Vegas to include the Strip and most developed areas, doubling the size of the city. The county commission then moved its offices to City Hall, but the next year the Supreme Court ruled the consolidation law unconstitutional. In 1978, city voters again approved consolidation, but county voters rejected it. In 1985, after years of hostile competition, the city and county signed a "Bury the Hatchet Agreement," a wide-ranging accord covering issues as diverse as sewage treatment, fire protection, and annexation. Since then, the community also has implemented a Regional Flood Control District and a Regional Transportation Commission for public transit. Most other municipal service agencies, however, remain fragmented. One of the few victories for area-wide service occurred in education when Clark County created a unified school district, though that involved action by the state legislature. The ninth largest District in the nation, the Clark County School District is now accused by some, however, of being too large and unresponsive to community needs and a move is underway to break it up. Henderson attempted to get the 1997 legislature to authorize residents to petition the state to form new school districts. Part of the problem in rapidly growing Henderson is that the school district doesn't build schools fast enough, even if the land is available: "Over the years we have requested that developers donate properties for the sole purpose of putting in elementary and junior high schools. But even though we have a good inventory of land, there is no guarantee from the school district when and if the properties will be used to build schools," said the city manager (Robiglio 1997).

Consolidation, or the actual merging of regional government, however, is not the only alternative and grows increasingly unlikely as the region expands. Much like other metropolitan areas in the country, no entity wants to lose its individual economic or power base in a fragmented region. A more practical alternative would be to establish comprehensive regional coordination in the area, given that water and air quality, chemical pollution, and the development of parks and other open space are all regional, county-wide concerns. In fact, due to the proximity of Las Vegas' businesses and residential areas to Lake Mead, threats they pose to water quality have an impact in at least three states, as we have seen. Thus far, however, regional cooperation has been limited, with competition between the city of Las Vegas and the county in particular a major factor in the failure to establish the kind of regional environmental controls that are characteristic of the Los Angeles area. This feature is one of the contradictions that have emerged with normalization and growth. The national anti-tax sentiment reflected in the local political culture is also a barrier to the public funding of amenities, like parks, that improve the quality of life (see next chapter). Although bond measures are theoretically a way out of government's fiscal dilemmas, there is increasing resistance to their passage from the growing number of permanent residents who perceive the mounting indebtedness as a threat. In short, these pressures fuel competition, not regional cooperation, and remain a contributor to the contradictions of the normalization process fueling contentious local politics.

Structural characteristics also strain relations among the various communities within the region. According to John Schlegel, director of advanced planning for Clark County, the building of Green Valley, away from the center of Henderson, and Summerlin, miles from the center of Las Vegas, have created examples of community development that contrast markedly with older areas (Schlegel 1998). These master-planned communities, with covenants, restrictions, and assessments for maintenance, have raised expectations everywhere in the region about the standards of neighborhood life by instituting architectural controls on housing, dedicating open land for parks or fee-based golf courses, having laws against graffiti and the neglect of lawns, and having aesthetically-pleasing landscaped common areas within their developments. The problem is that, by contrast, not all the new developments have these amenities. Outside the master-planned communities, many residential areas have no controls and no community-maintained landscaping. Residents in older neighborhoods often must contend with neighbors who pile junk on their lawns and live on streets that are less than aesthetically pleasing. As residents of more established neighborhoods watch the new master-planned developments receive new public-school buildings and libraries, along with community-controlled landscaping, they have created strong political pressures on elected officials to deal with resource inequalities. To date, however, these and other conflicts have resulted in far less regional and inter-community cooperation than is needed to foster better planning for future growth (see next chapter). The uneven development, characteristic of growth elsewhere as well as in Las Vegas, creates inequities that persist in fueling regional political conflicts.

In short, the normalization process, while producing a new political culture that plays off residents against business needs, also contains contradictory tendencies produced by the organization of separate political interests, conflicts over resources, factions of capital, fragmentation of social bases and political jurisdictions, and a fundamental clash between the increasing, multi-dimensional needs of local residents and a public ideology that limits local government to a weak role.

# 9 Las Vegas: An All-American Metropolis

We have argued throughout this book that, contrary to its reputation as the sinful "Other" in an otherwise moral society, Las Vegas is becoming a typical American metropolitan region in many ways. Our argument rests in part on an analysis of the changes the area itself has undergone during a prolonged period of rapid population growth. Discussed in previous chapters, these changes include the historical development of a corporate economic base, the physical construction of residential communities, the social construction of neighborhood life, the emergence of a citizen-involved local politics concerned with contentious quality-of-life issues, and the appearance of public amenities such as schools, libraries, art, and recreational programs. Profound changes over the last several decades also include, however, increasing social inequalities among local residents due to uneven development, exacerbated by a lack of effective local government and a public ideology resistant to government programs. A number of infrastructure and quality-of-life issues arising from rapid regional growth are also straining the ability of local government to deal with these problems in the future. In short, the normalization process fueled by the presence of large numbers of permanent residents also contains contradictions and dilemmas that could plague the region in the future.

Our other, equally significant, claim is that the rest of the nation has changed, and continues to change, in ways that make it more like Las Vegas. In this sense, Las Vegas is a harbinger of sorts, albeit sometimes in exaggerated form, of major transformations in contemporary urban economies, especially for cities struggling with economic revitalization after a period of deindustrialization. Several of these trends are best described in terms of the new urban-sociology approach presented in chapter 1. First, Las Vegas, like other metropolitan areas, is a region, not a city. Development is spread out and encompasses multi-centers, constituting a new form of settlement space (Gottdiener 1994b). Under these conditions of development there is no unified growth machine in Las Vegas that is responsible for development. Although the pursuit of growth is very much on the minds of elites, they are divided among themselves into different factions that compete with one another. As we have seen, development of the region occurred precisely because business interests used the political leverage of competing jurisdictions, especially between the city and the county, to produce several centers or growth poles. The main ones are downtown, or Glitter Gulch, and the Strip, and we have seen how their competition has affected the patterns of development. Thus, fragmentation and multi-centered growth characterize, the land-use pattern in Las Vegas. It is produced by competition for profit and power among factions of capital and government rather than a unified interest of elites, as suggested by more simplistic accounts of urban growth (see Logan and Molotch 1988). This same pattern of multi-centered regional development and political fragmentation increasingly characterizes urban areas elsewhere.

Secondly, metropolitan development in Las Vegas, as elsewhere, is dominated by the ebb and flow of money in real estate. This investment in the "second circuit of capital," which often assumes a speculative or venture-capital form, constitutes the leading edge of growth because it produces changes on the ground. Las Vegas' history has been characterized by a succession of individual boom and bust cycles, where risk-takers built casinos only to see them go bankrupt, with new owners arriving and investing again. Similar turnover in commercial land was also common. The true success of Las Vegas thus involved two separate social constructions. First, it became a tourist mecca, a national pleasure zone, based on legalized gambling, because of the sheer will of individual risk-takers prompted by the state of Nevada's free-wheeling legal structure. Secondly, the Las Vegas region became a prime housing market because of the vision of a few developers who took advantage of opportunities created by a combination of rapid population growth and cheap land. Most important for our argument, in both cases, is that investment in real estate was prompted and channeled by actors who remained, until passage of the Corporate Gaming Act of 1969, *outside* the spotlight of mainstream American business – Teamsters Union funds, small regional banks, mobsters from the Midwest and East Coast, small-time entrepreneurs moving to the West after World War II, and powerful politicians who skillfully maneuvered in Washington to obtain billions of federal dollars for the region.

The third, and most disturbing, trend in Las Vegas, as well as across the nation, concerns the contradictions and problems arising from uneven regional development. While many Las Vegans enjoy an enviable quality of life, including those who are retired and living on fixed incomes, there is cause for worry because of the many social and environmental problems in the area. Some of these issues are related to a heavy reliance on a gambling economy, such as the predominance of low-paying dead-end jobs, but others are the products of rapid growth, such as the overcrowding of schools, the class segregation of housing, poverty and homelessness, the environmental issues of air, water and land quality, the limitations of present government structures, and the increasing indebtedness required to meet the immense public costs of regional development.

Other important national trends here include the significant, even crucial, role of tourism for redeveloping urban economies, as well as the spread of casinos and other forms of gambling across the country. Older cities, such as New York, Baltimore, Detroit, and New Orleans, have renovated sections of their downtowns in an attempt to attract tourism and many of them feature nostalgic reconstructions of the sort first pioneered in Las Vegas' themed environments (Gottdiener 1997). In a sense, in fact, we can now speak of the *Las Vegasization* of city downtowns in the same way that we observe the spread of *McDonaldization* and theming across the American landscape.

Las Vegas-style reliance on gambling is not restricted to cities alone. Forty-eight states in the country now allow some form of legal wagering, with Utah and Hawaii the only remaining holdouts. Indian gambling enterprises are prospering everywhere. For example, in California Indian casinos alone attracted an estimated 1.6 million visitors in 1997, who spent approximately $1.4 billion (Berns 1998a). Forms of Lotto, a game of chance with very slim odds of winning, and Bingo are used by state governments across the nation to raise money. In these and other examples, regions reeling under the economic impact of deindustrialization have followed Las Vegas' lead and turned to legalized forms of gambling as a form of economic activity and job creation.

In their efforts to attract tourist dollars, municipal and state governments also are spending millions of marketing dollars on Las Vegas-style hype and boosterism to advertise themselves. Las Vegas hired the J. Walter Thompson advertising agency of Madison Avenue fame way back in 1945 to help shape its image in attracting tourists (Hess 1993). Now this sort of city self-promotion has become the national norm. Las Vegas may be viewed, in this sense, as the vanguard of an emerging postmodern socio-spatial culture where image, if not everything, certainly occupies an increasingly promising place. However one evaluates recent trends, and they do have a troubling side, one thing seems clear: that Las Vegas can no longer be dismissed as an aberration or "a loose thread in the American fabric" (Findlay 1990: 1). In many ways, and especially since the days of Venturi et al., people in the US have indeed been "learning from Las Vegas."

## The Metropolitan Future

The Las Vegas Valley continues to be the nation's fastest growing region, with Clark County's population increasing a phenomenal 6.8% in the period from July 1, 1996, to June 30, 1997 alone, gaining 76,260 new residents. Even more impressively, between 1990 and 1996 Henderson was the fastest growing American city, with a population of more than 100,000, increasing a whopping 88.4%, with the city of Las Vegas also among the top ten in the country with a 46% growth rate during the same period (Bowers 1998). Presently the area is a national leader in new-job creation, in business relocation, in new-home construction, in individual retirement relocation, and it remains, of course, a premier tourist destination. Such phenomenal growth over the last four decades, however, also presents a number of formidable challenges that must be met if the region is to continue to prosper. These include a range of issues that may be referred to collectively as growing pains, but which are amplified by several factors unique to the Las Vegas area, including its heavy reliance on tourism, its location in the middle of an arid desert, its fragile civic culture, and, most crucially, its weak and fragmented governmental structures.

## The Limits of Weak Government

A lively and multi-faceted debate is presently being conducted in urban policy circles, both within and outside of academia. Despite the complex nature of the issues and arguments in dispute, they tend to cluster around two general ideological poles. The first approach favors an interventionist public sector that supports state and local projects to improve business infrastructure and community quality of life and supports the public transfer of wealth to assuage uneven development. The second general view advocates a more *laissez-faire* approach, favoring minimal intervention in community affairs, primarily in the form of assistance to support business and economic development, with limited local regulation of business and the development process, along with cuts in public welfare spending. Nationally, these two alternatives have traditionally been identified with the Democratic and Republican parties respectively, but, as we have seen, this distinction has never been valid in Nevada politics, which has been dominated by Democrats who operate as anti-government fiscal conservatives, even while actively seeking all sorts of federal funding.

Our analysis of the effects of explosive growth in the Las Vegas

Valley strongly suggests an increasingly important role for state and local government in helping secure the future of the region. Las Vegas residents, however, historically have maintained a strong allegiance to what they term "Western-style individualism," which manifests itself politically as support for part-time and decentralized *laissez-faire* governmental structures.

Proponents of this view claim that the various governmental entities in the region, most of them headed by part-time elected officials, have done an admirable job, to date, of keeping pace with the area's incredible growth. They point especially to the area's regional flood-control and transportation accomplishments, where several major projects have been completed ahead of time with additional funding for future projects already in place, as well as the school and library districts. Additionally, the argument is put forth that part-time officials bring valuable skills from the private sector, reflecting many voters' aversion to "professional politicians."

Our analysis suggests, however, that the region has become too large, and its problems too complex, for part-time officials and weak fragmented government to be effective in dealing with the multiple problems created by such explosive growth. Both the city and county governments are adequately staffed with well-trained professionals, including a city and a county manager, each of whom earns a six-figure income, but these persons are advisory to the politicians, who have at times been unwilling to push for planning recommendations they receive from their more informed professional staffs. Furthermore, there are few teeth in government regulations to channel or rationalize private-sector growth even when development plans are approved.

Another criticism is that since most part-time elected officials also work in the private sector while performing their public duties, a conflict of interest is created. For example, in 1997 several county commissioners, including the Chair, Yvonne Atkinson Gates, were investigated by the State Ethics Commission. Gates was found guilty of violations for approaching casinos about possible leases for a frozen-daiquiri business. In the official report the Chair of the ethics committee told Gates: "The line between your public persona and your private interest is blurred. I think you knew that the position you occupy would give you access, and you used it" (S. Greene 1998). The ethics ruling carried only a reprimand, however, with neither fines nor a recommendation that Gates be removed from the commission. Six months later, Gates and fellow-commissioner Lance Malone were also found guilty of violating state ethics laws for awarding concessions at McCarran Airport to friends, family, and business associates (see chapter 8).

One local governmental entity, the Las Vegas city council, may be moving towards becoming full-time, in October 1998 appointing a committee to study whether their positions should be made full-time, as well as considering if two additional council seats should be created. The committee's recommendation could be presented to voters in a referendum in May 1999. The extensive use of referenda, however, has at times been an indicator of abrogation of leadership on the part of elected officials afraid of advocating policies that might be opposed by powerful local business interests or angry voters, another sign of weak government.

Even more potentially troublesome than the persistence of part-time government in an area the size of the Las Vegas Valley is the problem of fragmented government. As Moehring (1989) points out, politically and administratively Las Vegas is not one city but five, as different services throughout the valley are under the jurisdiction of Las Vegas, North Las Vegas, Henderson, Boulder City, and Clark County. Historically, as Moehring also notes, this fragmentation resulted from Las Vegas' inability to annex its suburbs, largely because the major Strip resorts successfully "repulsed all city attempts to tax their games and annex their property" (1989: 540). One result is the costly duplication of services at a time when sheer increase in population size presents an enormous strain. As early as 1968, urban consultants warned the region about this problem, and although some consolidation has taken place since that time, fragmentation continues to be the norm.

Planning consultants also deplored the unevenness of services, emphasizing how facilities and equipment varied in quality from one jurisdiction to the next, a problem exacerbated since 1968 with the construction of upscale enclaves such as Spring Valley, Green Valley, and Summerlin. A more recent study by the Urban Institute also emphasized the need for more efficient regional planning, and local officials set up the Southern Nevada Strategic Planning Authority, but they failed to grant the panel the power to override the city councils and county commission. The authority did, however, draft a plan for managing the effects of growth in Clark County over the next few years, putting together for the first time in a single document an outline of the issues the region's governmental agencies need to address (McKinnon 1998h).

The region's fragmented governmental structure also places it at a disadvantage in state politics, making it difficult for southern Nevada to put forth unified positions on important issues, as city and county governments continually squabble among themselves (Bowers 1998). Given the state of Nevada's historically antagonistic North–South split, this is indeed a problem as the Las Vegas area increasingly dwarfs the rest of the state in population size and generation of revenue.

In many respects the pattern of metropolitanization in the Las Vegas region is similar to that experienced by other large cities. Las Vegas' inner-city areas decline while its suburban areas boom and a greater diversity of people increases the difficulty of reaching political consensus. Growth of an active civic culture does not necessarily lead to a unified public voice. In two important aspects, however, Las Vegas is different. First, since the end of the Cold War, its economy has been almost completely dependent on tourism, especially legal gambling. Thus, without a greater push for increased economic diversification, the area will remain precariously reliant on national trends beyond its control.

Secondly, and perhaps even more importantly, despite the enormous growth in the number of permanent residents, Las Vegas is hampered by an outdated political culture that prevents it from dealing effectively with its many problems. As numerous observers have pointed out, the region's self-described Western-style individualism has always been something of a hypocritical myth, as Nevada in general and Las Vegas in particular have always been highly dependent on federal support, even while eschewing all forms of "big government." Regardless of its applicability in the past, today, in a town where the phrase "you get what you pay for" might be an appropriate municipal motto, the political legacy of part-time, fragmented government is perhaps better described by the phrase, "penny-wise, pound foolish." Simply put, anyone seriously concerned with controlling growth and the attendant social problems it creates or exacerbates must recognize that dealing with these issues costs money and requires more efficient regional coordination by the public sector.

Here again, the structure of state government in Nevada also poses significant barriers to dealing constructively with issues raised by Clark County's explosive growth. Although the state constitution declares that Nevada is a "home rule" state, the legislation required to allow city and county governments to exercise home rule was never passed by the state legislature, and state spending caps on local governments severely limit home rule (Schmidt and McGinnis 1998). Also, passage in 1996 of a "supermajority amendment" to the state constitution, requiring that tax increases be passed by a two thirds majority in both houses of the state legislature, makes it possible for lawmakers from Reno and the rural areas of the state to block any tax increases, even if Clark County officials come to recognize a need for them (Bowers 1998).

Many residents who are unwilling to bear the costs of more efficient government themselves, seek a solution in raising gambling taxes. Nevada currently has the lowest-gross-revenue gaming tax in the nation at 6.25%, compared with rates ranging from 9.25% to 20% in other states (Bowers 1998). The casino industry, however, argues that it already pays more than 40% of taxes in Nevada and, given its power as the state's largest industry and as a major source of campaign contributions, there is little support among state and local politicians for increasing gambling taxes.

Another possible source of revenue for dealing with growth-related issues in the valley is impact fees, paid by developers. Based on the idea that growth should pay for itself, impact fees require builders to help pay for roads, sewers, drainage projects, and water lines necessary for development (Parker 1997). Although impact-fees legislation was passed by the Nevada legislature in 1989, Reno is the only municipality to require them. In southern Nevada, builders instead pay approximately $5,000 in fees and permits per house. A proposal to implement impact fees, which would approximately double the price of fees for builders, failed to pass in 1993, largely due to an internal squabble between the city and county commissioners over including education expenses (Parker 1997). Here again, the region's fragmented governmental structure was a hindrance rather than a help in securing additional revenues to help pay for much-needed services.

## Growing Pains and Uneven Development

Given that the region's population is expected to continue to grow, one very basic question concerns where new residents and businesses will be located. The Las Vegas Valley sits in a bowl, with natural barriers to development to the west in the form of a federally-controlled mountain range, and to the east, the gigantic reservoir, Lake Mead. Basically then, there are only two directions the valley can grow, to the north and to the south along the Interstate Highway 15 corridor, and much of that arid desert land, like most of the state of Nevada, is owned by the federal government and can only be acquired through purchases or exchanges with the Bureau of Land Management (BLM). To the north, a commercial and industrial area is being developed at Apex, 17 miles away, and more than 40,000 acres of land near Moapa and Glendale, 45 miles northeast of Las Vegas, have been identified by the BLM as being available for exchange or sale. An additional 1,500 acres also is available closer in, at Indian Springs (McKinnon 1998f).

Additional opportunity for growth exists along Interstate Highway

15 south of the metropolitan area. Near Jean, less than 20 miles south, are 2,500 available acres of land, and further out, near the California border, an area of 6,000 acres has been obtained to build a freight-handling airport in the Ivanpah Valley that could create commercial development – and residential growth could follow. When McCarran Airport reaches full capacity of 60 million passengers a year, long-range planning includes the possibility that the proposed freight airport facility could be expanded to include passenger services.

Beyond the purely physical need for growing room are environmental concerns. Providing an adequate supply of water for residential and commercial use is of paramount importance for a booming desert metropolis like Las Vegas. An announcement in late 1997 by the Secretary of the Interior, Bruce Babbitt, that he will probably approve a plan by the state of Nevada to bank additional water from Lake Mead in Arizona's underground aquifers was greeted with a collective sigh of relief in Las Vegas because, if approved, it will allow the Las Vegas Valley to continue to grow until 2030 (Bowers 1998: 19–20). This, however, does not alter the fact that the region's principal ground-water aquifer is being reduced at an extremely high rate and, as critics such as Mike Davis (1995) rightly point out, the region's continued proliferation of grass lawns, golf courses, fountains, and mini-lakes is both environmentally and financially irresponsible. Similarly, with regard to air quality, although there has been significant progress in enforcing air-pollution-control regulations over the past two years, with fewer violations of national ambient air-quality standards (Schmidt 1998), much remains to be done in this area. Wind-blown dust due primarily to construction, and visible urban haze, mainly the result of automobile emissions, continue to be major issues that require a more active regional government.

No less important for an urban area growing as rapidly as the Las Vegas region is the need to provide the necessary infrastructural supports and services in the form of schools, roads, and fire and police protection. As we described earlier, the Clark County School District has done an admirable job to date, in meeting the Herculean task of providing schools for its burgeoning school-age population. The ninth largest district in the nation, Clark County operated 227 public schools with a 1998–9 enrollment of 203,777 (Clark County School District 1998), plus an additional 10,000 students enrolled in private schools (Metropolitan Research Association 1998). The school district's heavy reliance on bonds to finance new school construction could be a potential problem if current growth trends continue, although, in 1998, 65 percent of voters approved a bond issue that would provide $3.5 billion for school construction over the next decade. Some observers suggest that voter reluctance may grow stronger in the future, however, given the large influx of senior citizens who vote in disproportionately high numbers in local elections and who traditionally do not support school bonds.

One of the most common complaints voiced by residents in the Las Vegas area about their community is traffic congestion, a problem that directly affects the local quality of life. Local residents have seen their commuting times double, and in some cases even triple, in the past few years, and city and county officials are spending millions of dollars to expand and improve major thoroughfares, but their efforts are overwhelmed by the sheer increase in the volume of traffic. In addition, fragmentation makes it difficult to plan as several streets in the valley are at various locations controlled by the city, the county, or the state. There has been some coordination by these agencies on construction projects and Clark County now requires that no changes or digging be done on a street for five years after it is completed. However, the lack of sufficient regional coordination is characteristic of a city where planning by variance and yielding to developer interests have been at times more the rule than the exception. Consequently, despite public spending, the weakness of government to control growth remains a problem.

Another important area of infrastructural concern is the need to secure adequate police, fire, and emergency medical services. As with almost everything else in the Las Vegas area, each service is provided by a combination of county and various metropolitan agencies, making general assessments of these services difficult to compile. Regarding law enforcement, the three largest agencies, the Las Vegas Metropolitan Police Department, the Henderson Police Department, and the North Las Vegas Police Department, had a combined total of 1,791 officers plus 926 support-staff personnel to deal with a population of 1.25 million residents, and the more than 30 million annual visitors (Las Vegas Metropolitan Police Department Annual Report 1997; Henderson Police Department Annual Report 1997; North Las Vegas Police Department Annual Report 1997). The Las Vegas Valley is also served by five separate fire departments with approximately 1,300 firefighters, and by 300 emergency medical-service personnel. The exploding population in the valley has placed a significant strain on all these vital agencies, however, with fire department and emergency medical-service calls increasing by approximately 50 percent in the past five years (Shapiro 1998). With a fragmented government structure and without adequate funding, the quality of these vital public services will continue to be strained.

A final important quality-of-life issue is health care. The state of

Nevada as a whole ranks in the bottom one-third of the nation in regard to many health-care statistics, including access to primary care, public health spending, and per-capita Medicaid expenditures. While the data for Clark County are not quite as severe, they remain for the most part below the national average and are an area of major concern, especially for its less-affluent residents. Also, the record numbers of seniors moving to Las Vegas for their retirement years, along with the growing number of local retirees, has a tremendous potential to further strain health-care services and state Medicare funding when they are no longer relatively healthy or affluent. However, the community has yet to seriously confront these important issues. In sum, health care is an important area that needs to be more adequately addressed to improve the region's quality of life.

Problems associated with growing pains, formidable enough in themselves, are exacerbated when they have a disproportionate impact on certain segments of the population. As we discussed in chapter 5, the problem of uneven development is especially acute in the Las Vegas Valley, as the continued growth of upscale communities has resulted in an increasing concentration of poor and low-income minorities at the core of the urban area, especially in the cities of Las Vegas and North Las Vegas (Schmidt 1998). Schmidt has identified a number of factors contributing to uneven development including: the increasing median price of housing; private and public investment decisions by members of the real-estate investment and development industry; bank lending policies; the area's history of individual and institutional racism; and exclusionary zoning practices in some communities. Without more effective regional public-policy coordination and intervention, these trends, which have been in existence for decades, will result in an increasing segregation between the wealthy and poor citizens of the Las Vegas Valley.

## The Future of the Tourist-Based Economy

While projections into the next century see the Las Vegas area continuing to expand, a number of concerns have recently surfaced to challenge the region's extreme reliance on tourism. Las Vegas depends primarily on a single industry, with nearly one-third of the almost 700,000 workers in the valley employed directly by the casino industry. The area remains one of the nation's most popular tourist destinations, but Las Vegas Convention and Visitor Authority (LVCVA) statistics for 1997 indicate that visitor volume increased only a modest 2.8%, to about 30.5 million, not enough to compensate for the 6.3%

increase in room inventory that year. As Las Vegas' capacity grew from 99,000 rooms, at the end of 1996, to more than 105,000 with the opening of New York-New York and expansions at Harrah's, the Rio, and Caesars Palace, hotel and motel occupancy rates declined, with hotel occupancy down 3.1%, to 90.3%, and motel occupancy dropping 6.9 percentage points, to 68.8%. While other resort areas would love to have these year-round occupancy rates, as the US average was about 64% in 1997, the decline is cause for concern in Las Vegas, especially since an additional 20,000 rooms are scheduled to be added to the area's inventory within the next year or so due to the present mega-resort building boom on the Strip.

As an entertainment island in a sea of sand, the resort and gambling industry is heavily dependent on transportation arteries to bring in its lifeblood of visitors. However, problems are arising in the two primary ways visitors come to Las Vegas, by car and by plane, making it much less likely that they will come if they're caught in bumper-to-bumper traffic for ten hours or delayed or re-routed through three different airports. The economic future depends upon keeping the arteries of commerce open to allow the new megaresorts to attract new visitors.

Interstate Highway 15, the primary land-transportation route between Las Vegas and Los Angeles, is the main tourist pipeline to

**Figure 9.1**  New megaresort construction

southern California, the point of origin for 30 percent of southern Nevada's tourists. Because of increasing congestion and numerous construction projects, however, motorists often face lengthy drives both ways during holiday weekends, causing many of them to begin leaving Las Vegas resorts earlier to avoid the heavy traffic. More time on the road translates into less time in the casinos and therefore less money spent, and a miserable driving experience may prevent many of them from returning.

Federal highway authorities project that, by the year 2001, the average speed of vehicles traveling the clogged highway will be 42 to 50 mph, and possibly much slower during peak periods. To help ease congestion, Nevada's Department of Transportation was authorized in 1998 to contribute $10 million to California for a $140-million project to widen a 28-mile stretch of Interstate Highway 15 from four to six lanes between Victorville and Barstow, with Las Vegas' gambling interests reportedly contributing an additional $10 million (Ryan 1998). Also in 1998, Nevada was allocated $190 million per year for the next six years in federal funds for highway construction. The package totaled $1.1 billion and, through a joint effort by the Nevada and California congressional delegations, $24 million was dedicated to Interstate Highway 15 improvement in California. Nevada will also spend $2 million widening the highway from Las Vegas to the California state line.

Regarding air travel, despite McCarran International Airport's expansion, carriers have begun diverting planes to more lucrative routes, causing ticket prices to rise. The airport spent $1.1 billion in 1997 improving runways and building the new D-Gate terminal to increase passenger capacity from 30 million to 45 million passengers per year. However, as construction was in its final stage, passenger counts at McCarran flattened, with 1997 passenger volume declining 0.5% from 1996, which had been a year with aggressive airline advertising and promotional low fares. Meanwhile, room inventory grew by 6.3%, 3.5 times as quickly as the number of visitors.

One reason for the drop in airline passengers is recent business adjustments by the major carriers, as airlines can charge higher fares for non-tourist routes because business travelers typically pay more. Also, tourists shop for the best value and some trade in frequent-flier miles instead of purchasing their tickets to Las Vegas. Historically, McCarran has been a low-fare, high-frequency market since recreational travel is much more price-sensitive than business travel, as tourism is heavily affected by cost and availability. Consequently, some carriers are trimming their services to Las Vegas just when the city needs them most.

Another major source of concern for the future of the region is the recent decline from record high gambling profits in the Fiscal Year 1996. The 21 major Strip casinos, that each took in at least $72 million or more in gross gambling winnings, took in a total of $981.8 million in profits in Fiscal year 1996, a 16.2% return. In Fiscal year 1997, however, the major Strip resorts' earnings dropped to $909 million, a 14.1% profit (Nevada Gaming Control Board 1998). While a 14% profit would be the envy of many businesses, the relative decline causes concern for Las Vegas' gaming interests, especially during the present period of new casino construction.

Part of the decline in gambling profits no doubt comes from increased competition nationwide, a trend that has many Las Vegans worried about their economic future. While the growing social acceptance of gambling as a leisure activity led to a boom period in Las Vegas from 1989 through 1995, it also spurred the construction of casinos across the country, with nearly 300 new gambling venues built outside Nevada. Most ominously, Indian gaming expanded in nearby southern California, with large casinos now operating in San Diego and Palm Springs and dozens of other locations scattered across the state. A 1997 estimate of the take on "punch cards" in California, an illegal version of the slot machine, was $3 billion, representing additional money that might have been spent in Nevada casinos, as California is the principal feeder state to the Las Vegas region.

One unique feature of the Las Vegas megaresort boom period after 1989 was the ready availability of venture capital in the "second circuit" to the casino industry, as traditional investors and financial institutions historically did not view gaming as a legitimate investment. Today, however, concerns about loans to fund casino construction have been raised again because of the fear of overcapacity in Las Vegas and continuing unease over the reputation of the gambling industry, making investors wary about huge investments. Borrowing costs for gambling companies thus rose in 1998, driven up by concerns over market saturation and debt-load. For example, as the Bellagio opened in 1998, Mirage Resorts' corporate debt hit the $2.2-billion mark and its stock fell to half the selling price of the prior year (Berns 1998c).

Given these concerns, many local observers are wondering whether the four new megaresorts, the Bellagio, Mandalay Bay, the Venetian, and Paris, will reinvigorate faltering visitor volume or spark a brutal competition with room-price wars leading to a downward spiral in profits. The slack in visitor volume comes at the same time that these 20,000 highly leveraged hotel rooms are opening, raising the possibility of a price war. Before opening, the Bellagio slashed its projections for average daily room rates from $295 to $145, representing a decline in potential revenue of more than $150 million a year. Given that other Las Vegas resorts counted on the Bellagio to raise room prices across the board from an average rate of $81 in 1997, the ripple effect of its reduction in projected room rates could be disastrous for smaller, older resorts.

Since the 1980s Las Vegas has enjoyed a significant rise in visitor volume from international sources, with 19 percent of its 1997 visitors coming from other countries. A large fraction of these have traditionally been from Asian countries, however, making the current crisis among Asian economies another source of concern for the Las Vegas tourist economy.

Other variations in the global economy also have affected Las Vegas. Currency devaluations and exchange controls made travel to the United States more expensive in 1998, even though airfare prices remained level in dollar terms. Since an expanding Las Vegas will need more international visitors to help fill its additional hotel rooms, Nevada's congressional delegation and convention officials have successfully lobbied the White House, the Federal Aviation Administration and US Customs Service officials for direct international flights to Las Vegas, with non-stop flights from Japan beginning in 1998, though added capacity will count for naught if the present economic crisis in Asia continues.

Asian tourists are not the only ones subject to the potential barriers of a faltering economy. A similar downturn in the United States also could adversely affect Las Vegas just at the time the Bellagio, Paris, the Venetian, and Mandalay Bay open, as these new upscale resorts are counting heavily on the baby-boomer marketing niche, composed as it is of the most avid spenders in history. Following the lead of Caesars' Forum Shops, which produces the nation's highest annual revenue per square foot of shopping space at $1,200 (see chapter 4), retail space on the Strip will expand another 14% by the year 2000. Despite a leveling off in visitor volume and gambling revenue in 1997, spending on shopping and entertainment rose 8.9%. Thus, Las Vegas tourists increased their spending on shopping and shows while holding the line on gambling budgets. Also, the 1998 Las Vegas Convention and Visitors Authority survey found that entertainment, including shopping and fine dining, has displaced gambling as the number-one Las Vegas attraction, concluding that "the basic perceptions of Las Vegas are transforming to reflect more diverse offerings that appeal to a broader travel consumer audience" (H. Smith 1998a). Although the expansion of retailing and other commercial facilities is seen as a way to exploit this general spending trend, even the most optimistic projections see visitor volume growing at an insufficient rate to keep pace, cutting the ratio of visitors to total retail space in half when all the new resorts open. In short, we may have entered a phase of over-investment and over-capacity in all the dimensions of the casino/resort economy.

In 1997, only 13% of tourists polled by the Las Vegas Convention and Visitors Authority said that Las Vegas was too expensive, up from 5% in 1994 (Las Vegas Convention and Visitors Authority 1997: 78). However, with gambling increasingly available around the country, potential visitors may decide that it's more convenient and less expensive to gamble closer to home. Las Vegas has been able to compete successfully thus far because it has reinvented itself, with the spectacular archi-tainment of the megaresorts providing something not available elsewhere. A 1998 national study revealed that more than half the population, 56%, sees a lot more to do in Las Vegas than gamble, up from 34% in 1989. In the same time-frame, the number of people who view Las Vegas as an entertainment capital rose from 59% to 73%. This broader appeal of Las Vegas brought 29% more first-time visitors in 1997, up from 19% in 1988 (H. Smith 1998a), but the question remains whether those first-time visitors will return for subsequent vacations.

In addition, the Las Vegas tourist economy is threatened by increased government concern with the impact of gambling throughout the nation. The National Gambling Impact Study Commission is conducting a two-year study of the gambling industry, to be completed in 1999, which many believe could lead to calls for new federal taxes and regulation of casinos. This potential threatens to erode the profitability of the casino industry just as its earnings are most vulnerable.

A final troubling aspect of the region's extreme reliance on gambling and tourism concerns the nature and type of employment it provides. Although Las Vegas leads the nation in job creation, approximately half of all jobs in the area are poorly paid service occupations, most of them in the resort industry (Parker 1995). Most of these jobs require little formal education or training, with the most common occupations being waiter/waitress, retail salesperson, cashier, and maid (Nevada Employment Security Department 1992). According to the 1990 Census, Las Vegas was among the lowest-ranked metropolitan areas in the US in terms of the percentage of the workforce employed in skilled occupations such as executives, managers, and technicians (Ward 1994).

In sum, after years of unprecedented expansion, the southern Nevada tourist economy faces a number of challenges. Publicly, many casino executives and political leaders remain optimistic, challenging doomsday prophets and claiming that fears for the future of the Las Vegas economy are unfounded. Privately though, many acknowledge that the gambling industry nationwide is entering new territory, and wonder how well Las Vegas is prepared. Some acknowledge that legalized gambling and tourism has reached a new stage, one that will require different management strategies. In this view, the casino companies that fare best during the turbulent times ahead will be those whose management is prepared to deal with the shift from an industry characterized by explosive growth rates to one generating more normal returns for investors in a more stable environment. According to Las Vegas Convention and Visitors Authority president, Manny Cortez: "The fact is Las Vegas will change more in the next two years than it ever has" (H. Smith 1998a).

## The Future Quality of Life

Throughout this book we have attempted to document the emergence of a nascent civic culture with its own agenda that tempers the singular focus on economic growth. Master planning and the extensive development of suburban communities in particular have provided a growing number of residents in the region with a sense of place and a concept of everyday life that is independent of the gambling and tourist industry. Also, through its newly established Neighborhood Services Department, the city of Las Vegas is actively promoting local neighborhood associations in both older and newer non-master-planned areas, placing them on more equal footing with newer upscale residents (see chapter 6).

Other positive aspects of Las Vegas' residents' life include its libraries, community activities, and recreational sites. As we described earlier, though not without controversy the Clark County Library District has constructed an extensive network of architecturally impressive structures that also serve as neighborhood cultural centers, providing residents with access to plays, recitals, art exhibits, and other programs not attached to casino offerings. Although, overall, Las Vegas is deficient in parks (see chapter 8), public investment is improving. There are now approximately 150 parks in the Las Vegas Valley, many of which are new, while others have been extensively refurbished (Metropolitan Research Association 1998). The area also contains several other major sites for outdoor recreation within one hour's drive, including the Lake Mead Recreation Area, the Red Rock Canyon National Conservation Area, the Toiyabe National Forest, and the Valley of Fire State Park. In addition, although the state of Nevada consistently ranks near the bottom in terms of public funding of the arts (Bowers 1998), Las Vegas has a growing arts community serving local residents with performing arts centers, museums, art galleries, and locally-sponsored cultural events.

In other areas of community life, Las Vegas' emerging civic culture is more fragile. Most important among these is the quality of education, which, though improving, remains uneven. The area contains some excellent public schools, especially in the more upscale areas such as Green Valley and Summerlin, as well as some equally outstanding private schools for those who can afford them. Overall, however, education from kindergarten to grade 12 in the Las Vegas area leaves much to be desired. Most distressingly, Clark County schools continue to have an extremely high drop-out rate – 11.7 percent for students in grades 9–12 during the 1996–7 school year (Clark County School District 1998). Also, the scores of high school students on college entrance examinations such as the SAT and ACT hover around the national average (Clark County School District 1998), a disturbing fact given the increased spending on education.

A final area of educational concern that urgently needs to be addressed is the school district's woefully inadequate curriculum requirements. National political and educational leaders constantly emphasize the importance of language and maths/science skills to ensure success in an increasingly global economy, yet Nevada high schools (grades 9–12) require no foreign-language courses and only two courses each in maths and science, plus one-half of a credit in computers (Clark County School District 1998). While student achievement overall has been partially hampered by stresses from a near doubling of enrollments in the past ten years and a transiency rate that averages 43 percent (Clark County School District 1998), the need for a more academically rigorous curriculum should be a paramount concern of residents who wish to improve the local quality of life.

The presence of quality institutions of higher education is another important facet of building a viable civic culture and Las Vegas has made great strides in this area in the 1990s. Although state support for higher education has never been strong, legislative appropriation for the 1997–8 biennium was the single highest percentage increase in the nation (Bowers 1998). One major beneficiary of this increase is the Community College of Southern Nevada (CCSN), the fastest growing community college in the nation, with more than 32,000 students enrolled at five campuses around the valley (see chapter 6). The University of Nevada, Las Vegas (UNLV) also has experienced phenomenal growth. While the school is perhaps best known for its Hotel

Administration program, it has recently opened a School of Architecture and a new law school. The university also features a strong liberal-arts core curriculum and, since 1990, has initiated several Ph.D. programs in the humanities and the social and natural sciences.

Another important set of factors relevant for assessing the Las Vegas area's civic culture are lifestyle issues Here again, the overall picture is highly uneven. While many residents of southern Nevada take advantage of the area's warm, sunny climate to enjoy a variety of outdoor activities year round, others tend toward the less healthy aspects of the entertainment capital's binge culture (Parker 1995). In particular, Clark County residents have disproportionately high rates of smoking (28.5%), chronic drinking (4.8%), and being overweight (32.3%) (Nevada State Bureau of Health Planning and Statistics 1998). Other factors, such as suicide and crime, also remain unacceptably high in Clark County, although rates for both are exaggerated by the presence of more than 30 million visitors each year. Despite its rapidly growing population, violent-crime rates actually have declined in each of the past few years (Las Vegas Metropolitan Police Department 1997), but the *state* still has one of the highest incarceration rates in the country.

Finally, nowhere is the fragility of Las Vegas' quality of life more in evidence than in the area of family issues. Entry-level service positions provide the most numerous new jobs in the region, but they often do not pay enough for a family to establish or maintain itself, creating or exacerbating a number of family problems. The state overall continues to have the highest divorce rate in the nation and a recent study by the Children's Rights Council ranked Nevada only thirty-seventh nationally for raising a family, based largely on the state's unfavorable rankings in teen pregnancies, births out of wedlock, child-abuse rates, and provision of childcare (Bowers 1998; United Way of Southern Nevada 1998). As with most of the other statistics cited in this section, there exists a rather extreme class bifurcation between those living in the more upscale areas of the Las Vegas Valley and the rest of the population, which is a major cause for concern among those local citizens and government officials who are genuinely interested in improving the overall quality of life in the area.

## Conclusion

Many critics, no doubt, will continue to focus on the tacky exuberance of the Strip and Glitter Gulch as representative of an entire metropolis of more than a million people. Others, however, such as historian John Findlay (1990), suggest that the city's ascendance might more perceptively be considered as an artifact of a culture undergoing substantial change. Architectural critic Alan Hess makes essentially the same point, claiming that Las Vegas represents the emergence of a new urban form, what he calls the Strip City, "organized on a linear framework and tied to the car. The architecture and planning rules of Grid City, the city of sidewalks and squares, don't apply to Strip City, the city of parking lots and signs" (1993: 116). Put another way, Las Vegas is best described as a multi-centered metropolitan region (Gottdiener 1994b).

Throughout this book we have provided evidence that what we have called a normalization process is taking place in the Las Vegas metropolitan area, where the local agenda is increasingly being driven by residents as opposed to business concerns. We have also emphasized that, in order to address the all-important issues of economic diversification and improvement of the region's quality of life, this normalization process must be extended to the less prosperous areas of the community. Doing so, however, depends on a change in the local political culture and on improved regional cooperation and planning among the area's various governmental structures. Change also requires the continued development of an active civic culture, which will demand a more responsive and effective government to achieve a greater balance between business and social issues, the major contradiction that must be faced by the local community. Many professionals in local government also recognize this important point. According to a Las Vegas city planner speaking in support of the creation of the Neighborhood Services Department: "The basic premise ... is to give neighborhoods back to the community, to preserve and revitalize neighborhoods and to ultimately protect and provide a high quality of life for all citizens" (Hargrove 1995: 1). She goes on to add that, if this task is to be achieved, "it will be because of the commitment to active citizen participation and because the city listens to those citizens who participate" (Hargrove 1995: 1). In sum, in the past it was federal spending and the casinos that defined Las Vegas. Now, and in the future, it will be up to the people, the local citizens, to create the kind of community they want.

# References

Abbott, C. (1981) *The New Urban America: Growth and Politics in Sunbelt Cities*. Chapel Hill: University of North Carolina Press.

Anderson, K. (1994) "Las Vegas, USA." *Time*, 143, January 10: 42–51.

Associated Press (1998) "Dini defends his bill giving tax break to Steve Wynn, other art collectors." *Las Vegas Sun*, June 30.

—— (1997a) "Arizona going after wealthy seniors, affluent baby boomers." *Las Vegas Review-Journal*, January 7: 6D.

—— (1997b) "Las Vegas setting new standard for Labor Movement." *Las Vegas Sun*, February 12.

—— (1997c) "Employers slowly accepting seniors." *Las Vegas Review-Journal*, April 17: 4D.

Bailey, F. (1991) *Fall from Grace – The Untold Story of Michael Milken*. New York: Carol Publishing Group. In J. L. Smith 1995, ch. 2, p. 6.

Baudrillard, J. (1989) *America*. New York: Verso.

Bell, P. (1996a) "Las Vegas firms target Hispanic consumers." *Las Vegas Sun*, August 24.

—— (1996b) "Hispanic market: A burst of business." *Las Vegas Sun*, August 26.

Bennett, W. (1993) *Leading Index of Cultural Indicators*. New York: Simon & Schuster.

Berns, D. (1998a) "Tribal casinos hurting LV, study finds." *Las Vegas Review-Journal*, July 29.

—— (1998b) "Casino figures show a new LV emerging." *Las Vegas Review-Journal*, August 13.

—— (1998c) "Taking things to a new level." *Las Vegas Review-Journal*, October 11.

—— (1997a) "Gaming chips." *Las Vegas Review-Journal*, May 12.

—— (1997b) "Gaming chips." *Las Vegas Review-Journal*, October 20: 2D.

Best, K., and K. Hillyer (1995) "Fanciful Press Agency." In M. Tronnes (ed.), *Literary Las Vegas*, New York: Henry Holt Publishers, 1995, 119–26.

Bluestone, B., and B. Harrison (1982) *The Deindustrialization of America*. New York: Basic Books.

Bluethman, A. (1997) "New projects fanning craze for palm trees." *Las Vegas Review-Journal*, May 27.

Bowers, M (1998) 'The Sagebush State: 1997 Update." Unpublished manuscript, Department of Political Science, University of Nevada, Las Vegas.

—— (1996) *The Sagebush State: Nevada's History, Government, and Politics.* Reno and Las Vegas: University of Nevada Press.

Broadbent, R. (1997, February) Personal interview with authors.

Bureau of the Census (1960, 1980, 1990) Census of Population. Washington, DC: US Department of Commerce.

Calder, J. C. (1997) *Survey of the Migration of Nevada's Senior Population.* University of Nevada, Reno, Center for Applied Research.

Calkins, A. (1996) "Home-builders seek niches to market." *Las Vegas Sun*, July 30.

Cardinal, D. (1998) "Grass-roots views enter LV planning." *Las Vegas Sun*, June 13.

Carns, D. (1998) "Survey of Las Vegas Residents." Unpublished manuscript, Department of Sociology, University of Nevada, Las Vegas.

Caruso, M. (1998a) "All work and no workers." *Las Vegas Review-Journal*, January 18.

—— (1998b) "LV office inventory increases." *Las Vegas Review-Journal*, January 28.

—— (1998c) "Real estate professionals fear LV economy may soon decline." *Las Vegas Review-Journal*, July 17.

—— (1991) "Summerlin cuts time table, population." *Las Vegas Review-Journal*, April 28: 1K.

Castleman, D. (1996) *Las Vegas.* Oakland CA: Fodor's Travel Publications, Compass Guides.

Chase-Dunn, C. (1985) "The System of World Cities." In M. Timberlake (ed.), *Urbanization in the World Economy*, Orlando, FL: Academic Press.

Clark County School Duty (1998) *Annual Report.* Las Vegas: Clark County School District Public Information Office.

Cling, C. (1997) "Silver state on the silver screen." *Las Vegas Review-Journal*, November 30.

Collins, C. C. (1999) "A profile of Clark County's senior population." *Nevada Public Affairs Review* (in press).

—— (1993) "Reservation Roulette: Indian Gaming." Las Vegas: KLVX-TV.

—— (1987) "University of Nevada Las Vegas." Las Vegas: KLVX-TV.

—— (1986) "Gateway to Las Vegas: McCarran Airport." Las Vegas: KLVX-TV.

—— (1983a) "Las Vegas Paper Wars." Las Vegas: KLVX-TV.

—— (1983b) "Going for Broke: Compulsive Gambling." Las Vegas: KLVX-TV.

——(1982) "We Ought to Be in Pictures: Selling Las Vegas to Movies and TV." Las Vegas: KLVX-TV.

Davis, M. (1995) "House of cards." *Sierra*, 80: 36–41.

Debord, G. (1967) *The Society of the Spectacle*. Detroit: Black and Red Press.

Department of Housing and Urban Development (1993) *American Housing Survey*.

Doup, L. (1997) "More workers opt for early retirement." Knight Rider Newspapers, in *Las Vegas Review-Journal*, September 7: 1K.

Dunn, Reiber, Glenn, Marz (1997) press release, March 10.

Dunteman, D. (1993) "Health at what cost?" *Las Vegas Review-Journal/Sun*, May 9: 1D–5D.

Edwards, J. G. (1998a) "SOS: Stuck on Stocks." *Las Vegas Review-Journal*, June 2.

—— (1998b) "Citibank to increase LV staffing." *Las Vegas Review-Journal*, July 10.

Elliott, G. E. (1997 [1989]) "Senator Alan Bible and the Southern Nevada Water Project 1954–1971." In M. Green and G. E. Elliott, *Nevada Readings and Perspectives*, Reno: Nevada Historical Society, pp. 163–6.

FBI, US Department of Justice (1995, 1996) *Uniform Crime Reports for the United States*.

Feagin, J. R. (1998) *The New Urban Paradigm*. Boulder, CO: Rowan and Littlefield.

Feour, R. (1997) "Whitaker provided anxious moments for De La Hoya." *Las Vegas Review-Journal*, January 31.

Findlay, J. (1992) *Magic Lands: Western Landscapes and American Culture After 1940*. Berkeley: University of California Press.

—— (1990) "Suckers and Escapists? Interpreting Las Vegas and Postwar America." *Nevada Historical Society Quarterly*, vol. 33 (1) Spring: 1–16.

Fine, M. (1997, February and March; 1998, March) Personal interview with authors.

Fink, J. (1998) "UNLV serious about being a 'serious' school." *Las Vegas Sun*, August 31.

Fitzgerald, R. (1997 [1981]) "Blacks and the Boulder Dam Project." In *Nevada Readings and Perspectives*, M. Green and G. E. Elliott (eds), Reno: Nevada Historical Society, pp. 257–60.

Freiss, S. (1998) "Miller assails TV attack ads." *Las Vegas Review-Journal*, October 23: 1B.

Gabriel, T. (1991) "From vice to nice: The suburbanization of Las

Vegas." *New York Times Magazine*, December 1: Section 6, p. 68.

Gapp, P. (1992) "Vegas craps out: casino architecture finally loses its influence." *Chicago Tribune*, December 12, C-14.

Gerbner, G., et al. (1986) *Television's Mean World: Violence Profile 14–15.* Philadelphia: Annenberg School of Communications.

Goodman, R. (1995) *The Luck Business*, New York: Free Press.

Gottdiener, M. (1997) *The Theming of America: Dreams, Visions and Commercial Spaces.* Boulder, CO: Westview Press.

—— (1994a) *The Social Production of Urban Space*, 2nd edition, Austin: University of Texas Press.

—— (1994b) *The New Urban Sociology.* New York: McGraw-Hill.

—— (1977) *Planned Sprawl: Public and Private Interests in Suburbia.* Newbury Park, CA: Sage.

Gottdiener, M., and J. R. Feagin (1988) "The paradigm shift in urban analysis." *Urban Affairs Quarterly*, 24: 163–87.

Gottdiener, M., and N. Komninos (1987) *Capitalist Development and Crisis Theory.* London: Macmillan.

Green, Marian (1992) "Las Vegas is 38th most livable city in US." *Las Vegas Review-Journal*, February 18: 2B.

Green, Michael, and G. E. Elliott (1997) *Nevada Readings and Perspectives.* Reno: Nevada Historical Society.

Greene, J. (1994) "Nevada leads US in uninsured." *Las Vegas Review-Journal*, February 3: 1–3A.

Greene, S. (1998) "Ethics Commission finds Gates guilty.' *Las Vegas Review-Journal*, January 24.

—— (1997a) "Regional planning in sight." *Las Vegas Review-Journal*, May 27.

—— (1997b) "Poll: Voters want say on tax increase." *Las Vegas Review-Journal*, August 10.

—— (1997c) "Voters give commission poor marks." *Las Vegas Review-Journal*, August 11.

—— (1997d) "Pressure mounts as vote on sales tax increase nears." *Las Vegas Review-Journal*, November 9.

Guterson, D. (1992) "No place like home." *Harper's Magazine*, May: 55–61.

Hargrove, P. (1995) "Neighborhood Planning Ordinance." *Growth Watch*, 6 (1): 1

Harvey, D. (1989) *The Postmodern Condition.* Oxford, UK: Blackwell.

Havas, A. (1995) "Drug test company establishes LV office." *Las Vegas Business Press*, vol. 12 (4): 3.

—— (1992) "Taverns bring protest." *Las Vegas Sun*, April 5: C–1.

Hawley, A. (1981) *Urban Society: An Ecological Approach.* New York: J. Wiley.

Henderson Police Department (1997) *Annual Report.* Henderson, NV.

Hess, A. (1993) *Viva Las Vegas.* San Francisco: Chronicle Books.

Hoekstra, D. (1996) "EM guide to Las Vegas." *Electronic Media*, January 15: 36.

Holmstrom, D. (1993) "US is gambling as never before." *Christian Science Monitor*, US Section, January 26: 8.

Hopkins, A. D. (1997) "No more quickies." *Las Vegas Review-Journal*, March 9.

Horkheimer, M., and T. Adorno (1972 [1944]) *Dialectic of Enlightenment*, tr. by John Cumming. New York: Seabury Press.

Hunsberger, C. (1997, February) Personal interview with authors.

Hynes, M. (1997) "Growth: No slowdown for boomtown." *Las Vegas Review-Journal*, April 6.

Jones, J. (1992) "Caesars World keeps its appeal." *Investors Business Daily*, March 11: 34.

Judson, D. (1998) "Population Characteristics: Official Nevada Estimates (1997) and Projections (1998+)," Nevada State Demographer and Nevada Department of Taxation. Reno: University of Nevada, Reno.

Kamin, B. (1994) "Lessons from Las Vegas: Turning Casinoland into Disneyland with gambling." *Chicago Tribune*, Sunday Magazine, May 5: 10.

Kanigher, S. (1998) "Census charts changes in LV." *Las Vegas Sun*, September 10.

Katsilometes, J. (1997) "The big time: Winston Cup coming to LV." *Las Vegas Review-Journal*, August 13.

Las Vegas–Clark County Library District (undated) "Our Many Faces."

Las Vegas Convention and Visitors Authority (1998) Strategic and Market Research, "Las Vegas Redefined: An Analysis of the Competition, Air Service and Our Customers."

—— (1997) *1997 Las Vegas Visitor Profile Study*, San Francisco: GLS Research.

Las Vegas Metropolitan Police Department (1998) "Index of crimes reported to police, January through December, 1997."

—— (1997) *Annual Report.* Las Vegas, NV.

—— (1996) *Homicide Analysis Summary.* Las Vegas, NV.

*Las Vegas Review-Journal* (1997) "Major park set for Summerlin's newest village, the Arbors." August 10: 4P.

—— (1996) "Experts say Summerlin enjoys cooler temperatures, cleaner air." March 10: 1M.

—— (1991) "Summerlin cuts timetable, population." April 28: 1K.

—— (1989) "Las Vegas history outlined." July 20: 19AA–27AA.

*Las Vegas Sun* (1981) "Henderson cloud." November 1: 1.

Lefebvre, H. (1991a) *The Critique of Everyday Life*. New York: Verso, vol. 1.

—— (1991b) *The Social Production of Space*. Oxford, UK: Blackwell.

—— (1974) *La Production de l'espace*. Paris: Gallimard.

Logan, J., and H. Molotch (1988) *Urban Fortunes*. Berkeley, CA: University of California Press.

Longman, P. (1994) "Orlando becomes Vegas while Vegas becomes Orlando." *St Petersburg Times*, June 19: D–1.

Macy, R. (1997) "Work begins on $1.8 billion Venetian-themed hotel-casino." Associated Press, *Las Vegas Sun*, April 15.

Mandel, E. (1977) *Late Capitalism*. London: Verso.

Manning, M. (1998) "Water Forum will search for pollution sources." *Las Vegas Sun*, April 6.

—— (1990) "Mental Illness Report says Nevada stingy." *Las Vegas Sun*, September 11: 9A.

Martin, T. (1992) "Nevada: an area seen to be strong but still holding its own." *Southwest Real Estate News*, vol. 20 (1): 13.

McCarran International Airport (Clark County) (1996) *Past, Present and Future*. Airport Authority pamphlet.

McKinnon, S. (1998a) "Growing pains: Panel looks for solutions." *Las Vegas Review-Journal*, January 26.

—— (1998b) "Commissioners adopt plans to manage growth." *Las Vegas Review-Journal*, January 28.

—— (1998c) "Panel offers input to map city's future." *Las Vegas Review-Journal*, April 6.

——(1998d) "Growth panel sets goal for park acreage." *Las Vegas Review-Journal*, April 21.

—— (1998e) "Increase in visitors turning Red Rock into urban park." *Las Vegas Review-Journal*, May 10.

—— (1998f) "Drawing the line in the sand." *Las Vegas Review-Journal*, July 5.

—— (1998g) "Water may be woe of Mandalay Bay." *Las Vegas Review-Journal*, July 12.

—— (1998h) "Panel adopts plan to handle area's growth." *Las Vegas Review-Journal*, November 6.

—— (1998i) "Proceed with caution." *Las Vegas Review-Journal*, November 29.

—— (1989) "NLV new kid on the block to cash in on building boom." *Las Vegas Review-Journal*, November 19: 1A–20A.

Metropolitan Research Association (1997) *1997 Las Vegas Perspective*. Center for Business and Economic Research, University of Nevada, Las Vegas.

Metropolitan Research Association (1998) *1998 Las Vegas Perspective.* Center for Business and Economic Research, University of Nevada, Las Vegas.

Moehring, E. P. (1989) *Resort City in the Sun Belt: Las Vegas 1930–1970.* Reno/Las Vegas: University of Nevada Press.

Moody, E. N. (1997 [1994]) "Nevada's Legalization of Casino Gambling in 1931: Purely a Business Proposition." In M. Green and G. E. Elliott, *Nevada Readings and Perspectives*, Reno: Nevada Historical Society, pp. 169–77.

Morris, S. (1992) "Three winners back casino idea." *Chicago Tribune*, Business Section, August 15, p. 1.

Morrison, J. A. (1998a) "Atkinson Gates, Malone broke state ethics laws." *Las Vegas Review-Journal*, June 28.

—— (1998b) "Airport contracts won't be voided." *Las Vegas Review-Journal*, June 30.

Nadler, A. (1997) "Senior assisted-living residences multiply." *Las Vegas Sun*, April 26.

National Center for Health Statistics (1997) *Statistical Abstract for the US.*

Nevada Division of Aging Services (1994) *Clark County Senior Survey*, October.

Nevada Employment Security Department (1992) *Nevada Occupational Projections, 1991–96.* Carson City, NV: Nevada Employment Security Department.

Nevada State Bureau of Health Planning and Statistics (1998) *Behavioral Risk Factor Surveillance Survey.* Carson City, NV: Nevada State Health Division.

North Las Vegas Police Department (1997) *Annual Report.* North Las Vegas, NV.

O'Callaghan, M. (1998) "Where I stand: Las Vegas offers few excuses for not attending college." *Las Vegas Sun*, June 6.

O'Reilly, J. (1995) "In Las Vegas: Working Hard for the Money." In M. Tronnes (ed.), *Literary Las Vegas*, New York: Henry Holt Publishers: 25–39.

Packer, A. (1998a) "Boulder City residents keep a close eye on growth." *Las Vegas Sun*, June 27.

—— (1998b) "Henderson's most valuable tour guide." *Las Vegas Sun*, July 6.

Paher, S. (1971) *Las Vegas: As it Began – As it Grew.* Las Vegas: Nevada Publishers.

Parker, R. (forthcoming) "Las Vegas: Casino Gambling and Local Culture." In D. Judd and S. Fainstein (eds), *Places to Play: The Remaking of Cities for Tourists*, New Haven: Yale University Press:

chapter 7.

—— (1997) "Urban Growth Management in Southern Nevada." In D. Soden and E. Herzik (eds), *Towards 2000: Public Policy in Nevada*, Dubuque, IA: Kendall/Hunt Publishers: 201–14.

—— (1995) "Urbanites in Southern Nevada: Myths and Reality." Paper presented at the Midwest Sociological Society, Annual Meetings, Chicago, IL.

Patton, N. (1998a) "University regents ponder growing student population." *Las Vegas Review-Journal*, January 24.

—— (1998b) "Feeling the pulse." *Las Vegas Review-Journal*, July 20.

—— (1998c) "University welcomes 112 new professors to growing ranks." *Las Vegas Review-Journal*, August 21: 1B.

—— (1998d) "News report ranks UNLV in top 10." *Las Vegas Review-Journal*, August 22: 1–2B.

Postman, N. (1985) *Amusing Ourselves to Death*. New York: Viking Press.

Potters, M. (1996) "The women who built Las Vegas." *Las Vegas Sun*, August 27.

Przybys, J. (1998) "Seniors: Southern Nevada's new immigrants." *Las Vegas Review-Journal*, February 8: 1.

Puit, G. (1998a) "Growth, suicides linked." *Las Vegas Review-Journal*, April 3.

—— (1998b) "Statistics show crime drop." *Las Vegas Review-Journal*, August 28.

*Reno Gazzette Journal* (1996) "Latinos to make up more than one-fourth of residents by 2025." November 11.

Rizzo, J. (1992) "Ten ways to look at a library." *American Libraries Journal*, April 322–6.

Robiglio, D. (1997) "Cities want own school districts." *Las Vegas Review-Journal*, May 22.

Rodriguez, T. (1997) "A Profile of Hispanics in Nevada: 1997." Latin Chamber of Commerce.

Rogers, K. (1997a) "Eroding wetlands may affect water quality." *Las Vegas Review-Journal*, January 20.

—— (1997b) "Tainted water turns up." *Las Vegas Review-Journal*, September 5.

Ryan, C. (1998) "Nevada to contribute $10 million to widen I-15 in California." *Las Vegas Sun*, May 13.

Sassen, S. (1991) *The Global City*. Princeton, NJ: Princeton University Press.

Sawyer, G., G. E. Elliott, and R. T. King (1993) *Hang Tough! Grant Sawyer: An Activist in the Governor's Mansion*. Reno: University of Nevada Oral History Program.

Schlegel, J. (1998, March) Personal interview with authors.

Schmidt, R. (1998) "Costs and Consequences of Urban Sprawl in the Las Vegas Valley." Unpublished Ph.D. dissertation, Department of Sociology, University of Nevada, Las Vegas.

Schmidt, R., and T. McGinnis (1998) "The State's Role in Managing Regional Growth." In *The Las Vegas Metropolitan Area Project: Studies of Selected Quality of Life Issues*, pp. 255–95, Las Vegas: University of Nevada, Las Vegas.

Schweers, J. (1997a) "Resorts battle holds up Strip frontage road." *Las Vegas Sun*, March 5.

—— (1997b) "Bally's chairman criticizes county on Caesars air rights." *Las Vegas Sun*, April 8.

Scott, C. (1996) "Sheriff says Vegas high crime rating 'erroneous'." *Las Vegas Sun*, May 7.

Sebelius, S. (1996) "New maps balance populations but come under fire." *Las Vegas Sun*, April 12.

Segerblom, S. (1998, August 25) Personal interview with authors.

Shapiro, P. (1998) "Southern Nevada Fire Department and EMS Statistics." Unpublished report, Department of Sociology, University of Nevada, Las Vegas.

Smith, H. (1998a) "Study shows evolution of LV visitors." *Las Vegas Review-Journal*, July 15.

—— (1998b) "Convention competition drives building." *Las Vegas Review-Journal*, July 20.

—— (1998c) "Las Vegas offers businesses chances to thrive." *Las Vegas Review-Journal*, July 23.

Smith, J. L. (1998a) "Operation Button-Down: Mafia's Equal Opportunity destroyer." *Las Vegas Review-Journal*, February 4.

—— (1998b) "Pity the poor, huddled masses without pals who are county pols." *Las Vegas Review-Journal*, June 30.

—— (1998c) "One 'ordinary' Las Vegas very extraordinary for community." *Las Vegas Review-Journal*, July 14.

—— (1997) Column: "Casino's signature leaves Wall Streeters whining." *Las Vegas Review-Journal*, May 28.

—— (1995) *Running Scared: The Life and Treacherous Times of Las Vegas Casino King Steve Wynn*. New York: Barricade Books.

Smith, R. (1994) "A Report Card on Entry Level Workers." *Las Vegas Business Press*, February 7, vol. 11 (5): 1.

Spanier, D. (1992) *Welcome to the Pleasuredome*. Reno, NV: University of Nevada Press.

Steinhauer, A. (1997a) "Their Kind of Town." *Las Vegas Review-Journal*, June 30.

—— (1997b) "Rev up the hype: Vegas marketing machine puts pedal to the metal." *Las Vegas Review-Journal*, August 13.

Thompson, H. (1971) *Fear and Loathing in Las Vegas*. New York: Random House.

Timmons, H. (1996) "A juggernaut of growth in the desert shows no signs of slowing down yet." *American Banker*, March 15: 9.

Tronnes, M. (ed.) (1995) *Literary Las Vegas*. New York: Henry Holt Publishers.

United Way of Southern Nevada (1998) *The Human Side of Growth*.

USAF, Nellis Air Force Base (1997) *Economic Resources Impact Statement, Fiscal Year 1996*.

Venturi, R., D. S. Brown, and S. Izenour (1972) *Learning from Las Vegas*. Cambridge, MA: MIT Press.

Ward, S. (1994) "Mostly unskilled." *USA Today*, March 11: 1B.

Warner, G. (1995) "Will revamped Glitter Gulch shine as bright." *Pittsburgh Post Gazette*, November 12: 4G.

Whaley, S. (1993) "Nevada still ranks 5th in US for cost of typical hospital stay." *Las Vegas Review-Journal*, February 10: 1A.

Wolfe, T. (1995) "Las Vegas (What?) Las Vegas (Can't Hear You! Too Noisy) Las Vegas!!!" In Mike Tronnes (ed.), *Literary Las Vegas*, New York: Henry Holt Publishers (1995), 1–24.

—— (1965) *The Kandy-Kolored Tangerine-Flake Streamline Baby*. New York: Farrar, Straus and Giroux.

Woo, G. (1998) *UNLV Las Vegas Metropolitan Poll*, Cannon Center for Survey Research.

Zapler, M (1998a) "Fremont not quite that free." *Las Vegas Review-Journal*, January 21.

—— (1998b) "City finds weeds in parks cost audit." *Las Vegas Review-Journal*, July 13.

—— (1998c) "Trail to-do." *Las Vegas Review-Journal*, July 13.

—— (1997a) "LV OKs downtown bank deal.' *Las Vegas Review-Journal*, February 6.

—— (1997b) "Growth hot topic for elections." *Las Vegas Review-Journal*, March 23.

—— (1997c) "Thrill of victory comes at a price." *Las Vegas Review-Journal*, June 8.

—— (1997d) "LV Valley lagging in parks." *Las Vegas Review-Journal*, July 6.

# Index